Taxation

1990–91 Edition

Bill Pritchard, BA, FTII

Pitman

Pitman Publishing
128 Long Acre, London WC2E 9AN

A Division of Longman Group UK Limited

First published in 1980

A CIP catalogue record for this book is available from the British Library

ISBN 0 273 03336 0

Typeset, printed and bound in Great Britain

Contents

Author's Preface

For this eleventh edition, *Taxation* has been revised and updated to incorporate the provisions of the Finance Act, 1990.

My secretary, Mrs Joan Orrell, has again done the typing, and as always,. she deserves my eternal thanks.

The book is once more dedicated to my children Kate, Mark and Philip who ensure that I never see the royalties!

W.E. Pritchard
September, 1990.

Revision Questions

Try the questions indicated when you have read the following chapters:

a) At the end of Chapter 7 try the "Income Tax" questions:
   7, 11 to 15, 21, 24, 28, 29, 30, 31.
b) At the end of Chapter 10 try the "Income Tax" questions:
   4, 5, 6, 20, 22.
c) At the end of Chapter 13 try the "Income Tax" questions:
   9, 18, 23, 25, 27.
d) At the end of Chapter 14 try the "Corporation Tax" questions.
e) At the end of Chapter 15 try the "Capital Gains Tax" questions.

Chapter One

General Principles and Administration

Introduction

Income tax is an annual tax levied by Parliament through the medium of the Budget and the resultant Finance Act. It is administered by the Treasury through the Inland Revenue.

The main law on taxation has been consolidated in the following Acts of Parliament:

1. Income and Corporation Taxes Act, 1988 (ICTA, 1988).
2. Taxes Management Act, 1970 (TMA, 1970).
3. Capital Allowances Act, 1990 (CAA, 1990).
4. Capital Gains Tax Act, 1979 (CGTA, 1979).

These are supplemented and extended by the subsequent annual Finance Acts. Many points of detailed law and interpretation have been considered by the Courts at all levels and a supplementary body of case law has been built up over the years that supplements the statute law. In addition, the Inland Revenue often publish their opinions on certain points through Press Releases and Statements of Practice. They have also published Concessions on points where they are prepared to relax the strict interpretion of the law.

The main body administering direct taxation is the Inland Revenue who are responsible for income tax, corporation tax and capital gains tax. These are administered by the Board of Inland Revenue (consisting of a number of Commissioners of Inland Revenue) situated in London. The detailed routine of administration is however mainly carried out by "Districts" into which the whole country is divided. Each District is in the charge of an Inspector of Taxes who has the necessary clerical staff to help. The Inspector's main job is to quantify the liability. Collection of the taxes is the responsibility of the Collector of Taxes who is separate from the Inspector. Curiously, repayments are made by the Inspector.

Inheritance Tax is dealt with by a specialist office in London.

The Inland Revenue also have specialised branches to advise on specialist matters and provide the necessary administrative back up to Inspectors and Collectors. See appendix 1 for more details regarding the duties of an Inspector.

Liability to income tax

Individuals and trustees are liable to income tax if they are either:

1. RESIDENT in the UK when basically they are liable to UK tax on income derived from anywhere in the world.
2. If they are not resident in the UK, they can be liable to UK tax on income derived from the UK.

Liability and the amount of liability often depend on whether an individual is "resident", "ordinarily resident" or "domiciled" in or out of the UK. These terms are therefore important and are defined in appendix 2.

Assessment of liability

Income tax is levied for a fiscal year (sometimes known as the year of assessment) which runs from 6th April to the following 5th April. The fiscal year 1990/91 for example runs from 6th April, 1990 to 5th April, 1991. The amount of tax reliefs known as PERSONAL ALLOWANCES and the rates of tax are set in the Budget and the Finance Act each year. However, the amount of income on which tax is levied is not determined by the year of assessment, but by the BASIS PERIOD which may or may not coincide with the year of assessment.

"Income" is not defined in general terms. Instead, sources of income (known as SCHEDULES, two of which are subdivided into CASES) are identified, and if money is derived from one of these sources it is assessed to income tax.

The schedules and cases are of basic importance and should be known thoroughly for the following reasons:

1. They are, as already stated, the source of assessable income.
2. Each has a different basis period to quantify the income assessable in a particular year of assessment.
3. Each has different rules as to measurement of income and allowable deductions.

The schedules and cases are analysed in detail in appendix 3.

Mechanics of administration and assessment

The Inland Revenue have three basic annual duties:

1. To identify taxpayers and their sources of income.
2. To quantify the amount of income assessable, allowing the correct deductions and reliefs.
3. To assess and collect the tax due.

These duties are discharged mainly by the use of two procedures:

1. The issue of an annual tax return to each taxpayer which he has to complete and return to the local Inspector within thirty days of its issue. They are normally sent out each April, just after the beginning of the new tax year.
2. The quantification of income and the calculation of tax payable is normally due (apart from income subject to PAYE) by the preparation of an annual

ASSESSMENT. This is in effect an annual bill showing the taxpayer his gross income, the allowable deductions, and the rates of tax applied.

A thorough understanding of the annual administrative procedure and the detailed layout of the assessment gives a good grounding in basic income tax. Readers are advised to note the next part carefully, as much of the rest of this book uses the concepts and layouts about to be described.

Procedure

The annual administrative procedure is as follows:

1. The Inspector, having identified a taxpayer, sends him a tax return for the year. The RETURN is basically divided into three parts:
   a) A return of income for the fiscal year just ending.
   b) A return of certain payments known as ANNUAL CHARGES for the fiscal year just ending. An annual charge is an annual legal obligation to pay money on which the taxpayer may or may not get tax relief. He may also have to deduct and pay to the Inland Revenue basic rate tax (known as deduction at source).
   c) A claim for personal allowances for the fiscal year about to begin.
2. Having received the completed return (together with any supporting documents such as accounts from the self-employed) the Inspector examines it and calculates the taxable income and the amount payable on an assessment.
3. If the Inspector does not receive the return or has reason to doubt its validity he can estimate the assessable income and issue the assessment accordingly. If he has reason to believe income may have been underassessed for a previous year he can issue an additional assessment.
4. The taxpayer can either accept the assessment and pay the tax on the appropriate day or appeal against it within thirty days of its issue. Late appeals are rarely accepted.

If he does appeal, the Inspector has a duty to try and informally settle the outstanding points with the taxpayer or his professional representative. If he cannot, the matter is placed before an independent tribunal known as the COMMISSIONERS for determination (see appendix 1 for a detailed description). Either side can appeal on a point of law to the High Court and thence to the Court of Appeal and House of Lords.

Payment of income tax

When the liability is finally agreed the tax can be paid in one of several ways:

1. Tax can be deducted at source by the payer, in whole or in part:
   a) PAYE should, in theory, deduct the whole of the correct amount of tax from wages and salaries under Schedule E.
   b) Basic rate tax only can be deducted at source. Examples are company dividends (Sch.F), certain government stock and local authority loan

interest (Sch.C), payments to unregistered subcontractors in the building industry (Sch.D, Case I), and income from trusts and settlements.

c) Certain income is deemed to have already borne basic rate tax (such as building society interest). The difference between "deemed" tax and an actual basic rate deduction is that whilst both types of credit can offset tax payable a surplus of "deemed" credit can never be repaid, whereas a surplus of "actual" credit can.

As from 6th April, 1985 this system of "deemed" tax (officially known as the "composite rate") has been extended to bank interest with certain exceptions:

i) Interest paid to companies, charities, pension funds, etc.
ii) Interest paid to individuals not resident in the UK.
iii) Interest on certain certificates of deposit and time deposits of not less than £50,000 and a term of not less than 28 days.
iv) Interest on National Savings.

From 6th April, 1986 the scheme has also extended to:

i) Certain interest paid by local authorities.
ii) Interest on deposits held in foreign currency.

N.B. The composite rate scheme is to be abolished from 6th April, 1991 (see later).

2. Tax payable direct is due on the 1st January in the year of assessment, or 1st July or 1st December following the year of assessment. The detailed division is:

a) On trading profits (Sch.D, Cases I and II) two equal instalments 1st January and 1st July.
b) On other income not subject to deduction at source (bank interest Sch.D, Case III, overseas income Sch.D, Cases IV & V, miscellaneous sources, Sch.D, Case VI and woodlands Sch.B) on 1st January.
c) Higher rates on income subject to deduction at source (government interest Sch.C, company dividends, Sch.F, building society and trust income) on 1st December.

If an assessment is not raised within thirty days of the above dates the tax is due thirty days after the issue of the assessment. When an original estimated assessment is increased on settlement of the appeal, interest is charged on all the tax due (including the increase) from the original date interest is charged (the so-called "reckonable date").

Interest is charged on overdue tax. The interest payment can be postponed for up to a maximum of six months by appealing against the whole or part of the tax payable. This postponement cannot apply to the second part of tax on business profits (1st July instalment). The rate changes from time to time.

When a repayment of over £25 is made more than twelve months after the end of the year of assessment to which it relates interest is paid by the Inland Revenue from the end of the relevant year of assessment to the date of repayment. Again, the rate is amended from time to time.

There follows an example of the calculation of assessable income and tax payable. Before attempting it, readers would be well advised to read appendices 3 and 4.

Assessment: a worked example

George and Jean Winterbottom give the following details on income tax returns:

Income tax returns for	**1990–91**	**1991–92**
Returning income for	Year ended 5/4/90	Year ended 5/4/91
Business profits (George as retail butcher). Accounting date 30th September.	y/e 30/9/89 25,000	y/e 30/9/90 10,642
Capital allowances claimed	644	597
Salary (Jean as a teacher)	2,940	6,900
(Tax deducted under PAYE)	(300)	(500)
Dividends received (George)	5,610	5,717
National Savings Bank interest (deposit A/c) – Jean	225	209
Building society interest (Jean)	291	298
Allowable bank interest paid (gross amount) (paid jointly)	470	370
Covenant paid to charity (gross amount) (paid by George)	150	150

An income tax return for 1990/91 would be sent to the taxpayer about April, 1990. The tax return requires:

1. A return of income for the tax year just ending, i.e. the 1990/91 return asks for details of income received for the year ended 5th April, 1990.
2. A return of annual charges paid in the tax year just ended, i.e. 1990/91 return requires details of annual charges paid in year ended 5th April, 1990.
3. A claim for personal allowances for the tax year about to begin, i.e. the 1990/91 return requires claims for personal allowances for year ended 5th April, 1991.
4. The return may also require details of capital assets acquired and disposed of in the year just ended.

The important point for the example of George and Jean Winterbottom is the return of income for the PREVIOUS year. Thus, to calculate the income for 1990/91 we need details from the 1990/91 return if the basis period is preceding year (year ended 5th April, 1990) and details from the 1991–92 return if the basis year is current year (year ended 5th April, 1991).

Calculation

The tax assessment for 1990–91 based on this example would be as follows:

Husband				Wife		
Sch.D Case I			25,000	Sch.E		6,900
Capital allowances			(644)	*BSI	298	
			24,356	298 × ⅓ ($^{25}/_{75}$)=	99	397
*Sch.F		5,717				
5,717 × ⅓ ($^{25}/_{75}$)=		1,905	7,622	Sch.D, Case III		225
			31,978			7,522
Bank interest 370 × ½ =		185		Bank interest 370 × ½ =		(185)
Covenant		150	(335)			
			31,643			7,337
SPA	3,005			SPA		(3,005)
MCA	1,720		(4,725)			
			26,918			4,332
20,700 × 25% =			5,175.00	4,332 × 25% =		1,083.00
6,218 × 40% =			2,487.20			
26,918			7,662.20			
Tax deducted from covenant (150 × 25%)=			37.50			
Tax payable December, 1991/January/July, 1992			7,699.70			

Notes on calculation

1. This two column layout separates the income of husband and wife, who are assessed as two separate individuals.

2. The four stages illustrated below should be followed in strict order to achieve the correct result:

Stage I Calculate the gross income, but deduct at this stage various allowances from trading income (Sch.D, Cases I & II) and salaries (Sch.E).
The main ones, (all of which are explained in detail later) are:

a) From trading income:
   i) capital allowances;
   ii) retirement annuity relief.

b) From salaries and wages:
   i) superannuation contributions of the employee.
   ii) necessary expenses of doing the job incurred by the employee.

Stage II Deduct the annual charges, if allowable.

Stage III Deduct the personal allowances.

Stage IV Calculate the tax payable, allowing for the various credits.

While this is not the only possible layout, students are recommended to follow it and it is used throughout this book.

3. Dividends and building society interest received are less tax deducted at source. As it is *gross* income which is assessable to tax, the tax has to be added to the net amount received. The fraction used of ⅓ (applied to the net figure) calculates the tax deducted at 25% of the gross.

4. Covenants paid to charity are an allowable deduction, with no limit. However, up to 5th April, 1986 the amount deductible was limited in amount – for example, for 1985/86 it was £10,000. However, the tax deducted at source from such payments has to be accounted for to the Inland Revenue.

Income surcharge

Up to 5th April, 1984 in addition to basic and higher rates of tax, unearned or investment income was subjected to a surcharge. It was payable on net investment income after the deduction of certain annual charges (not all annual charges were allowable for this purpose – See Chapter 3 on annual charges), but before the deduction of personal reliefs.

The investment surcharge has been abolished since 6th April, 1984, except for the income of discretionary trusts. For 1990/91 it is at a rate of 10%.

Appendix 1 – Inspectors and Commissioners

Inspectors

Inspectors of Taxes have the following duties:

1. To issue tax returns.
2. To receive completed returns.
3. To issue assessments.
4. To receive appeals.
5. To present the Revenue's case at appeal meetings.
6. To make repayments of tax.

Appeals

When a taxpayer appeals and cannot agree the matter informally with the Inspector, the matter has to be decided by the Appeal Commissioners, an independent tribunal body.

There are two bodies of Commissioners, the Generals and the Specials. The Generals are organised in local Divisions and consist of unpaid local businessmen who are not tax experts.

The Specials are fulltime, paid civil servants who are acknowledged tax experts. The taxpayer can appeal to the Specials as an alternative to the Generals, but certain appeals on specialised topics must go to the Specials.

The decision of the Commissioners on a point of fact is final, but either side can appeal to the High Court on a question of law.

Appendix 2 – Definition of Residence, Ordinary Residence and Domicile

RESIDENCE is a question of fact, and is simply the country in which you happen to be living even though only temporarily. It applies for one tax year at a time, and the Inland Revenue have issued guidelines on residence:

1. A visitor is ''resident'' in the UK in any tax year in which he is in the UK for more than 182 days.
2. If habitual visits are made to the UK (on average three months or more per year over a period of four years) the visitor will be regarded as resident in the UK.

ORDINARY RESIDENCE introduces an element of regularity into residence and is the country in which the taxpayer normally resides.

DOMICILE is the country which the taxpayer regards as his home. ''Domicile of origin'' is acquired at birth and remains with the person until he so alters his lifestyle to acquire another domicile of choice.

Appendix 3 – Schedules and Cases

Schedule and Case	Types of income	Deductions allowed	Basis period
Schedule A	Rents from property premiums on short leases.	Costs of maintenance Capital allowances.	Current year. Assessable.
Schedule B	Commercial woodlands.	Abolished from 6th April 1988	
Schedule C	Interest from certain Government and local authority loans. Interest from the National Savings Bank.	None	Current year. Deduction at source.
Schedule D Cases I & II	Profits of trade, professions and vocations.	Allowable business expenses. Capital allowances. Retirement annuity relief.	Preceding year based on accounting date. Assessable.
Case III	Some bank interest. Interest on government securities paid gross. Small maintenance payments.	None.	Preceding year. Assessable.

Cases IV & V	Foreign income.	Depends on the type of income.	Preceding year. Assessable.
Case VI	Miscellaneous profits.	Depends on the type of income.	Current year. Assessable.
Schedule E	Emoluments from employment.	Expenses necessarily incurred.	Current year. PAYE.
Schedule F	Company distributions.	None.	Current year. Deduction at source.
Building society & bank interest	–	None.	Current year. Taxed as composite rate (abolished from 6/4/91).
Trust income	Distributions by trustees.	None.	Current year.

Note that the first five cases of Sch.D (trading profits, bank interest and foreign income) are the only ones which use the preceding year basis period.

Appendix 4 – Personal Allowances and Rates of Tax for 1989–90 and 1990–91

Personal relief:		**1989–90**	**1990–91**
Single		2,785	3,005
Married man		4,375	–
Married couple		–	1,720
Monthly reduction in year of marriage		124.17	143.33
Wife's earned income		2,785	–
Age allowance:			
65–74	Single	3,400	3,670
	Married	5,385	–
	Married couple	–	2,145
75 and over	Single	3,540	3,820
	Married	5,565	–
	Married couple	–	2,185
Income limit for age allowance		11,400	12,300
Widow's bereavement		1,590	1,720
Additional personal		1,590	1,720
Blind persons		540	1,080

Rates of tax (1989–90 and 1990–91):

Up to £20,700	25%
Over £20,700	40%

Chapter Two

Personal Allowances

Introduction

Personal allowances are reliefs from taxation as slices of income according to an individual's status and responsibilities.

Up to 5th April, 1990 every single individual, male or female, received a **single person's allowance**. A married man living with his wife received a larger personal allowance known as the **marriage allowance**. A married woman living with her husband did not receive a separate personal allowance; her status as an individual for tax purposes disappeared on marriage. In effect, the whole of her income was taxed as if received by her husband, with a few specific exceptions. See the chapter on Husband and Wife (Chapter 4). One of these exceptions was that if a wife was in receipt of earned income, from employment or self-employment, she qualified for a special alolowance known as **wife's earned income allowance**. This was equivalent in amount to the single person's allowance, but could only be utilised against earned income of a working wife. If the earned income was less in amount than the wife's earned income, the balance of the allowance could not be offset against investment income of her own, or against any income of the husband.

The system was changed as from 6th April, 1990, under what is called the **independent system of taxation**. Under this system, a wife is treated for tax purposes as a separate and single individual from her husband. See Chapter 4 for more details.

Personal allowance

Every individual, male or female, single or married, irrespective of age, who is resident in the United Kingdom in a tax year, receives a **personal allowance** (PA). This is an amount of income they can receive without having to pay tax on it. For 1990–91 the amount is £3,005 for single people.

Married couple's allowance

A **married couple's allowance** (MCA) is an additional relief granted to a married couple who are legally married at some time in the relevant tax year. It is not available to an unmarried couple who live together, even if they are common law man and wife. The amount of the allowance is £1,720 for 1990–91.

The allowance is granted to the husband initially, and only the unused balance can be transferred to the wife. In determining the amount of any unused MCA the deduction of MIRAS interest paid and business expansion scheme relief (BES) from the husband's income is ignored. The transfer of any surplus allowance is not given automatically by the Inland Revenue, it has to be claimed by making a written election to the relevant tax office within six years of the end of the relevant tax year. If in the tax year itself, a husband estimates his income will be insufficient to absorb all the MCA, he can write to the tax office and they will estimate his income and transfer under the PAYE system, if his wife is in employment, an estimated amount of the MCA to his wife.

Example
Bernard and Nellie Murgatroyd in 1990–91 have the following details:

Bernard – earnings	£ 3,500
Nellie – earnings	£10,000
Investment income	£2,000

They pay jointly mortgage interest of £1,000 gross (under MIRAS).
Calculation of tax liability for 1990–91:

Bernard			**Nellie**			
Earnings		3,500	Earnings		10,000	
–			Investment income		2,000	
					12,000	
MIRAS relief		(500)*			(500)×25%	
						= 125.00
		3,000			11,500	
PA	3,005		PA	3,005		
MCA	495*	(3,500)	MCA (1,720–495)=	1,225	(4,230)	
		Nil			7,270 ×25%	
						=1,817.50
Total tax due						1,942.50

* Note: MIRAS relief is ignored in deciding how much of the MCA is transferable to the wife.

It is not possible to allocate the MCA to the wife first, for tax planning purposes, for example.

In the year of marriage the MCA is restricted if the couple are married for less than 12 months in the particular tax year, that is they marry on or after 6th May (in fiscal years, months start on 6th April and run to 5th April, etc.). The restriction is one twelfth of the allowance for each complete tax month they are not married.

Example
A man and woman get married on 7th June, 1990. Their allowances for 1990–91 are:

She	– PA	3,005
He	– PA	3,005
MCA	– $1{,}720 \times \frac{10}{12}$ =	1,434
Total allowances		7,444

In the tax year the marriage takes place, a man cannot claim both the MCA and the additional personal allowance (APA) (equivalent in amount to MCA) given to single parent families (see later for a detailed explanation). However, a woman getting married can continue to claim the APA in the year the marriage takes place. The man can however make an election to claim APA instead of MCA in the year of marriage if it is to his advantage.

Example
Don Duckworth and Minnie Mousehold get married on 11th November, 1990. Donald has an earned income of £20,000 and Minnie an investment income of £6,000. Both are widowed and have charge of dependent children.
Tax liability for 1990–91 would be:

	Donald			**Minnie**		
Earned income			20,000	Investment income		6,000
PA		3,005		PA	3,005	
MCA $1{,}720 \times \frac{5}{12}$ =	717 OR			APA	1,720	(4,725)
But APA could be claimed instead.	1,720					
Therefore:						
APA		1,720	(4,725)			
			15,275			1,275

15,275×25%=3,818.75 1,275×25%=318.75

In later tax years (1991–92 onwards in the above example), neither the husband nor wife can claim APA in tax years whilst they remain married and live together. In the year of death of the husband the widow can claim APA (in full) in the year of widowhood (or year of separation if permanent) for the remainder of the year in which the death/separation takes place. The husband cannot claim APA in the year of death of his wife or year of separation. He continues to get full

MCA for the whole of the relevant tax year. See Chapter 4 (Husband and Wife) for further details.

Age allowance

For individuals aged 65 or over in a particular tax year the amount of personal allowance is increased. If they are aged 75 or over in the tax year the amount increases again. Husband and wife qualify for age allowance as separate individuals. Since the advent of personal taxation, qualification for age allowance depends on the age of husband and wife individually. The rate for each individual for 1990–91 is £3,670 for the year, and £3,820 if aged 75 or over.

For married couples the MCA is also increased if *either* spouse is aged 65 or over or 75 or over in a particular tax year. The rates for 1990–91 are:

65 or over	£2,145
75 or over	£2,185

Example
Joe Blundell is aged 60 in 1990–91. Jean, his wife, is aged 65 on 5th April, 1990. They have income as follows:

Joe, earned income	7,000
Jean, earned income	5,000
investment income	1,500

Tax liability:

Earned		7,000	Earned	5,000
PA	3,005		Investment	1,500
MCA (AA)*	2,145	(5,150)		6,500
		1,850 ×25%	PA (AA)	(3,670)
		=462.50		2,830 ×25%
				=707.50

* Note: Joe is not 65 in the tax year, and therefore does not qualify for AA. Jean, however, is 65 at the end of the tax year (on 5th April, 1990), and therefore qualifies for AA individually. Because Jean is also 65 in the tax year they qualify for MCA at the higher rate, given initially of course to Joe.

In the year of marriage the MCA (AA) is restricted in the same way as the ordinary MCA.

Restriction of age allowance by level of total income

If an individual's income exceeds a certain level, the amount of AA can be restricted by half the excess income, but not below the ordinary level of PA.

In the case of a married couple, the MCA is only restricted by the level of the husband's income (but not below the ordinary level of MCA). The husband's PA is restricted first, and if it is restricted to its ordinary level, any surplus excess income over the limit then restricts the MCA next.

The income level for 1990–91 is £12,300.

Example

Bert and Ethel Nicholas are both aged 67 in 1990–91. They have the following income for 1990–91:

Bert	– earned income	10,620
	investment income	3,300
Ethel	– earned income	10,500
	investment income	1,000

They pay joint mortgage interest of £400 paid gross, not under MIRAS. Tax liability for 1990–91:

				Bert		Ethel
		Earnings		10,620	Earnings	10,500
		Investment		3,300	Investment	1,000
				13,920		11,500
		Mortgage interest		(200)	Mortgage interest	(200)
				13,720		11,300
PA (AA)		3,670			PA (AA)	(3,670)
Income	13,720					
Limit	(12,300)					7,630
	1,420 × ½					
	=710					
But limited to	665	(665)	3,005			
Excess limitation (set against MCA)	45					
MCA		2,145				
Excess limitation		(45)	2,100	(5,105)		
				8,615		

8,615×25%=2,153.75 7,630×25%=1,907.50

Notes:

1. If Ethel's total income exceeded the limit it could only restrict her personal SPA, not the MCA.

2. By making an election to allocate the whole of the mortgage interest to Bert, the restriction on Bert's income could have been reduced by £100 (200 × ½).

Additional personal allowance (APA)

The relief benefits mainly single parent families by giving them the same total of allowances as a married man. Those who can claim are:

1. Anybody other than a married man who has a qualifying child living with them for the whole or part of the year.
2. A married man whose wife is totally incapacitated.

A "qualifying child" is either:

1. A child under 16 at the beginning of the tax year (or if over 16 and in full time education) who is the claimant's own, adopted stepchild, an illegitimate child (for a man who has married the mother).
2. Any other child aged under 18 at the beginning of the tax year who is maintained by the claimant for the whole or part of the tax year.

If two or more people claim for the same child the allowance is apportioned between them as they agree or in proportion to the time the child is resident with each of them in the tax year.

Dependent relative relief

This relief was abolished from 6th April, 1988.

Widower's housekeeper allowance

This relief was abolished from 6th April, 1988.

Son's or daughter's services

This relief was abolished from 6th April, 1988.

Blind person's relief

A registered blind person can claim £1,080 allowance and a married couple where both partners are blind £2,160. The allowance was doubled from its 1989/90 figure.

Widow's bereavement allowance

In the tax year a married man dies and the following tax year, his widow is entitled to an additional allowance equivalent to the difference between the married and single allowance. The allowance is given in addition to her full single person's allowance and additional personal allowance (if she has a dependent child). The rate for 1990/91 is £1,720.

Example

A man died on 17th August, 1990, having earned £9,600 from 6th April, 1990. His widow receives total pensions of £6,800 from 17th August, 1990 until 5th April, 1991.

Husband

Sch.E		9,600		
SPA	3,005			
MCA	1,720	(4,725)		
		4,875	×25% =	1,218.75

Widow

Sch.E		6,800		
SPA	3,005			
WBA	1,720	(4,725)		
		2,075	×25% =	518.75

The widow would also receive the widow's bereavement allowance in 1991/92.

Life assurance relief

Tax relief is given on premiums paid by UK resident holders of qualifying life assurance policies made on or before 13th March, 1984. The relief is not given on policies taken out on or after 14th March, 1984.

The relief is given by way of reduction of the premiums paid to the insurer who then recovers the tax from the Inland Revenue. Relief can only be had up to a maximum in any one year of £1,500 or one sixth of total income whichever is the greater.

When the terms of qualifying policy are varied after 13th March, 1984 so as either to increase the benefits or extend the term, the insurance is treated as made after 13th March, 1984 and the premiums will cease to qualify for relief.

The rate of relief was 15% of qualifying premiums up to 5th April, 1989, but 12.5% from 6th April, 1989.

Residence and allowances

To qualify for a personal allowance an individual has to be resident for tax purposes in the relevant fiscal year.

Personal allowance can also be claimed by other categories if they are not resident in the relevant fiscal year. They are:

1. UK and Irish citizens.
2. Residents of the Channel Islands and the Isle of Man.
3. Individuals (or their widows) who are or have been in the service of the Crown.
4. Citizens of certain countries under double taxation agreements.

Up to 5th April, 1990 those individuals who were non-resident and qualified for personal allowance only obtained the benefit of a proportion of personal allowance, roughly approximating to their UK taxable income in the proportion to their total income worldwide. This apportionment was abolished from 6th April, 1990.

Chapter Three

Annual Payments and Interest

Introduction

Annual charges, a contract under which one person pledges to pay an annual sum of money to another person, plus interest, sometimes reduce for tax purposes the payer's income and increase the recipient's.

Example
Berman has an income of £32,000 and pays mortgage interest of £2,000 on a mortgage of £20,000. He is married.

Gross income		32,000		
Mortgage interest		(2,000)	Tax deducted	500.00
		30,000		
SPA	3,005			
MCA	1,720	(4,725)		
		25,275		
20,700×25%			=	5,175.00
4,575×40%			=	1,830.00
Total tax payable				7,505.00

Having deducted £500.00 tax under the so-called MIRAS (mortgage interest relief at source) Berman will only pay £1,500.00 to the building society. Such payments are sometimes paid with basic rate tax deducted at source, and sometimes not.

Annual charges

Only two types of payment now unreservedly attract tax relief:

1. Covenants to charity.

2. Payments made in connection with a business such as copyright royalties, patent royalties, and covenants paid in connection with the purchase of a business.

3. Covenants to individuals taken out before 15th March, 1988 and not connected with divorce or separation, e.g. student covenants. However, these do not attract tax relief to the payer but the recipient can claim basic rate tax repayment if his income is not taxable or not wholly taxable. The payer deducts basic rate income tax and only pays over the net amount.

Example

David, the father, has an income of £32,000, is married, and pays his son, Jonathan, a student, a covenant of £2,000 (gross) a year. The covenant was enacted before 15th March, 1988.

Gross income		32,000		
Covenant		(2,000)	Tax deducted	500.00
		30,000		
SPA	3,005			
MCA	1,720	(4,725)		
		25,275		
20,700×25%			=	5,175.00
4,575×40%			=	1,830.00
25,275				
2,000 (covenant)×15% (40%−25% already paid)			=	300.00
Total tax				7,805.00

Jonathan receives £1,500.00 (net) from the covenant and can also reclaim the £500.00 tax from the Inland Revenue if he is not otherwise liable to tax.

Covenants to individuals taken out after 14th March, 1988 do not attract tax relief.

Gift aid

From 1st October, 1990, there is relief on gifts of cash to charities by individuals that are not made by way of covenant.

The relief is due on gifts of amounts between £600 and £5 million. The gift is made net of basic rate income tax, and the donor qualifies for higher rate relief if appropriate. The charity, as with a covenant, can claim repayment of the basic rate tax deducted.

Maintenance

Maintenance payments in connection with divorce or separation used to attract full tax relief, but major changes were made in March 1988, depending on whether:

1. The order was made before 15th March, 1988 or applied for before 16th March, 1988 and granted before the end of June 1988, and:
2. Those applied for and granted after 16th March, 1988.

Orders made before 15th March, 1988: Tax relief is granted to the payer on the full payments and the recipient is exempt from tax on the first £1,720 (equivalent to MCA for 1990/91). This covers *both* payments to an ex-spouse and to dependent children of the marriage. From 6th April, 1989 all payments are made gross. Before then, certain larger payments had basic rate tax deducted at source (i.e. by the payer).

Example
David pays his ex-wife Dorothy £3,000 a year maintenance. He has an income of £28,000 in 1990–91. Dorothy has an independent income of £5,000. The court order was made before March, 1988.

Gross income	28,000		
Maintenance	(3,000)		
	25,000		
SPA	(3,005)		
	21,995		
20,700×25%		=	5,175.00
1,295×40%		=	518.00
21,995			
Total tax paid			5,693.00

Dorothy:				
Maintenance	3,000			
Exempt from tax	(1,720)	1,280		
Other income		5,000		
		6,280		
SPA		(3,005)		
		3,275 ×25%	=	818.75

1. The payer gets the same tax relief (but no more) as before the change.
2. All payments are made gross, from 6th April, 1989.

3. The recipient is taxed on the same amount (no more) as in 1988/89, but also gets the equivalent of the married couple's allowance free of tax (£1,720 for 1990–91).

Orders made on or after 16th March, 1988: The payer only gets tax relief equivalent to the married couple's allowance (£1,720 for 1990/91). The payments are made gross, without deduction of tax, and the recipient is exempt from tax on all the maintenance.

Example

Jeffrey and Joan are divorced in July 1990. The maintenance order is made in August 1990. Jeffrey has an income of £28,000 and pays £250 a month to Joan from 1st August, 1990.

Joan gets a job and earns £6,000 from 1st August, 1990 to 5th April, 1991.

Jeffrey:

Gross income			28,000
Relief on maintenance			(1,720)
			26,280
SPA	3,005		
MCA	1,720*		(4,725)
			21,555
	20,700×25%	=	5,175.00
	855×40%	=	342.00
			5,517.00

*Jeffrey qualifies for full MCA up to 5th April, 1991.

Joan:

Earnings			6,000
Maintenance (taxable)			Nil
			6,000
SPA			(3,005)
			2,995
	2,995×25%	=	748.75

Interest

Persons (excluding companies) must pay annual interest (on borrowed money) gross, that is, without deducting basic rate tax unless:

1. It is paid under the MIRAS (mortgage interest relief at source) scheme, on a mortgage to buy a house, or:
2. It is paid to someone not resident in the UK.

Whether the interest payments are allowable as a deduction against taxable income depends on how the money was spent. However, interest on overdrafts is never allowable unless it is a business overdraft and the interest is then a business expense.

Allowable interest

The following types of interest attract tax relief:

1. Interest which is a business expense and therefore allowed in the accounts. If the business ceases any interest on outstanding loans is no longer allowable.
2. Interest on a loan to purchase shares in a close company (unquoted companies) or to lend as working capital to such a company, provided the borrower has over 5% of the ordinary shares. A full-time employee can have an interest of less than 5%.
3. Interest on a loan to acquire shares of an employee-controlled company, provided certain conditions are satisfied. Such a company is one in which more than 50% of both issued ordinary share capital and voting power are owned by full-time employees.
4. Interest paid by active partners on borrowing to buy a share in a partnership or to buy machinery and plant to be used in the business.
5. Interest on a loan to pay inheritance tax.
6. Interest on a loan to purchase land and buildings, caravan or houseboat used as:

a) The borrower's only or main resident at the time the interest is paid or is paid within 12 months of the property being used as a residence.
b) The only or main residence of a dependent relative or spouse, but not if the loan was first taken out from 6th April, 1988 onwards.
c) Interest to be used, in due course, as the borrower's only or main residence if he is occupying "job-related" accommodation, which is accommodation required to be occupied by an employee as an essential element of his job, under an arm's length contract of service.

The accommodation must not be provided by a company in which the borrower and spouse have a "material interest" (over 50%) or by a business partner. The occupier can be employed or self-employed.

Note that the relief is only given on loans to purchase property, not to improve it. The interest on loans to improve property do still qualify if they were first taken out before 6th April, 1988.

The limit of relief is the interest on the first £30,000 of borrowing on loans taken out before 1st August, 1988. The £30,000 was per individual, provided they were not married. Thus, an unmarried couple living together could have relief on the interest on £60,000 of borrowing. For new loans taken out from 1st August, 1988 the restriction is £30,000 per dwelling.

The interest on most such borrowing is paid under MIRAS under which the interest is paid net of basic rate tax if the borrowing is £30,000 or less. However, if the borrowing is in excess of that figure interest on the £30,000 may be under MIRAS, the rest paid gross and tax relief given in a tax assessment.

Example

Mr. and Mrs. Home have borrowed £50,000 to buy their family house. Interest is paid at 10% (gross). He has an earned income of £29,000 and she an earned income of £7,000. They have made an election for the husband to receive the entire tax relief on the mortgage interest.

Sch.E		29,000	Sch.E	7,000
Mortgage interest limited to 30,000×10% =		(3,000)		
		26,000		
SPA	3,005			
MCA	1,720	(4,725)	SPA	(3,005)
		21,275		3,995

3,995×25% =	998.75
20,700×25% =	5,175.00
575×40% =	230.00
Total tax on income	5,405.00

If paid under MIRAS they will pay:

Interest on	30,000×10% =	3,000.00	
Tax relief	3,000×25% =	(750.00)	2,250.00
Interest on	20,000×10% =		2,000.00
			4,250.00

The total tax would be

Total as before	5,405.00
Tax relief on 3,000×25%	750.00
Total tax payable	6,155.00

Otherwise, tax relief would be obtained twice at the basic rate (i.e. deduction of gross income from taxable income, and only paying £2,250 net interest, not £3,000 to the building society/bank).

7. Interest on a loan to purchase other land and buildings provided the property is available for commercial letting throughout any continuous period of 52 weeks and is actually let for either 26 weeks or more, or is available for letting throughout

the period. Interest on borrowing to buy let property can only be offset against rents received, not against other income.

8. Home remortgage schemes are eligible for relief in respect of interest on a loan, provided at least 90% of it is used to buy a single joint life annuity, if the annuitants are aged 65 or more.

Private medical insurance

From 6th April, 1990 (1990/91 onwards) tax relief is given to individuals paying private medical insurance for those aged 60 and over. The relief is due when premiums are paid either by the insured or by another individual on their behalf.

Relief is due at the payer's marginal rate of tax, with basic rate relief being given by deduction at source. Higher rate tax relief will be given in a tax assessment.

Benefits and treatments permitted under eligible medical insurance contracts cover the full range of hospital treatments available under the NHS, as well as operations and treatments by general practitioners.

Chapter Four

Husband and Wife

General

Up to 5th April, 1990 a husband and wife were taxed on the general principle of being one unit. Their income was added together and taxed basically as one, with the husband being legally responsible for completing a married couple's tax return and paying any tax due.

Only one personal allowance was given, the marriage allowance to the husband, equivalent in amount to the single person's allowance plus the married couple's allowance. However, if the wife had earned income from self employment, a job as an employee, or a pension earned in her own right, then she could claim a wife's earned income allowance which could only be set against her earned income, not against investment income. No unused balance could be transferred to the husband. The net taxable income was then subject to tax at one set of basic rates, the balance of income being liable at the higher rate.

Over the years the harsh effects of this system on the taxation of married women was gradually softened by the introduction of reliefs towards women. The more important ones were:

1. Separate assessment, a claim that could be made by either spouse and made a wife legally responsible for completing her own tax return and paying her own tax.
2. Separate taxation of wife's earnings, a claim that could be made jointly by a married couple. If they did, then a wife was treated as a separate single person for tax, receiving her own single person's allowance, and her own basic rate band of tax. The bad news was:
   (a) it did not apply to the wife's investment income, and
   (b) the husband lost the marriage allowance, he only received the single person's allowance.

Thus the loss of marriage relief had to be set against the gains of the wife, and the claim was only worth making by couples on a large, combined earned income.

This of course was all swept away from 6th April, 1990 and replaced by the independent system of taxation, under which a married woman is treated as a separate person from her husband for the purposes of income tax.

Under the independent taxation system:

1. A wife is responsible for completing her own tax return and paying her own tax liabilities.
2. Her income, both earned and investment, is taxed quite separately from her husband. For the treatment of investment income from jointly held properties, see later.
3. Payments such as annual charges and interest which are paid by the wife and qualify for tax relief are dealt with separately from her husband. For amounts paid jointly (e.g. interest on a joint mortgage) see later.
4. She gets a single person's allowance separate from her husband but no unused balance of that allowance can be transferred to her husband.
5. The husband also gets a single person's allowance. The couple also qualify for a married couple's allowance, which must be given to the husband first, and only any unused balance can be transferred to the wife. See Chapter 2 on Personal Allowances for further details.

Transitional relief

Because a husband who cannot utilise the whole of his single person's allowance against taxable income for 1990–91 onwards under independent taxation, cannot transfer it to his wife, he may be worse off than under the old system, when automatically all the husband's allowances were offset against the combined income of husband and wife.

Therefore, to ensure that no married couple are worse off under independent taxation, transitional relief may be due. Under this, additional transitional personal relief may be due to a couple in 1990–91 and future tax years, to ensure they get at least the same total of personal allowances in those years as they did in 1989–90, but also to ensure they do not get any extra relief from transitional relief over the total level of allowances for 1989–90. In other words, transitional relief freezes the level of allowances in 1990–91 onwards to a minimum of the total granted in 1989–90.

Example

A man and wife have the following income in 1989–90, the man £2,000 and the wife £15,000.

The 1989–90 assessment would be:

Husband		2,000
Wife		15,000
		17,000
MA	4,375	
WEIA	2,785	(7,160)
		9,840 ×25%
		= 2,460.00

In 1990–91 the husband could not use the whole of his single person's allowance, but could not transfer the balance to his wife, he could only transfer the married couple's allowance. Therefore the couple would only get, without any transitional relief:

Husband	– SPA	2,000	(if income level same as for 1989–90)
Wife	– SPA	3,005	
	MCA	1,720	
		6,725	

Therefore, the shortfall of allowances compared with 1989–90 would be 7,160 − 6,725 = 435. Therefore transitional relief would be given to the wife of £435 in 1990–91.

Assuming income levels remained the same as in 1989–90 the assessment for 1990–91 would be:

Husband		**Wife**		
Income	2,000	Income		15,000
SPA	(2,000)	SPA	3,005	
		MCA	1,720	
	Nil			
		Transitional relief	435	(5,160)
				9,840 ×25%
				= 2,460.00

Therefore, transitional relief may also be due in other circumstances, notably for older couples, when the wife is 65 or over, and the husband under 65. Under the old system the husband would qualify for the marriage allowance at the higher rate in 1989–90; £5,385 instead of £4,375. However, in 1990–91 he would only get the married couple's allowance at the higher rate £2,145 instead of £1,720, but not the single person's allowance, only getting £3,005 not the higher rate of £3,670. Again they should be no better off as a couple under the new system than under the old system.

Example

1989–90 allowances		**1990–91 allowances**	
MA	5,385	SPA (husband – ordinary rate)	3,005
WEIA (if applicable)	2,785	MCA (higher rate)	2,145
		SPA (wife – higher rate)	3,670
	8,170		
			8,820

However, if allowances had been at the same level in 1990–91 as 1989–90, the couple would only have got:

SPA (husband)	2,785	(lower rate)
MCA	1,935	(5,385–3,400) (higher rate)
SPA (wife)	3,400	(higher rate)
	8,170	

Instead of:

SPA (husband)	3,400	all higher rate
MCA	1,985	all higher rate
SPA (wife)	3,400	all higher rate
	8,785	

Thus, transitional relief will be due in 1990–91 of 8,785–8,170=£615.

Jointly held property

When income-producing property is jointly owned between husband and wife the income will be assumed to be received equally, unless:

1. the property, as well as the income, is actually owned in a different ratio than half each, and
2. an appropriate declaration is made to the effect that income is owned other than half each and ownership of the underlying property is in the same proportion as the income. The Inspector of Taxes must be informed of the declaration within 60 days of making the declaration. Once made, a declaration is irrevocable for that tax year, and will continue to operate for future tax years until another declaration is made. Declarations cannot be backdated.
3. gifts of income only without an equivalent gift of capital are ineffective for tax purposes, with the exception of earned income, e.g. partnerships, pension rights. Thus, gifts of annuities and covenants betweeen husband and wife are ineffective for tax purposes.

Example

Jonah and Janice Jones have rents from a jointly owned block of flats, amounting to £4,000 in 1990–91. Janice has no other income, but Jonah has an earned income of £24,000.

Without any transfer of income, tax liability for 1990–91 would be:

Jonah				
Earned income			24,000	
Sch.A (rents)		4,000 × ½ =	2,000	
			26,000	
PA	3,005			
MCA	1,720		(4,725)	
			21,275	
		20,700 × 25% = 5,175.00		
		575 × 40% = 230.00		5,405.00
Janice				
Sch.A (rents)		4,000 × ½ =	2,000	
PA			(2,000)	
			Nil	Nil
Total liability				5,405.00

By physically transferring (say) an amount of income to Janice, and of course giving her the appropriate share of ownership of the flats, making a declaration, and then informing the Inspector within 60 days of the declaration, there may be a tax saving. By gifting Janice (say) 95% of the flats, Jonah retaining a 5% interest then:

Jonah				
Earned income			24,000	
Sch.A		4,000 × 5% =	200	
			24,200	
PA	3,005			
MCA	1,720		(4,725)	
			19,475	
		19,475 × 25% =		4,868.75
Janice				
Sch.A		4,000 × 95% =	3,800	
PA			(3,005)	
			795	
		795 × 25% =		198.75
Total liability				5,067.50

There could therefore be a tax saving of	5,405.00
	5,067.50
Tax saving	337.50

Allocation of mortgage interest between spouses

With tax relief given to a married couple on mortgage interest paid on their family home, and if the house and mortgage are in joint names, then normally the tax relief on interest paid would be allocated equally between them. If the house and mortgage were in one spouse's name only, the relief would be given wholly to that spouse.

However, provided the couple are living together as man and wife, they can divide the interest tax relief between them in any proportion they wish. They can do this by making a written election to the Inland Revenue (on form 15(1990)), which must be jointly signed and sent to the Inland Revenue within twelve months of the end of the relevant tax year. This is known as an 'allocation of interest'.

This could be used in tax planning to reduce the tax payable between them. Remember, however, that in allocating unused MCA from husband to wife interest paid under MIRAS is ignored.

Example

Ronald Rogan is disabled, and only has a taxable income of £3,500. Nancy Rogan earns a salary of £27,000. They have a house in joint names and a joint mortgage (paid under MIRAS) on which they paid £2,400 (gross) interest in 1990–91.

Without an allocation of interest election the tax position would be:

Ronald

Income		3,500
Interest relief	2,400 × ½ =	(1,200)
		2,300
PA		(2,300)
		Nil

BUT in allocating MCA to Nancy income is deemed to be

		3,500 (ignoring MIRAS)
PA	3,005	
MCA	495	(3,500)
		Nil

Therefore only MCA of (1,720 − 495) = 1,225 could be transferred to Nancy.

Nancy

Income		28,000	
Interest relief	2,400 × ½	= (1,200) × 25% =	300.00
		26,800	
PA	3,005		
Transferred MCA	1,225	(4,230)	20,700 × 25% = 5,175.00
Assessable		22,570	1,870 × 40% = 748.00
			6,223.00

If, however, they made an election to transfer all the mortgage interest to Nancy the tax liability would become:

Ronald

Income		3,500
PA	3,005	
MCA	495	(3,500)
		Nil

Nancy

Income		28,000	
Interest relief		(2,400) × 25 % =	600.00
		25,600	
PA	3,005		
Transferred MCA	1,225	(4,230)	20,700 × 25% = 5,175.00
Assessable		21,370	570 × 40% = 268.00
			6,443.00

Separation and divorce

In the tax year a marriage permanently breaks up because of separation or divorce, there are certain tax consequences. These generally take effect from the year of permanent separation; nothing new happens when the divorce is granted. When the husband and wife separate, from then on they are treated as two separate individuals for tax purposes, not that this makes much different under independent taxation. However:

1. Married couple's allowance is granted in full for the tax year of separation. There is no restriction as in the year of marriage. However, no married couple's allowance will be due for tax years they are not married at the start of the year.
2. If either parent has charge of dependent children after the separation, they can qualify for the additional personal allowance for the remainder of that tax year and following tax years.

Example

Alan and Di Vorce separate permanently on 30th June, 1990. She goes to live with her mother, taking with her young Euriah, the only child of the marriage.

For 1990–91 Alan earns £2,000 a month and is provided by his employer with a car, scale benefit being £2,200. Up to 30th June Di earned £700 a month, but from 1st July, she takes a part-time job to spend more time with Euriah and earns £400 a month. Alan agrees to pay maintenance of £100 a month from 1st August, 1990, confirmed by a court order.

They had a joint mortgage involving payment of £150 (gross) a month interest on a mortgage of less than £30,000. From 1st August Alan takes over responsibility for the mortgage.

Assessments for 1990–91:

Alan			Di	
Sch.E – salary 2,000×12 =		24,000	Sch.E – 700×3 =	2,100
Scale benefit		2,200	400×9 =	3,600
		26,200		5,700
Mortgage interest relief			Mortgage interest relief	
4×150 = 600×½ =	300			
8×150 =	1,200	(1,500)	4×150 = 600×½ =	(300)
		24,700		5,400
Relief on maintenance paid				
100×9 =		(900)		
		23,800		
SPA	3,005		SPA 3,005	
MCA	1,720*	(4,725)	APA 1,720*	(4,725)
		19,075		675
19,075×25% = 4,768.75			675×25% = 168.75	

* Note: The additional personal allowance is given in full in spite of Di being separated for only part of the year. The same principle applies to the married couple's allowance. It is granted in full, even though they are only married for part of the year.

Widowhood

When a husband dies part way through a tax year, the widow can qualify for an additional widow's bereavement allowance for the remainder of the tax year after her husband's death, and the following tax year, but not for any tax years after that. She may also qualify for additional personal allowance if she is left with dependent children.

Example
Brian Quinn was killed in a car crash on 31st August, 1990. Up to then he had earned £3,000 a month. Susan Quinn, his widow, has a job which paid £700 a month. After his death, from 1st September, she also receives £500 a month private pension and £2,600 state pension in 1990–91. She is left with their two children aged 10 and 7. Up to 31st August, 1990 they paid joint mortgage interest of £200 (gross) a month (mortgage less than £30,000), but it was fully paid up by insurance on Brian's death. No apportionment election was made on the mortgage interest.

Tax calculations 1990–91:

Brian		**Susan**	
Sch.E – 3,000×5 =	15,000	Sch.E – earnings 700×12 =	8,400
Mortgage interest		Private pension 500×7 =	3,500
200×5 = 1,000×½ =	(500)	State pension =	2,600
	14,500		14,500
SPA 3,005		Mortgage interest	
MCA 1,720	(4,725)	200×5=1000×½ =	(500)
	9,775		14,000
		SPA 3,005	
		WBA 1,720	
		APA 1,720	(6,445)
			7,555
9,775×25% = 2,443.75		7,555×25% = 1,888.75	

If a man is widowed, he does not qualify for widow's bereavement allowance on his wife's death. In the tax year of his wife's death, he cannot also qualify for additional personal allowance as well as marriage allowance, if he is left with young children. However, for following tax years, he would no longer qualify for the married couple's allowance, being a single man, but would get additional personal allowance if left with dependent children.

Chapter Five

Trades, Professions and Vocations

Introduction

The profits of the self-employed are assessed to tax under the rules of Sch.D, Cases I & II. The assessable profit for a fiscal year is that computed for the "basis period", and the tax is payable in two equal instalments on the 1st January in the year and 1st July following the fiscal year. The "basis period" is generally the trader's twelve month period of account ended in the previous fiscal year except on the commencement or cessation of trade or if the trader's accounting date is altered.

Example
A self-employed garage proprietor who has been in business for a number of years and has 30th September as his accounting date will, for 1990/91, be assessed to tax on the profit he makes in the period of account 1st October, 1988 to 30th September, 1989. The tax is payable in two equal instalments on 1st January, 1991 and 1st July, 1991.

"Trade" and profits of trading are not defined in the legislation. To find guidance in cases of doubt you have to turn to case law.

The following conclusions emerge:

1. A trade can include an isolated transaction, one purchase and one sale.

2. The deciding factor is motivation on purchase. If something is purchased with the specific intention of selling it at a profit then the profit is from trading. Profits from the sale of assets which were originally purchased for personal consumption for the pleasure of personal possession or aesthetic appeal, or because they yield an income from investment are capital and are not trading profits.

3. How to you recognise the profit motive? Guidance can be obtained by applying the so-called "badges of trade":

a) The nature of the asset e.g. the purchase of a large quantity of silver bullion.
b) The quantity purchased e.g. very large purchases of toilet paper (say 1 million rolls) would hardly be for personal use!
c) The number of transactions in a certain period of time. The faster the turnover, the more likely it is it will be interpreted as trading.

d) Expertise by the purchaser in dealing with that asset e.g. a builder who buys and sells building plots.
e) If the asset is made more attractive to a potential purchaser – is it repaired, renovated, improved, etc.
f) The method of disposal. If the asset is advertised for sale, it points towards trading.

Computation of the taxable profit

If we have a trade, the trader's accounting profit may not be the taxable profit. The statutes and case law lay down rules as to what income should be included as trading profit and what expenditure is deductible.

Income

Only trading income is relevant to Cases I & II. Any form of investment income or capital profit included in the accounts has to be eliminated, although in practice small amounts of bank interest and rents may be left in a trading profit. From 18th March, 1986, any trader in receipt of the enterprise allowance is taxable on it under Schedule D, Case VI, and it is therefore assessed on the current year basis and thus is only taxed once, and not included in the first twelve months trading profit and assessed two or three times (see later, regarding "commencing basis").

Expenditure

The rules on deductible expenditure can be summarised as anything is allowable if it is accepted accounting practice to treat such expenditure as revenue expenditure. Then in addition there are a small number of special disallowances or allowances on specific types for tax purposes.

Pre-trading expenditure incurred within five years prior to the commencement of trading can be treated:

1. For income tax as a trading loss incurred in the first year of trading.
2. For corporation tax as expenditure incurred in the first period of account.

For trades commenced from 1st April, 1989 the period is five years (previously 3 years).

Adjustment of the accounting profit

The accounting profit is unlikely to be the same as the taxable profit, not only because of the differing definitions of trading income, but also because of different rules of deductible expenditure.

For tax purposes only trading income is included in the Sch.D, Cases I & II computation although in practice small amounts of bank interest and rent may be retained in the taxable trading profit.

Tax law does not have a list of allowable expenditure. Instead, the courts have decided that anything is allowable under current accounting practice as revenue expenditure unless specifically prohibited by tax law.

Disallowed expenditure

The following categories of expenditure are disallowed:

1. Expenditure not wholly and exclusively for business purposes. This can be specifically applied to:

a) An expense incurred for a dual private and business reason, e.g. a business trip that was partly to attend a business conference and partly to take a holiday. The *whole* expense would be disallowed, there would be no apportionment. This is known as the concept of "duality".

b) When an annual item of expenditure can be divided between exclusive business use and exclusive private use, an apportionment is made e.g. expenditure on petrol can be divided between business journeys and private travel. Again, journeys with a dual motive are wholly disallowed. Similar apportionments occur with telephone bills, rates and rent of premises used partly as business premises and also as private living accommodation. Fuel bills can be similarly apportioned.

c) When stock is extracted from the business for the private use or consumption of the proprietor, family or friends, it has to be accounted for tax purposes at the retail selling price, not at anything less. The rule is tax has to be paid on the profit element of stock whether it is sold or consumed e.g. a grocer takes a tin of meat from his shelves for which he paid 30p wholesale, the retail selling price being 50p. If he credits sales by 30p, 20p has to be added to the taxable profit. If no record of the extraction is made 50p has to be added to the taxable profit.

2. Capital and ancillary expenditure is disallowed. This includes:

a) Purchases, disposals and improvements of capital assets, including the ancillary costs such as legal fees, valuation and advertising expenses. Only the legal costs of *renewing* a lease of fifty years or less in length are allowable. "Improvement" can include the replacement of or reconstruction of an "entirety", which can be defined as an asset which exists or is identifiable as itself e.g. a boilerhouse which is physically separate from the factory it heats.

b) Substantial and basic repairs to a secondhand asset bought in a defective state.

c) The costs of disposal of an asset are disallowed.

d) When a repair improves an asset, e.g. replacing a rotted single pane window frame with double glazing, the cost would in general be apportioned and only the cost of replacing a single pane window would be allowed – the "improvement element" would be disallowed.

3. Costs not directly incurred in running the business are not allowed. This is really a variant of the "wholly and exclusively" rule. This includes:

a) Fines and legal costs incurred in breaking the law – it is assumed the business must be run within the law even if it is an illegal business. Basically only legal costs of collecting trade debts or hiring and disposing of staff are allowable.

b) Donations to charity when there is no business advantage e.g. purchase of advertising. However, *covenants* to charity are allowable within certain limits (see the chapter on covenants and interest). Non-close companies can, from 1st April, 1986, claim "one-off" gifts, provided they do not exceed 3% of the ordinary dividends paid by the company. Basic rate tax has to be deducted from such payments.

c) Bad and doubtful debts are only allowable if they are *trade* debts specifically written off or a reasonable specific reserve is made. Write offs of capital debts, non-trade debts (e.g. a loan to an employee) and general bad debts reserves are not allowable.

Example

A bad debts account shows:

Written off:		Reserves brought forward:	
Trade debts	6,000	General reserve	10,000
Outstanding debt on sale of machinery	1,000	Specific reserves	8,400
Loan to employee	500	Carried to profit and loss account	10,100
Reserves carried forward:			
General reserve	12,000		
Specific reserves	9,000		
	28,500		28,500

Add back to the taxable profit:

Increase in general reserve (12,000 − 10,000)	2,000
Loan to employee written off	500
Debt on sale of machinery	1,000
	3,500

d) Expenditure connected with changes of ownership or financial structure of the business:

i) Cost of increasing or amending share capital.

ii) Compensation for loss of office paid to directors on a take-over bid or sell-out.

e) Expenditure concerned with determining the taxable profit of the company other than those of a routine nature e.g. the costs related to the conduct of a tax appeal.

4. Gifts to and entertainment of customers. No deduction can be claimed for:

a) Business entertainment

b) Gifts to customers of:

i) Food, drink or tobacco or vouchers for such items unless the donor deals with such items in his trade and they are offered free to the general public (e.g. an advertising promotion), therefore gifts of drink and hampers at Christmas are not allowed for example.

ii) Other gifts to customers do not qualify as an allowable deduction unless they contain an advertisement for the donor and the cost per gift (cost to the donor) does not exceed £10 per item for 1985/86 onwards (previously £2 per item).

5. Certain items of expenditure are specifically allowed as deductions:

a) From 1985/86 onwards, an individual may deduct half his Class 4 National Insurance contributions liability from his total income.

b) The cost of obtaining or renewing a patent.

c) Payments for technical education.

6. Normally income and expenditure is dealt with ignoring VAT (net of VAT). However, if VAT on expenditure cannot be claimed as input tax, for income tax and corporation tax, relief is granted on the gross expenditure, e.g. a business which is classified as 'exempt' for VAT purposes expends £115 (£100 plus VAT) for business purposes. The allowable deduction would be £115.

Penalties, interest and surcharges imposed under VAT regulations are not allowable expenses for income tax or corporation tax.

A summary of receipts and expenditure

Receipts

Add to taxable profit	Deduct from taxable profit
Retail profit on extractions of stock by proprietor and family (if charged out at wholesale price, or not charged at all). Voluntary contributions by customers (tips, etc.).	Investment income (bank interest, rents, dividends, etc.). Capital profit on sales of assets.

Expenditure

Add to taxable profit	Allowable expenditure
Preliminary expenses of setting up the trade.	Cost of stock.
Depreciation.	Wages and salaries (but not excessive payments to members of family).
Appropriations of profit by proprietor – salary, interest on capital.	Rent, rates, heat and light of business premises.
General bad debts reserves.	Business transport costs.
Loans to staff written off.	Advertising.
Legal costs of obtaining leases, renewing long leases.	Business telephone.
Tax appeals and contraventions of the law.	Accountancy costs of drawing up accounts.
Private expenditure on rent, rates, motoring, telephone.	Office expenses – paper, etc.
Entertainment of customers, whether resident in the UK or abroad (from 15th March 1988).	Maintenance and repair costs.
Gifts of food and drink and tobacco or other gifts that cost the donor over £10 per article to buy.	Staff defalcations.
	Legal costs of renewing a short lease and recovering trade debts.
	Removal costs.
	Trade debts written off and reasonable specific reserves.

50% of Class 4 national insurance contributions.

Donations to charity (as from 1st April, 1980), if connected with the trade, or paid by non-close companies (subject to limitations).

From 1st April, 1982, for a ten year period, contributions to approved local enterprise agencies.

As from April 1987 the costs to an employer of retraining in new skills employees who have been employed for a minimum of two years.

Example

Allen has been in business as a manufacturer of holiday souvenir novelties for many years. His trading and profit and loss accounts for a particular year show:

Opening stock	50,000		Sales	260,000
Purchases	140,000			
	190,000			
Less:				
Closing stock	70,000	120,000		
Wages		77,000		
Gross profit		63,000		
		260,000		260,000
Administration costs		4,000	Gross profit	63,000
Cost of premises (rent, rates, heat & light, etc.)		6,000	Rents received	1,000
Royalties payable (note 2)		1,000	Bank interest	50
Repairs & renewals (note 3)		6,700	Profit on sale of car	600
Transport costs (note 4)		3,300	Grants received (note 1)	400
Selling and distribution		2,900		
Entertaining (note 5)		1,000		
Loan interest (note 6)		1,500		
Subscriptions (note 7)		700		
Legal and other professional costs (note 8)		2,000		
Bad debts (note 9)		350		
General expenses (note 10)		1,500		
Depreciation		10,000		
Net profit		24,100		
		65,050		65,050

Notes:

1. Grants received from:

Under Industry Act, 1972	300
Contribution by supplier to advertising campaign	100
	400

2. Patent royalties actually paid

Patent royalties actually paid	700
Royalties accrued but not paid to end of accounting period	300
	1,000

3. Repairs and renewals:

Machinery repairs	4,000
Repairs to building	1,000
Cost of office extension	1,700
	6,700

4. Transport costs:

Lorries and vans	1,500
Salesman	1,500
Proprietor (agreed with Inland Revenue 30% is private)	300
	3,300

5. Entertaining costs:

UK customers	200
Overseas customers	500
Gift to customers of ballpoint pens costing £5.00 each	300
	1,000

6. Loan interest was payable to a finance company, but only 1,200 had actually been paid at the accounting date, the remaining 300 was accrued

7. These consist of:

Chamber of Commerce	100
Trade association	200
Local golf club	100
Local conservative association	300
	700

8. Legal and professional costs:

Collecting trade debts	500
Prosecution over contravention of industrial safety regulations	400
Renewal of factory lease (30 year lease) (short lease)	200
Breach of contract dispute	900
	2,000

9. Bad debts account:

Trade debts written off		800	Reserves brought forward:		
Non-trade debts written off		100	General	700	
			Specific	300	1,000
Loan to ex-employee written off		150			
Reserves to carry forward:			Trade debts previously written off, now recovered		800
General	600		Profit and loss account		350
Specific	500	1,100			
		2,150			2,150

10. General expenses:

Staff Christmas party	400
Gifts to retiring staff	100
Contributions to local charities	300
Other allowable expenses	700
	1,500

11. Capital allowances have been agreed with the Inland Revenue at 6,400.

The task is to compute the taxable trading profit for the accounting period.

Computation of taxable profit:

Profit per the accounts			24,100
Add:			
Depreciation		10,000	
General expenses		300	
Bad debts	100		
(see explanatory note in appendix)	150		
700 − 600 =	(100)	150	
Legal costs, etc.		400	
Subscriptions	100		
	300	400	
Entertaining		700	
Transport 300×30% =		90	
Repairs and renewals		1,700	
Royalties		1,000	14,740
			38,840

Deduct:		
Grants	300	
Rents	1,000	
Bank interest	50	
Profit on sale of car	600	(1,950)
		36,890
Capital allowances		(6,400)
		30,490
Annual charges:		
Royalties		(700)
		29,790

Basis periods

Normally the twelve month period of account ended in the previous fiscal year is the basis period. However, special rules are needed in commencement, cessation, or a permanent change of accounting date.

Commencement of trade

When a trader commences the "preceding year basis" cannot be used as there are no previous profits. Therefore:

1. In the first fiscal year the profits are those from the date trade commences to the following 5th April.
2. The profit for the second fiscal year is that of the first twelve months' trading.
3. The profit of the third fiscal year is generally again that of the first twelve months' trading unless by then there is a complete twelve months period of account ending in the second fiscal year.

If the taxpayer elects (within seven years of the end of the second year) the profit of the second and third years can be amended to the profits actually earned in those years (from April to April). Both years must be amended together, not just one.

The profits are apportioned arithmetically as necessary.

Example

A shopkeeper began to trade on 1st October, 1984 and drew up the following accounts:

	Tax adjusted profit
1/10/86 to 30/9/87	18,000
1/10/87 to 30/9/88	6,000
1/10/88 to 30/9/89	32,000

Original assessments

1986/87 (1/10/86 to 5/4/87)	18,000×6/12=	9,000	
1987/88 /1/10/86 to 30/9/87)			18,000
1988/89 (1/10/86 to 30/9/87)			18,000
Total of second and third years			36,000
1989/90 (1/10/87 to 30/9/88)		6,000	
1990/91 (1/10/88 to 30/9/89)		32,000	

Revised assessments if taxpayer so elects

1986/87		9,000	
1987/88 (6/4/87 to 5/4/88)	18,000×6/12=	9,000	
	6,000×6/12=	3,000	12,000
1988/89 (6/4/88 to 5/4/89)	6,000×6/12=	3,000	
	32,000×6/12=	16,000	19,000
Total of second and third years			31,000
1989/90		6,000	
1990/91		32,000	

In this case the taxpayer would be well advised to make the appropriate election. This could be represented pictorially:

Periods of account:

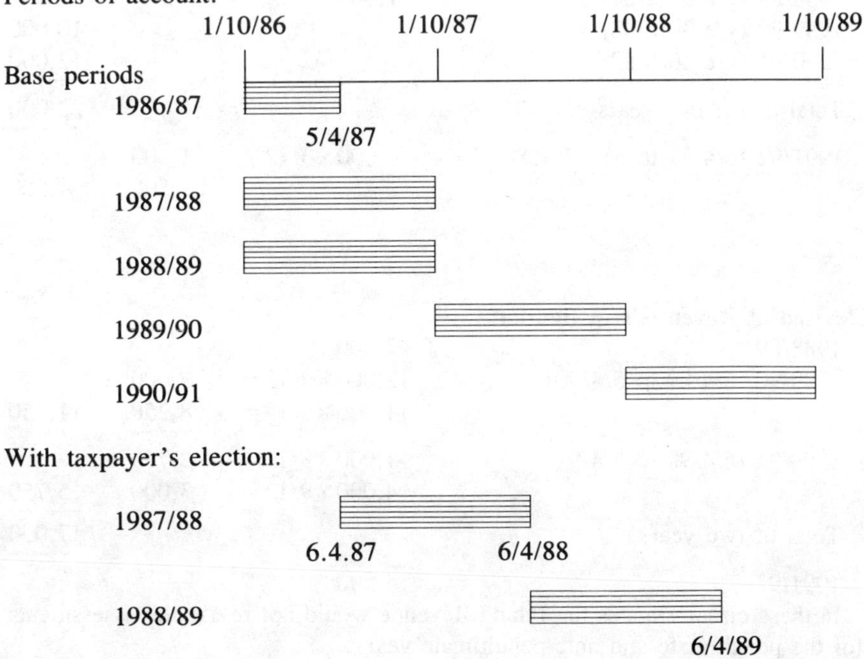

Cessation of trade

On cessation of trade the final year's basis period runs from the previous 6th April to the date of cessation. The previous two fiscal years' basis periods may be amended by the Inland Revenue to current year (April to April) from preceding year. Again, they can only amend the two years together, not one on its own. They are generally known as the penultimate and ante-penultimate years.

Example

A shopkeeper who has been in business for many years ceases trading on 31st December, 1991 having had these results (his accounting date had been 30th June):

	Tax adjusted profit
1/7/86 to 30/6/87	7,000
1/7/87 to 30/6/88	10,000
1/7/88 to 30/6/89	12,000
1/7/89 to 30/6/90	11,000
1/7/90 to 30/6/91	4,000
1/7/91 to 31/12/91	3,500

Assessments:

Original

1988/89 (y/e 30/6/87)	7,000		
1989/90 (y/e 30/6/88)			10,000
1990/91 (y/e 30/6/89)			12,000
Total of the two years			22,000
1991/92 (6/4/91 to 31/12/91)	4,000×3/12=	1,000	
		3,500	4,500

Revised at Revenue's instigation

1988/89	7,000		
1989/90 (6/4/89 to 5/4/90)	12,000×3/12=	3,000	
	11,000×9/12=	8,250	11,250
1990/91 (6/4/90 to 5/4/91)	11,000×3/12=	2,750	
	4,000×9/12=	3,000	5,750
Total of two years			17,000
1991/92	4,500		

In these circumstances the Inland Revenue would not revise the assessments for the penultimate and ante-penultimate years.

This could be illustrated graphically:
Periods of account:

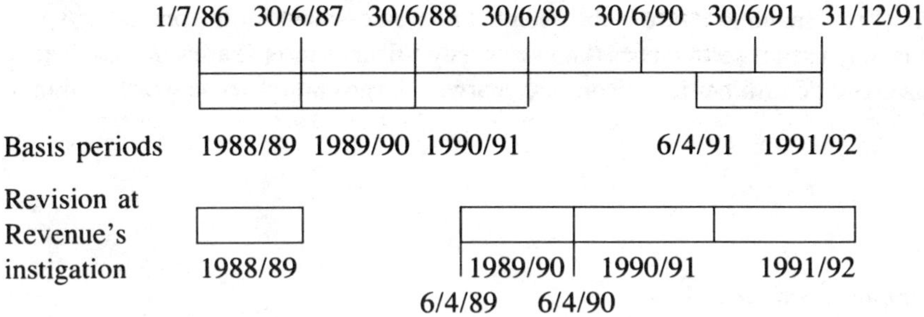

Change of accounting date

When a trader permanently changes his accounting date it confuses the basis periods for the relevant fiscal years. Therefore, in the first fiscal year affected by the change the Inland Revenue are entitled to choose their own basis period and normally take the twelve months ended on the new accounting date.

Example

A garage proprietor changes his accounting date in 1991 from 31st March to 30th September with these results:

1/4/89 to 31/3/90	16,000
1/4/90 to 31/3/91	10,000
1/4/91 to 30/9/91	12,000

Assessments:

1990/91 (y/e 31/3/90)			16,000
1991/92 (y/e 31/3/91)			10,000
1992/93 (base period chosen by Inland Revenue, 1/10/90 to 30/9/91)	10,000×6/12=	5,000 12,000	17,000

In this example the same period of account (1/10/90 to 31/3/91) is used twice. In different circumstances a period of account may not be assessed at all. This may lead to distortions in the assessed profit which are unfair to either Revenue or taxpayer. To rectify this there can be a revision of the assessment of the "preceding year", the fiscal year preceding the one for whom the Revenue have chosen the basis period.

The accepted method of revising the preceding year's assessment is laid down in Revenue statements of practice, but the taxpayer does have a right of appeal to the Commissioners. The method is to take the periods of account before the period itself and periods after, up to the new accounting date, convert the total profit to the same proportionate profit for the total fiscal years using the periods of account as basis periods, and deduct all the assessments apart from the preceding year. The remaining figure is the potential new assessment for the preceding year, but is only used if certain tests (known as "significance tests") are satisfied. These tests are to determine if the proposed charge is large enough to be worth making.

Example (continued)
Continuing the above example the preceding year is 1991/92. The first task is to work out the total equivalent profit for the fiscal years based on the profit of the periods of account as follows:

Relevant periods of account	Profit	Fiscal years using the periods of account as basis periods
1/4/89 to 31/3/90*	16,000	1990/91
1/4/90 to 31/3/91	10,000	1991/92
1/4/91 to 30/9/91	12,000	1992/93
30 months	38,000	36 months

* Note: The first relevant period of account is found by going back two years from the new accounting date and taking the period of account you end up in i.e. in this case 30/9/89 in year ended 31/3/90.

Find the same equivalent average profit for three fiscal years:

$$\text{Total profit} \times \frac{\text{Fiscal years}}{\text{Periods of account}}$$

$$38{,}000 \times 36/30 = 45{,}600$$

Deduct the total of the other assessments leaving the potential new preceding year assessment.

		45,600
1990/91	16,000	
1992/93	17,000	33,000
Potential new assessment 1991/92		12,600

This new assessment is not used unless it fulfils two significance tests:

1. The original and new assessments for the preceding year differ by more than £1,000 (which they do 12,600 − 10,000 = 2,600).

OR If the difference is less than £1,000 it is greater than 10% of the "mean average" – the average profit of the "corresponding period" plus the next year's assessment. The "corresponding period" is a basis period for the preceding year to the new accounting date:

1991/92 (1/10/89 to 30/9/90)	16,000×6/12=	8,000	
	10,000×6/12=	5,000	13,000
1992/93			17,000
			30,000

30,000×½ = 15,000×10% = 1,500 – the difference (2,600) is greater, although having already passed the 1,000 test it is unnecessary in this case.

2. The potential new assessment for the preceding year (12,600) has to be intermediate between the old assessment (10,000) and the profit of the corresponding period (£13,000), which it is in this particular case.

Therefore, in this example the assessment for 1991/92 would be revised from 10,000 to 12,600.

The number of fiscal years and the length of relevant periods of account vary according to the particular circumstances of a case. The following table may be helpful.

Length of period of account from old to new accounting date	Denominator of conversion fraction (in months)	Numerator (fiscal years, in months)
1. Less than twelve months.		
a) Crossing 5th April	24–36	36
b) Not crossing 5th April	24–36	24
2. Longer than twelve months.		
a) Crossing 5th April once	24–36	24
b) Crossing 5th April twice	36–48	48

The particular method described here is not used when one or more special circumstances are relevant:

1. The trade is seasonal.
2. The change of accounting date is within the first three fiscal years from the commencement of trading.
3. There are losses involved.

Appendix: bad debts accounts

Students can have special problems with bad debts accounts adjustments.

Allowable as deductions against taxable profit are trade debts written off, and specific reserves reasonably made against potential bad trade debts. Any bad debts previously written off and later recovered are taxable income in the year of recovery.

Not allowable as deductions against the taxable profit are:

1. General bad debts reserves.
2. Loans to staff written off.
3. Any debt that is not a genuine trade debt.

Therefore, in adjusting a bad debts account for tax purposes, the student should add to the trading profit:

1. Increases in the general bad debts reserve (or deduct from the profit any decrease in the reserve).
2. Loans to staff and any non-trade debt that has been written off.

Example

Bad debts account

Trade debts written off	556	General reserve brought forward (2% of debtors)	765
Loan to member of staff written off	100	Specific reserves brought forward	810
General reserve carried forward (2% of debts)	728	Trade debts previously written off and now recovered	104
Specific reserves carried forward	892	Charge to profit & loss account	597
	2,276		2,276

Adjustments for tax:

Add back loan to staff member		100
Deduct decrease in general reserve	765	
	728	(37)
Add to taxable profit		63

Chapter Six

Capital Allowances

Introduction

A trader cannot write off capital expenditure against income. Further, when he depreciates his fixed assets, that depreciation is not allowable as a deduction against trading profit. Instead, tax law allows standardised depreciation allowances known as "capital allowances" to be set against the trading profit. For individuals and partnerships such allowances are a separate and distinct class of deduction, but for companies they are treated as a trade expense.

The rules are contained in the Capital Allowances Act, 1968, the Finance Act, 1981 and subsequent Finance Acts. Capital allowances cannot be claimed on any capital expenditure, only on certain defined categories:

1. Plant and machinery.
2. Industrial buildings and hotels.
3. Agricultural land and buildings.
4. Patents and know-how.
5. Mines and oil wells.
6. Dredging.
7. Crematoria.

From 13th March, 1984 there has been a phased withdrawal of what had been generous rates of allowances on expenditure on plant and machinery (first year allowances) and industrial and agricultural buildings (initial allowances), leaving only a claim for comparatively small annual allowances (writing down allowances). This phased withdrawal was completed by 31st March, 1986. Details are described in each individual section.

Plant and Machinery

Definition

The legislation does not define the meaning of "plant and machinery". This has been left to case law. The phrase has been defined as including "assets of a durable nature purchased by the trader for use in his trade". More specifically, the asset has to have an active function in the trade, that is, be directly involved in the actual trading process, rather than simply be part of the "setting" or background against or in which the trade takes place such as the building in which a trade is conducted. One of the largest areas of uncertainty is whether an asset is a building or part of a building, or whether it might be plant or machinery.

It has been decided that a boat used as a restaurant, prefabricated classrooms in a school, ceiling tiles, and a petrol station canopy are not plant and machinery. However, a swimming pool at a holiday camp and fixtures and fittings in hotels, such as central heating, air conditioning, etc., do qualify. The definition also includes motor vehicles, the reference books of professional people, furniture in offices, hotels, etc. and the cost of altering buildings to accommodate machinery.

Availability and types of allowances

Allowances are first available in the basis period (income tax) or chargeable accounting period (corporation tax) when expenditure is incurred on the provision of plant and machinery, irrespective of whether it is then or at any time actually used in the trade.

Expenditure is deemed to have been incurred when there exists an unconditional obligation to pay the purchase price, that is when delivery is taken of the asset, even though the actual date of payment may be later. If expenditure is incurred before trading commences it is deemed to have been incurred on the date trading commences.

In recent years there have been three basic types of allowance/adjustment:

1. FIRST YEAR ALLOWANCE (FYA) which used to be given in the year of purchase of plant and machinery (except for motor cars of a type which can be used privately) but was phased out on 31st March, 1986. The rate varied over the years from 100% to 50%. It is now of historical significance only.

2. WRITING DOWN ALLOWANCE (WDA). This is now the main allowance. It is given at the rate 25% per annum on the reducing balance method, that is, an expenditure brought forward and not relieved in previous periods, plus purchased in the year, less sales of machinery.

Normally the WDA is calculated on a "pool" of unallowed expenditure, which includes all plant and machinery purchased, with three notable exceptions:

a) Cars costing in excess of £8,000, each one of which is dealt with individually. The maximum WDA allowed is £2,000 p.a. (25% ×8,000).
b) Assets used for purposes other than wholly and exclusively in the trade, such as private use. In practice this usually means private cars costing under £8,000 which form a "pool" of their own.

   See later in chapter for a more detailed comment on private cars.
c) An election can be made to keep "short-life" assets out of the pool and calculate allowances individually. They are items of plant and machinery with an estimated useful life of less than 5 years, used wholly and exclusively

in the trade, and cannot include motor cars, ships, leased plant, rented television sets, or any asset used privately.

If the asset is not disposed of within 4 years of the end of the period of purchase, the unused balance of expenditure is transferred automatically to the general pool.

See later in the chapter for a more detailed treatment of this.

3. DISPOSALS OF PLANT AND MACHINERY: When an asset is disposed of the sale price (or market value in certain circumstances) is deducted from the pool (after adding the cost of purchases) and WDA calculated on the net balance.

On the disposal of assets, the maximum deduction there can be is the original cost of the items sold. If an asset is sold for more than cost, the amount received above cost is a possible capital gain (see the chapter on capital gains tax for further clarification).

If the disposal proceeds exceed the value of the pool the excess is a BALANCING CHARGE, a clawback of capital allowances previously granted. It is added to the trading profit in strictness, but in practice normally reduces the capital allowances given for the year.

A disposal value less than the value of the pool leads to a BALANCING ALLOWANCE (a capital allowance) of the difference and the pool then has a nil carry forward value, until there are more purchases in future periods.

Before looking at an arithmetic example, remember the order of doing things:

1. Bring forward the value of the pool.
2. Add on the cost of new purchases.
3. Deduct the cost of sales.
4. If there is still a positive value to the pool, calculate a 25% WDA.

In the year of cessation of trade, assets are deemed to be disposed of at market value, and a balancing adjustment arises.

Example

Mr. Bullock, a self-employed farmer, previously leased all his equipment, but now decides to buy it. His accounting date is 31st December and he is assessed on the preceding basis in Sch.D, Case I income tax.

Y/e 31 December, 1989:

1/2/89 purchased machinery	6,000
30/6/89 purchased a car	9,000
(agreed with the inspector it is used 60% for business use)	9,000
1/10/89 purchased a secondhand van	5,000

His trading profit in the accounting period was £28,000.

1990–91:

Sch.D. Case I					28,000
Capital allowances:					
Pool			**Expensive car (over £8,000)**		
Cost	6,000		Cost	9,000	
	5,000*	11,000			
WDA (25%)		(2,750)	WDA (restricted)	(2,000)	
Carry forward		8,250	Carry forward	7,000	
			(2,000)×60% =	(1,200)	
		Total allowances 2,750+1,200 =			(3,950)
					24,050

Notes:

1. *A commercial vehicle is included in the general pool.
2. The date an asset is purchased has no effect on the size of the WDA. Only the length of the basis period matters (e.g. the basis period in which trade commences, if less than 12 months).

Y/e 31st December, 1990:

1/3/90	buys two cars costing £6,000 for use by members of staff	12,000
1/5/90	purchased a machine for	3,000
1/7/90	sold a machine for	1,600

His trading profit in the accounting period was £22,000.

1991/92

Sch.D, Case I						22,000
Capital allowances:						
Pool		**Expensive car**		**Lower priced cars**		
B/F	8,250	B/F	7,000	Cost	12,000	
Cost	3,000					
	11,250					
Sales	(1,600)					
	9,650					
WDA (25%)	(2,413)	WDA (25%)	(1,750)*	WDA (25%)	(3,000)*	
	7,237		5,250		9,000	
		(1,750×60% =	(1,050)			
Total allowances 2,413+1,050+3,000 =						(6,463)
						15,537

Notes:

1. *Once the written down value of the expensive car drops below 8,000 the WDA becomes 25% of the written down value.

2. The 8,000 limitation on private cars only applies to *individual* cars which cost over 8,000.

3. The private use of cars by *employees* does not affect the capital allowances of the *employer*. Private use for the employees is a Schedule E benefit-in-kind. It is only private use of cars by a business proprietor which affects the size of the allowable WDA.

Y/e 31st December, 1991:
1/5/91 sells the employees' cars for 10,000.
1/5/91 buys a machine for 4,000.
1/8/91 sells a machine for 2,800.
His trading profit in the accounting period was £38,000.

1992/93:

Sch.D, Case I						38,000
Pool		**Expensive car**		**Lower priced cars**		
B/F	7,237		5,250		9,000	
Cost	4,000					
	11,237					
Sales	(2,800)			Sales	(10,000)	
	8,437			Balancing		
WDA (25%)	(2,109)	WDA (25%)	(1,313)	charge	1,000	
	6,328		3,937			38,000
		(1,313)×60%	= 788			
Total allowances 2,109+788	= (2,897)−1,000					= (1,897)
						37,103

Assets qualifying as plant and machinery
Some items of expenditure qualify specially as plant and machinery, when they would not qualify on ordinary definitions in the year of purchase.

The items of expenditure which qualify for this treatment are:
1. Thermal insulation of trading premises.
2. Fire safety in hotels and boarding houses.
3. Safety measures to protect the public, e.g. at sports grounds.

Plant and machinery which are fixtures
Plant and machinery installed in buildings which become fixtures in the building, (e.g. a lift) which are for the use of tenants, can be the subject of a claim for

capital allowances by the landlord. He can elect to transfer the benefit of those allowances to the tenant.

Short life assets
The trader can elect to have assets which will be disposed of within 4 years of the end of the period of purchase to be treated separately from the pool. The advantage of this is an enhancement of any possible balancing allowance when the asset is disposed of rather than the disposal just evaporating in the general pool.

Example
A company elects to have a short life asset dealt with separately.

General pool (including short-life asset)			**Short life asset**
B/F (say)	10,000		
Accounting period 1:			
Cost	4,000		4,000
	14,000		
WDA (25%)	3,500	(1,000 S/L asset)	(1,000)
	10,500		3,000
Accounting period 2:			
WDA (25%)	(2,625)	(750 S/L asset)	(750)
	7,875		2,250
Accounting period 3:			
Short life asset sold	(1,200)		(1,200)
	6,675		
WDA (25%)	(1,669)	Balancing allowance	1,050
	5,006		

If a short life asset is not sold four years after the end of the year of purchase, the written down value is then transferred to the main pool.

Ships
WDAs on ships are granted by way of "free depreciation" – they can be claimed but not utilised, but carried forward to future accounting periods.

Example
A ship is purchased by a company for £800,000 in y/e 31st March, 1990, when it makes a loss, and does not wish to utilise the WDA, but carry it forward to y/e 31st March, 1991 when it does make a profit of £900,000.

Y/e 31/3/90:			
Trade profit			Nil
Capital allowances:			
Cost of ship	800,000		
WDA (carried forward)	(200,000)		Nil
	600,000		Nil

Y/e 31/3/91:			
Trade profit			900,000
Brought forward	600,000		
WDA	(150,000)	150,000	
	450,000		
B/F		200,000	(350,000)
			550,000

Restriction of claim

A taxpayer does not have to claim all the capital allowances to which he is entitled in a year. He can, if he wishes, restrict the claim. This would happen, possibly, mainly with a self-employed individual, where small trading profits might well be covered by personal allowances, and a claim for capital allowances would be a waste of time.

Example

Mr. Bird is a self-employed chicken breeder. In y/e 30th September, 1989 (basis period for 1990/91) he makes a trading profit of 7,000 (having no other income) and is married. His capital allowances are:

Pool brought forward 10,000.
Private car brought forward 6,000 (private use 40%).
He buys machinery in the year at a cost of 4,000.

Sch.D, Case I					7,000
	Pool		**Car**		
	10,000		6,000		
Cost	4,000	WDA (25%)	(1,500)×60%	= 900	
	14,000		4,500		
WDA (restricted)	(1,385)				
	12,615				

Total allowances 1,385+900 =		(2,275)
SPA	3,005	4,725
MCA	1,720	(4,725)
		Nil

He could have claimed a WDA on the pool of up to 3,500.

Basis periods (income tax)

In a trade carried on by an individual or a partnership and subject therefore to income tax, Sch.D, Cases I & II, preceding year basis of assessment applies ordinarily. However, with the special circumstances of commencement and cessation special rules apply to capital allowances.

Commencement of trade

In the opening years, the basis periods can overlap. Assets purchased first qualify for allowances in the basis period of the earliest tax year they are purchased, and then qualify for allowances for future tax year.

If the basis period of the very first tax year is less than 12 months in length, WDA is proportionately reduced.

Equipment purchased before the date of commencement of trade is deemed to be purchased on the day trading starts.

Example

A trader commenced trading on 1st October, 1988 and drew up his accounts to 30th June. His purchases of equipment were:

1/9/88	machinery	3,000
1/2/89	machinery	2,000
1/7/89	machinery	4,000
1/11/89	machinery	1,000
1/6/90	machinery	5,000

1988/89 (1/10/88 to 5/4/89):

Cost (1/9/88)	3,000	
(1/2/89)	2,000	5,000
WDA (restricted to 6 months)		
$5{,}000 \times 25\% = 1{,}250 \times \frac{6}{12} =$		(625)
		4,375

1989/90 (1/10/88 to 30/9/89)*:
*But only new purchases from 6/4/89 to 30/9/89 are brought in for the first time.

		4,375
Cost (1/7/89)		4,000
		8,375
WDA (25%)		(2,094)
		6,281

1990/91 (1/10/88 to 30/9/89)*:
*This is repeating the second year basis period, so no new purchases can be included.

		6,281
WDA (25%)		(1,571)
		4,710

1991/92 (1/7/89 to 30/6/90):

		4,710
(1/11/89)	1,000	
Cost (1/6/90)	5,000	6,000
		10,710
WDA (25%)		(2,678)
		8,032)

However if the taxpayer exercised his alternative choice and claimed the second and third tax years on the current year April to April basis, this would mean different basis periods for capital allowances as well, and generally purchases of machinery would be dealt with in earlier tax years.

Example
In the example above 1989/90 and 1990/91 allowances are claimed on the current year basis by the taxpayer.

1988/89 (1/10/88 to 5/4/89 (first tax year unchanged)):

Cost (1/9/88)	3,000	
(1/2/89)	2,000	5,000
WDA (restricted)		
$5{,}000 \times 25\% = 1{,}250 \times \frac{6}{12} =$		(625)
		4,375

1989/90 (6/4/89 to 5/4/90):

			4,375	
Cost	(1/7/89)	4,000		
	(1/11/89)	1,000	5,000	Previously first included 1991/92
			9,375	
WDA (25%)			(2,344)	
			7,031	

1990/91 (6/4/90 to 5/4/91):

		7,031	
Cost	(1/8/90)	5,000	Previously first included 1991/92
		12,031	
WDA (25%)		(3,008)	
		9,023	

1991/92 (1/10/89 to 30/9/90):

	9,023
WDA (25%)	(2,256)
	6,767

Cessation of trade

On termination of trade there is always an unassessed period in the basis periods. The Inland Revenue have the right to alter the basis periods of the last two but one years of assessment (the penultimate and ante-penultimate tax years) from preceding to current year basis. The final tax year is always current year (from 6th April to the date of cessation of trade).

In the final tax year there can be no WDA, only balancing allowances or charges. If machinery is retained on the last day of trade is it deemed to be sold for its market value.

If any sales or purchases take place in a basis period not assessed for capital allowance purposes only:

1. If the Inland Revenue retain preceding year basis, the transactions in the unused period are deemed to take place in the penultimate tax year.

2. If the Inland Revenue choose current year basis, the unused period is shifted to an earlier period, and transactions are deemed to take place in the ante-penultimate tax year.

Example

A trader ceases in business on 30th June, 1991. His accounting date had been 31st March, 1988 (end of basis period for 1988/89) the pool of machinery stood at 10,000. He then had these transactions:

1/5/87	bought machinery for	3,000
1/5/88	sold machinery for	1,000
1/5/89	sold machinery for	2,000
1/5/90	sold machinery for	2,400
30/6/91	retained machinery worth	1,800

Assuming the Inland Revenue retain preceding year basis:

1988/89 (1/4/87 to 31/3/88):

		Pool
		10,000
Cost		3,000
		13,000
WDA (25%)		(3,250)
		9,750

1989/90 (1/4/88 to 31/3/89):

Sale 1/5/88)		(1,000)
		8,750
WDA (25%)		(2,188)
		6,562

1990/91 (1/4/89 to 31/3/90) – but including any transactions between 1/4/90 and 5/4/91 (unused period)

		6,562
Sales (1/5/89)	2,000	
(1/5/90)	2,400	(4,400)
		2,162
WDA (25%)		(541)
		1,621

1991/92 (6/4/91 to 30/6/91) – no WDA

Value of machinery retained	(1,800)	
Balancing charge	179	– added to trading profit

If the Inland Revenue had chosen the current year (April to April) basis for 1989/90 and 1990/91 then:

1988/89 (unchanged) (1/4/87 to 31/3/88)

		10,000
Cost		3,000
		13,000
WDA (25%)		(3,250)
		9,750

1989/90 (6/4/89 to 5/4/90) – but including unused period 1/4/88 to 5/4/89

		9,750
Sales (1/5/88)	1,000	
(1/5/89)	2,000	(3,000)
		6,750
WDA (25%)		(1,688)
		5,062

1990/91 (6/4/90 to 5/4/91):

Sales (1/5/90)	(2,400)
	2,662
WDA (25%)	(666)
	1,996

1991/92 (6/4/91 to 30/6/92) – unchanged, no WDA

Value of machinery retained	(1,800)
Balancing allowance	(196)

If the business ceases because it is transferred to another trader who is connected (e.g. a sole trader converting his business to limited status) then the second trader, if they are connected, can elect to transfer equipment retained at written down value in the final year, and not suffer balancing adjustments.

Industrial buildings and hotels

Allowances can be claimed as follows:

1. On a new industrial building or improvement or extension of an old one (you do not get any allowances on the cost of the land):
   a) An INITIAL ALLOWANCE (IA) of a percentage of qualifying cost expended in the basis period. "Qualifying cost" is the cost of building.

The initial allowance is being phased out from 13th March, 1984 as follows:

Expenditure incurred	**Rate**
Up to 13th March, 1984	75%
14th March, 1984 to 31st March, 1985	50%
1st April, 1985 to 31st March, 1986	25%
From 1st April, 1986	Nil

Payments made after 13th March, 1984 but before 1st April, 1987 under a contract agreed on or before 13th March, 1984 continued to qualify for the IA at 75%.

b) A WRITING DOWN ALLOWANCE (WDA) of 4% of total qualifying cost (straight line method) from the year the building is completed and brought into use and subsequent years when it is still owned and used as an industrial building on the last day of the basis period.

c) On buildings completed prior to 6th November, 1962 and still owned a writing down allowance of 2% is still given.

2. On a secondhand industrial building a writing down allowance is given based on the qualifying cost (which cannot exceed the historic cost of construction) and this is spread equally over the years until the twenty-fifth (or fiftieth if the building was completed before 6th November, 1962) anniversary of completion.
3. For expenditure incurred from 26th March, 1980 to 26th March, 1983, capital expenditure on the construction, extension or improvement of industrial buildings there is an allowance of 100% providing the working space does not exceed 2,500 sq. ft. after the work has been completed. The allowance can be disclaimed in whole or in part, the balance being given (up to a total cost) as a 25% annual allowance (based on cost).

   After 26th March, 1983 the scheme was extended for a further two years (to 26th March, 1985) for expenditure on "very small workshops" defined as buildings whose floor space does not exceed 1,250 sq. ft.
4. In the so-called enterprise zones, a 100% initial allowance on the construction, extension or improvement of any industrial or commercial building. The allowance can be restricted and the balance of expenditure allowed as a 25% initial allowance.
5. On a new hotel or improvement or extension of an old one:

   a) An INITIAL ALLOWANCE (IA) of 20% of qualifying cost expended in the basis period. This was reduced to nil from 1st April, 1986.

   b) A WRITING DOWN ALLOWANCE (WDA) of 4% of qualifying cost from the year of completion (straight line method).

   Only in rare circumstances are allowances given on secondhand hotels.
6. For expenditure incurred on or after 10th March, 1982 and before 1st April, 1987 a new allowance has been introduced for property built and used for letting under the assured tenancies scheme introduced by the Housing Act, 1980. The allowance is 75% in the first year, and 4% WDA thereafter.

Example

A joiner has 31st March as his accounting date and expends money on a new manufacturing unit which was completed and brought into use on 31st October, 1990.

Y/E 31st March, 1989:

Cost of land 1/5/88	100,000
Spent on building	42,000

Y/E 31st March, 1990:

Spent on building	30,000

Y/E 31st March, 1991:

Spent on building	15,000

His allowances would be:

1991/92 (y/e 31/3/91) and yearly thereafter until total cost written off:

WDA (4%) 42,000+30,000+15,000 = 87,000×4% = 3,480

If the building was sold on 30th June, 1993 for 250,000 (including 120,000 for land) then:

1992/93 (y/e 31/3/90)	WDA	3,480
1993/94 (y/e 31/3/91)	WDA	3,480
Total allowances given		10,440
1994/95 (y/e 31/3/94)	Balancing charge	10,440

There would also be a capital gain based on the profit over historic cost of both land and building.

If the purchaser uses it as an industrial building he will only qualify for a WDA of:

Qualifying cost (limited to historic cost) 87,000

Spread over remaining time from date of sale to twenty-fifth anniversary (fiftieth anniversary if completed prior to 6th November, 1962) of completion:

Completed 31st October, 1990

25th anniversary 31st October, 2015

Purchased 30th June, 1993 this gives a remaining qualifying life of 22.33 years.

$$\text{WDA} \quad \frac{87{,}000}{22.33} = 3{,}896$$

Definition of an industrial building

An industrial building is one that is used:

1. As a mill, factory or other manufacturing process.
2. For storage of manufactured goods or raw materials.
3. For transport, dock, water, tunnelling or hydraulic power.
4. For working of mines, oil wells or other mineral resources.
5. For ploughing, cultivating or other agricultural operations which are not the occupation of the trader.
6. For catching shellfish.

7. From 10th March, 1982 for repairing and servicing goods or mterials except where such activities are part of a retail trade or a wider ''non-industrial'' business.
8. For warehousing and storage by traders and wholesalers (not retailers) when the goods stored are to be used for an industrial process.
9. As a sports pavilion for the employees of any trade.

The building itself cannot include the cost of the land it stands on and also excludes retail shops, houses, showrooms or offices, but workers' canteens and other buildings used for staff welfare are included. However, if these do not form more than 25% of the total (in cost) (10% when expenditure incurred before 16th March, 1983) of a comprehensive building they can be included as part of an industrial building. Whilst expenditure on land is disqualified, the cost of preparing, levelling and tunnelling is allowed.

Example
Land is purchased for 200,000 and one building constructed:

Factory portion	270,000
Office portion	90,000
Total cost of building	360,000

As office is not more than 25% of the total, allowances will be given on 360,000.

A hotel qualifies if:

1. The service provided is sleeping accommodation, not normally for more than one month at a time, and breakfast, evening meal, making of beds and room cleaning.

AND

2. The hotel is open for at least four months in the season which is April to October inclusive.

AND

3. The hotel has at least ten letting bedrooms.

Basis periods for industrial buildings and hotels allowances are the same as for plant and machinery.

Industrial buildings which are let or on licence can still attract allowances for the lessor if he incurs the expenditure of construction. The allowances are given to the person who has the ''relevant interest'' in relation to the expenditure. Say, for example, an investment company builds a factory for £100,000 on land of which it owns the freehold. It is let on lease to a manufacturer who immediately extends it (with the landlord's permission) at a cost of £40,000. The landlord would get allowances on £100,000 and the lessee would get allowances on £40,000.

Agricultural land and buildings

General

Capital allowances are given on qualifying expenditure on the construction of farmhouses, farm or forestry buildings, cottages, fences, and improvements to agricultural or forestry land (such as drainage work) incurred for the purposes of husbandry or forestry on agricultural or forestry land.

"Husbandry" is the production of food for human or commercial animal consumption, including the intensive rearing of livestock and fish farming.

Expenditure on farmhouses qualifying for allowances is restricted to a maximum of one third of the total expenditure.

The rate of allowance depends on whether it was incurred before 1st April, 1986 or after that date.

Expenditure incurred on or after 1st April, 1986

The only allowance given is a 4% writing down allowance on a straightline basis. The allowance is first due in the accounting year in which, or the year of assessment in the basis period of which, the expenditure is incurred, and is expressed as being given over a writing down period of 25 years.

When ownership changes hands the new owner takes over the allowances still to be given for the remainder of the 25 year period beginning with the date of acquisition. If the purchase occurs in the middle of a chargeable period the allowance is apportioned between the two owners.

Example

Gurney spends £20,000 on agricultural buildings in y/e 30th June, 1988. On 30th September, 1990 his farm is purchased by Cobley who makes up his accounts to 31st December.

Thus Gurney ceases trading in 1990/91 (final basis period 6/4/90 to 30/9/90). Cobley commences trading on 1/10/90.

Gurney:				
1989/90 (y/e 30/6/88)	20,000×4%		=	800
1990/91 (6/4/90 to 30/9/90)	20,000×4% =	$800 \times {}^{3}/_{12}$	=	200
Cobley:				
1990/91		800−200	=	600
1991/92, etc.	20,000×4%		=	800

However, the old and new owners can make a joint election to the Inspector within 2 years of the end of the accounting period or year of assessment in which ownership is transferred for a balancing adjustment to apply. If there is destruction or demolition of an asset only the previous owner makes the election.

The allowance given to the new owner is a writing down allowance of the original cost or price paid (whichever is the lower) in equal instalments over the remainder of the 25 years.

A further example

Burlington, making up his accounts to 31st December, spends £40,000 on agricultural buildings in June, 1988. He ceases trading on 30th September, 1991 and sells his farm to Canning for £22,000. They make the appropriate election before 5th April, 1994. Canning is extending his farming activities and thus is on preceding year basis of assessment. He makes up his account to 31st March.

Burlington:

1989/90	(y/e 31/12/88)	Cost	40,000
		WDA (4%)	(1,600)
			38,400
1990/91	(1/1/89 to 5/4/91 assuming no Revenue charge to current year basis)	WDA (4%)	(1,600)
			36,800
1991/92	(6/4/91 to 30/9/91)	Sale price	(22,000)
		Balancing allowance	(14,800)

Canning:
Purchased 30/9/91 (y/e 31/3/92) – first allowance 1992/93
Writing down period 6/4/89 to 5/4/2014
Remaining writing down period 1/10/91 to 5/4/2014 – 22.5 years
Writing down allowance each year:

Sale price $22{,}000 \times {}^{1}/_{22.5} = 978$

An election can be made to transfer the asset at written down value instead of sale price, but this is not available when the two parties are connected. The transfer is deemed to take place at open market value.

Expenditure incurred before 1st April, 1986

Other rules apply to expenditure on assets incurred before 1st April, 1986 or to expenditure incurred before 1st April, 1987 under contracts entered into before 13th March, 1984. Two allowances are given:

1. An initial allowance of up to 20% of cost. Less could be claimed if required.
2. A writing down allowance of 10% of cost per year or accounting period until the entire expenditure has been allowed.
3. On sale there is no balancing adjustment, the new owner takes over the remaining allowances, assuming he continues to use the building, etc. for agricultural purposes.

Normally any claims for allowances are based on the expenditure, etc. in the year ended the previous 31st March, but the farmer's accounting period can be used if the Inland Revenue agree.

Example

Smith built a barn at a cost of £20,000 in September, 1985. He sells it to Jones on 30th June, 1988. Smith's accounting period is to 30th September, Jones' to

31st March. Smith ceases trade on 30th June, 1988. Jones commences farming on 1st July, 1988.

Smith:

1986/87 (y/e 30/9/85)	Cost 20,000		
	IA (20%)	4,000	
	WDA (10%)	2,000	6,000
1987/88 (y/e 30/6/86)	WDA		2,000
1988/89 (6/4/88 to 30/6/88)	WDA $2,000 \times {}^{3}/_{12}$ =		500

Jones:

1988/89 (1/7/88 to 5/4/89)	WDA $2,000 \times {}^{9}/_{12}$ =	1,500
1989/90, etc.	WDA	2,000

Patent rights and know-how

Capital expenditure on patent rights used to be allowed in equal instalments for the remaining useful life of the patent up to the maximum life for a new patent which is 17 years.

Relief for capital expenditure on know-how was given in six equal annual instalments.

Both of these were replaced from 1st April, 1986 by a writing down allowance at a rate of 25% calculated on the reducing balance method.

On a sale of patent rights or know-how a balancing allowance or balancing charge applies to the disposal. If any profit is made over original cost, the balance is assessed as income under Sch.D. It can, if appropriate, be assessed as a trading profit under Case I, otherwise under Case VI.

Example

An engineering company buys brand new patent rights from the investor for 17,000. It sells them 2½ years later for 18,500.

If expenditure incurred prior to 1st April, 1986:

		Cost		17,000
Accounting period	1	WDA	$17,000 \times {}^{1}/_{17}$ =	(1,000)
				16,000
	2	WDA		(1,000)
				15,000
	3	Sale price (restricted)		17,000
		Balancing charge		(2,000)
		Sch.D, Case VI 18,500−17,000	= 1,500	

If expenditure incurred on or after 1st April, 1986:

		Cost	17,000
Accounting period	1	WDA (25%)	(4,250)
			12,750
	2	WDA (25%)	(3,188)
			9,562
	3	Sale price (restricted)	17,000
		Balancing charge	(7,438)
		Sch.D, Case VI 18,500 − 17,000 = 1,500	

The income charge on the profit over cost is spread over 6 equal annual amounts if the taxpayer does not elect to have it all assessed in the year of receipt.

Scientific research
Capital expenditure qualifies for a 100% allowance in the year of purchase and there are no balancing adjustments.

Mines and oil wells

Allowances can be claimed for expenditure on mines, oil wells, etc. for searching for, discovering, testing, etc. deposits and works which will be of little value when the source is no longer used.

The allowances are an initial allowance of 40% (100% in development areas). WDA is the greater of 5% of capital expenditure or output for year divided by estimated output of source multiplied by capital expenditure. Balancing adjustments apply on sale.

Depletion of minerals

For expenditure on or after 1st April, 1986, a writing down allowance of 10% on a reducing balance basis is given for minerals and mineral rights. For expenditure on other assets the WDA rate is 25%.

Ships

Ships qualify for "free depreciation". This means the claimant can claim the cost as and when he likes, and does not have to put any expenditure waived in the year of purchase into the pool.

The maximum rate of writing down allowance is 25%.

Chapter Seven

Trading Stock and Farming

Trading stock

In taxation stock in trade is valued at the lower of cost or market value. This only varies on cessation of the trade when the stock is valued at:

1. Sale price if disposed of to another trader who will in his turn use it as trading stock.
2. Otherwise at market value on the termination of trade.

When a trader appropriates stock for the private use of himself or his family, adjustments have to be made to ensure that the equivalent of the retail profit is added to the taxable profit.

Example
A grocer appropriates in a year food for his family's consumption that cost £500 wholesale. It could have been sold retail for £850. If no entry was made in the books £850 would have to be added to the profit. If the food was entered at £500 in the proprietor's capital account, £350 would have to be added to the profit.

Farming

Farmers' averaging of profit

Individuals and partnerships (not companies) carrying on a trade of farming or marketk gardening can, in certain circumstances, make a claim to average their Schedule D, Case I & II profits over two years if this is advantageous.

Averaging can only be claimed if the difference between the two profits is 30% or more of the higher of the two profits. It is calculated before capital allowances and losses. The profit used is the profit for the year of assessment and not necessarily that of the basis period. This means, for instance, if the profit of a third year is then averaged, it is the "averaged" profit of the second year that is used.

When there has been an averaging claim, however, previous claims for capital allowances can be amended in the light of the averaged profit.

Example

Barleycorn, a farmer, has been in business for a number of years. He has these results:

	y/e 31/12/92 (assessable 1993–94)	**y/e 31/12/93** (assessable 1994–95)	**y/e 31/12/94** (assessable 1995–96)	**y/e 31/12/95** (assessable 1996–97)
Gross tax adjusted profits from farming	13,700	20,170	8,450	12,400
Farming losses brought forward	(4,630)	–	–	–
Capital allowances	2,840	1,960	1,760	2,770

Averaging 1993–94

	y/e 31/12/93		20,170		
	y/e 31/12/92		(13,700)		
	Difference		6,470		
	20,170×30%	=	6,051		
Average:	20,170+13,700	=	33,870 × ½	=	16,935
−Capital allowances					(2,840)
					14,095
−Loss B/F					(4,630)
					9,465

Averaging 1994–95

	First averaged profit 1994–95		16,935		
	y/e 31/12/93		(8,450)		
	Difference		8,485		
	16,935×30%	=	5,080		
Average:	16,935+8,450	=	25,385 × ½	=	12,692
−Capital allowances					(1,960)
					10,732

Averaging 1995–96

y/e 31/12/94		12,400	
Second averaged profit 1994–95		12,692	
		292	
12,692×30%	=	3,807	

Therefore no averaging

Assessable profit	12,692
−Capital allowances	(1,760)
	10,932

Averaging is not allowed for either the first or last years of assessment, including a technical cessation on a change of partners. In this situation therefore, averaging is only available when an election for the continuation of the preceding year basis has been made under S.154. Averaging is also disregarded for the purpose of the Revenue's alternative in cessation to convert the penultimate and ante-penultimate years to current year basis.

A trading loss in the basis period for any year of assessment is treated for averaging purposes as a nil profit, but is still available for relief under any of the various provisions.

Example

Tennant commenced farming on 1/1/93 and makes up his accounts to 30th June. His results have been:

6 months	1/1/93 to 30/6/93	1,200
	1/7/93 to 30/6/94	5,800
	1/7/94 to 30/6/95	2,240
	1/7/95 to 30/6/96	(3,600)

Assessments:

1992/93 (1/1/93 to 5/4/93)

$1{,}200 \times {}^{3}/_{6} =$ 600

Alternative:

1993/94 (1/1/93 to 30/12/93)			1993/94 (6/4/93 to 5/4/94)		
	1,200		$1{,}200 \times {}^{3}/_{6} =$	600	
$+5{,}800 \times {}^{6}/_{12} =$	2,900	4,100	$+5{,}800 \times {}^{9}/_{12} =$	4,350	4,950
1994/95 (1/1/93 to 31/12/93)			1994/95 (6/4/94 to 5/4/95)		
	1,200		$5{,}800 \times {}^{3}/_{12} =$	1,450	
$+5{,}800 \times {}^{6}/_{12} =$	2,900	4,100	$2{,}240 \times {}^{9}/_{12} =$	1,680	3,130
		8,200			8,080

As the tax payers' alternative is more beneficial he could also average for 1993/94:

1993/94	4,950
−1994/95	3,130
Difference	1,820 (30% ×4,950 = 1,485)

Therefore claim assessable profit 4,950+3,130 = 8,080× ½ = 4,040 for both 1993/94 and 1994/95.

For 1995/96.

Normal basis period (y/e 30/6/94)	5,800
−Assessment for 1994/95	4,040
Difference	1,760 (30% ×5,800 = 1,740)

Therefore could claim averaged profit for 1995/96:

4,040		
+5,800		
9,840 × ½ =		4,920

1994/95 would also have to be revised to 4,290 if 1995/96 claimed (an increase of 4,920 − 4,040 = 880).

For 1996/97:

Normal basis period (y/e 30/6/95)	2,240	
−Assessment for 1995/96	4,920	
Difference	2,680	(30% × 4,920 = 1,476)

Therefore could claim assessable profit for 1996/97 (and 1995/96):

2,240		
+4,920		
7,160 × ½ =		3,580

1995/96 would also be revised to 3,580.

Summary of final assessments to date:

1992/93	600
1993/94	4,040
1994/95	4,920
1995/96	3,580
1996/97	3,580

1997/98:

Normal basis period (y/e 30/6/96) (3,600) =	Nil	
Assessment 1996/97	3,580	
Difference	3,580	(30% × 3,580 = 1,074)

Therefore could claim assessable profit for 1997/98 (and 1996/97):

3,580		
+ Nil		
3,580 × ½ =		1,790

Revised assessments to date:

1992/93	600
1993/94	4,040
1994/95	4,920
1995/96	3,580
1996/97	1,790
1997/98	1,790

The loss of (3,600) could be claimed against all income for 1996/97 and/or

1997/98, and any unused balance carried forward against profits of the same trade for 1998/99 onwards.

Marginal relief

When the difference between the two years' profits is less than 30% but more than 25% (of the higher of the two profits) a marginal relief is due by increasing the lower profit and lowering the higher profit by the same amount. That amount is three times the sum of 75% of the higher profit minus the lower profit.

Example

The profit assessable on a farm is £10,000 for 1995/96 and £7,200 for 1996/97. The difference is £2,800 and £10,000×30%=£3,000, and £10,000×25% =£2,500, and therefore marginal relief applies.

The marginal relief is:

10,000×75% =	7,500	
−Lower profit	7,200	
Difference	300	×3 = 900

	1995/96		**1996/97**
	10,000		7,200
	− 900		+ 900
Average profit	9,100	Average profit	8,100

Strictly the relief should be expressed as an amount equal to three times the difference between the two profit figures and 75% of the higher profit.

Example

Given the facts in the previous example:

	10,000	
	− 7,200	
	2,800×3=	8,400
−75%×	10,000 =	7,500
Difference		900

Marginal relief ceases to be effective when the difference between the two profits is 25% or less.

Example

The profit for 1995/96 is 10,000 and for 1996/97 7,500

10,000×75% =	7,500
−Lower profit	7,500
Difference	Nil

The claim is optional on the taxpayer, and has to be claimed within two years of the end of the second year of assessment.

In the case of a partnership it is the joint partnership profits which are averaged, and therefore all partners have to sign a joint claim if it is required. Company partners cannot claim averaging relief.

No claim is available for a year before a year already included in a claim, as well as a year of commencement or cessation.

Example

A claim is made to average the profits of the years 1995/96 and 1996/97. Before 6/4/98 a claim is made to average the profits of 1994/95 and 1995/96.

As 1995/96 has already been averaged with a later year (1996/97) it cannot now be averaged with an earlier year (1994/95).

Restriction of loss relief

Relief by setting a loss against other income is restricted to trades carried on on a commercial basis and thus affording a reasonable prospect of profit. Hobby farms, etc. are being aimed at here.

Also, for farming and market gardening losses, no relief is due if losses have been made in each of the previous five years unless the activities were carried on (in the year of claim) in such a way as to have a reasonable expectation of profit if the activities were carried on by a competent farmer or market gardener.

This does not apply to farming or market gardening carried on ancillary to a larger trade.

The herd basis method of valuing farm stock

Animals are normally treated as trading stock and dealt with as such in the accounts. However, farmers can make a special election to have them dealt with on the herd basis (which effectively deals with them as capital assets) if they are members of a production herd, i.e. livestock kept for the sake of products obtainable from the living animal, e.g. dairy herds but not beef herds.

Form of the election. The election must be in writing and once made is irrevocable. It must be made within two years of the end of the year of assessment in the basis period for which a production herd was first kept. It must be claimed afresh whenever there is a change of proprietorship, including a change of partners, even when continuation applies.

An election can also be made where compulsory slaughter of a herd takes place and compensation is received. It must be made within two years after the end of the first year of assessment which included compensation.

Method of valuation. In effect, the herd is treated as a capital asset, and initial cost and additions are capitalised. Transfers from trading stock are made at initial cost or cost of breeding plus the cost of rearing to maturity.

However, with small sales and replacements such as one or two animals at a time, receipts and cost of replacement (limited to REPLACEMENT cost – not including any improvement element) are treated as revenue items. They are dealt with on renewals basis. To claim an animal as a replacement the Revenue require it to be purchased within twelve months of the disposal of the animal it replaces.

Where single animals are sold without replacement the profit or loss is brought into revenue account.

The sale of the whole herd at one time or over twelve months, the proceeds are not treated as revenue. However, if the herd is replaced within five years, the proceeds are brought into account and the cost of the new animals is a charge against profits.

You should now attempt the "Income Tax" Questions 7, 11 to 15, 21, 24, 28, 29, 30, 31 (*see* pages 249–62).

Chapter Eight

Relief for Pension Contributions

Introduction

Tax relief is available, subject to the satisfaction of certain conditions, for contributions to pension schemes by both the employed and self-employed.

The schemes can be roughly divided as follows:

1. Retirement benefit schemes set up by employers for their employees.

2. Personal pension schemes for the self-employed, or employees on non-pensionable earnings.

These are subdivided into:

(a) Those set up before 1st July, 1988, known as retirement annuities.

(b) Those set up on or after 1st July, 1988 known as personal pension schemes.

Retirement benefit schemes

To ensure that:

1. Contributions by the employer are not treated as a taxable benefit-in-kind on the employees; and

2. Contributions by employees attract tax relief.

A scheme has to be approved by the Superannuation Funds Office of the Inland Revenue and comply with certain conditions.

The main conditions which affect employees are:

1. Employers and employees only get tax relief on contributions to provide pensions and commuted lump sums up to certain limits which:

(a) For schemes established for new employees joining after 14th March, 1989 the maximum pension will be calculated by reference to maximum earnings. The maximum pension will be calculated by reference to earnings of £60,000, and calculated as 1/6th of final remuneration for each year of service up to 40 years maximum, e.g. maximum pension of £40,000. A lump sum of up to a maximum of £90,000 can be commuted. These figures will be index-linked.

(b) For schemes established before 14th March, 1988 the pension must not exceed 1/60th of final remuneration for each year of service up to a maximum of 40 years (widow's pension limited to 2/3rds of husband's pension), and a lump sum up to 3/80ths of final remuneration up to a maximum of 40 (i.e. 1.5 times final salary). "Final remuneration" for entrants after 16th March, 1987 is limited to £100,000, making the maximum lump sum of £150,000.

2. Employer's contributions are allowable as a deduction against income.
3. The scheme is not liable to tax on its income or capital gains.
4. Up to 15% of the remuneration attracts tax relief as employees' contributions.

Personal pensions schemes set up on or after 1st July, 1988

The Inland Revenue can approve such schemes, if certain conditions are satisfied, and contributions, within limits, will attract tax relief.

The main points are:

1. Contributions do not attract relief if related to earnings or income in excess of £64,800 from 6th April, 1990, a figure which is indexed for inflation. The lump sum is restricted to 25% of the total fund.

2. The contributions attract tax relief for the self-employed and employed, in non-pensionable income, e.g. you cannot include earnings from an employer already providing a pension scheme.

3. Tax relief can be claimed as a percentage of "net relevant earnings" (see later for definition) as follows:

Age	Percentage of relevant earnings
35 or less	17.5
36 to 45	20
46 to 50	25
51 to 55	30
56 or over	35

Relief is given on contributions paid in the current year.

4. No more than 5% of net relevant earnings can be allocated to provide death before retirement life cover.

5. Contributions paid in a year can be carried back one tax year, or the year before that, if there were no net relevant earnings in the previous tax year. To carry back contributions, an election has to be made not later than 3 months after the end of the tax year in which the contributions were actually paid.

6. If there is unused relief in any tax year, it can be carried forward and utilised for up to 6 tax years if contributions are paid in future tax years excess of the current year's relief.

7. Contributions by an employer to an approved pension scheme are not taxable on the employee.

8. Income and capital gains of such a scheme are free of tax.

Retirement annuity plans set up before 1st July, 1988

These are much the same as personal pension schemes, except that the benefits that can be derived differ, and the contributions that qualify for relief differ.

They are still relevant, in that plans taken out before 1st July, 1988 can still continue to maturity.

The relief available is like personal pension plans, a percentage of "net relevant income" as follows:

Age at beginning of tax year (6th April)	Percentage of net relevant earnings
Up to 50	17.5
51 to 55	20
56 to 60	22.5
61 or over	27.5

Net relevant earnings

These are defined as being from non-pensionable employment, or from a trade, profession or vocation. The income of spouses are kept separate, so that each can make separate qualifying pension contributions.

Qualifying earnings are the tax adjusted income less:

1. Capital allowances.
2. Trade losses.
3. Annual charges incurred for business purposes (copyright and patent royalties, etc.), apart from annual business interest not deducted as a trade expense.

General interest and charges such as house mortgage interest, qualifying maintenance payments, etc., are not deducted.

4. Taxable benefits-in-kind are included for the employed, but earnings from pensionable employment are excluded.

Calculation of relief

Assuming relief available at 17.5% maximum of net relevant earnings, the relief is calculated as follows:

Example

A trader for a twelve-month period of account has:

Gross trading profit	14,320
Capital allowances	690
Unused losses brought forward	(1,750)

He pays a retirement annuity premium in the year of assessment of £2,500.

Gross profit		14,320
Capital allowances	(690)	
Loss relief	(1,750)	(2,440)
		11,880
Retirement annuity premium	2,500	
Maximum of relief 11,880×17.5% =	(2,079)	(2,079)
Unrelieved premiums	421	
Net taxable profit		9,801

However, if the relief available in a particular year is not utilised, it can be carried forward and used against excess premiums paid in future years. The current year relief is used first, then the earliest relief brought forward. In no circumstances can unused relief be carried forward for more than six years.

	Year 1	Year 2	Year 3
Trading profit	22,900	15,600	19,400
Capital allowances	790	1,220	860
Retirement annuity premiums paid	3,900	1,326	4,200

Year 1

Sch.D, Case I		22,900
Capital allowances		790
		22,110
Premiums paid	3,900	
Relief available 22,110×17.5% =	3,870	3,870
Unrelieved premiums	30	18,240

Year 2

Sch.D, Case I		15,600
Capital allowances		1,220
		14,380
Maximum relief 14,380×17.5% =	2,517	
Premiums paid	1,326	1,326
Unused relief carried forward	1,191	13,054

Year 3

Sch.D, Case I				19,400
Capital allowances				860
				18,540
Premiums allowed				4,200
				14,340
Relief available:				
		Current year	Unused relief brought forward	
18,540×17.5% =		3,245		1,191
Premiums paid	4,200			
Current year relief	3,245	3,245		
	955	Nil		
Relief from previous years	955			955
	Nil		Carry forward	236

Allowable premiums can be paid up to one year after the end of the relevant year and, if there is no income in the following year, up to two years after the relevant year, i.e. for 1990/91, allowable premiums could be paid up to 5th April, 1992 and exceptionally up to 5th April, 1993.

As mentioned above, the relief for widows', etc., annuities are calculated according to their own special limit: 5 per cent of net relevant earnings. The payment of such premiums can affect the amount of relief for a retirement annuity in that any widows', etc. annuity allowed for tax is deducted from the maximum relief available on a retirement annuity. The maximum limit for dependant's benefits contributions is 5% per annum of net relevant income.

Example

A self-employed man has an assessable profit of £16,000 and capital allowances of £2,000. He pays a retirement annuity premium of £2,200 and a widow's annuity premium of £600.

Sch.D, Case I			16,000
Capital allowances			2,000
Maximum relief available	14,000×17.5% =	2,450	14,000
			600
Widow's annuity allowed		600	13,400
Retirement annuity paid	2,200		
Allowed	1,850	1,850	1,850
	350	Nil	
Net taxable profit			11,550

Chapter Nine

Relief for Trade Losses

Introduction

Having discussed the taxation of trading profits at some length, what effect does a trading loss have? It can reduce the taxable income of the trader in one of several alternative ways. Not more than the total loss can be utilised to reduce income. The alternatives available are:

1. The simplest way is to carry the loss forward from the loss-making period of account to reduce trading profits from the same trade of future years. This relief is available under S.385, Taxes Act 1988.

2. The main alternative is to offset the loss against all other income (both earned and unearned) of the year of assessment in which the loss-making period of account ends, and the following year of assessment. This is available under S.380, and is a voluntary relief – the taxpayer has to make a written claim if he wants to have it.

3. If the trade loss occurs in any of the first three years of assessment after commencement of trade the loss can be offset against all types of income of the three years of assessment preceding the loss year.

4. Unrelieved trade losses of the final twelve months preceding cessation of trade can be offset against the taxable profits of the same trade in the three years of assessment preceding the final year. This is known as terminal loss relief.

Finally there are several miscellaneous rules regarding losses, mainly to prevent their abuse.

Carry forward of losses – S.385 relief

When a loss is made in a trade, profession or vocation it can be carried forward (or the balance after claiming S.380 relief) and offset against the first available future profit of the same trade. The carry forward is without time limit but the maximum possible loss MUST be offset against the first available profit without regard to the effect on personal allowances, as the loss must be offset prior to the claiming of personal allowances.

Example

Leak, an old established plumber, has these results:

	Profit (loss)	Capital allowances claimed
Year ended 30th September, 1987	5,000	215
Year ended 30th September, 1988	(3,150)	Nil
Year ended 30th September, 1989	9,400	376

He is married, received £500 per annum from rents and pays mortgage interest of £200 per annum.

Tax assessments:

1988/89:

Sch.A	500	Sch.D, Case I		5,000
		Capital allowances		(215)
Mortgage interest	(200)			4,785
	300			
			5,085	
		AM	(4,095)	
Taxable income			990	

1989/90:

Sch.A	500	Sch.D, Case I	Nil
Mortgage interest	(200)		
	300		
AM	(4,375)		
	Nil		

1990/91:

Sch.A	500	Sch.D, Case I		9,400
		Capital allowances		(376)
				9,024
		Loss relief		(3,150)
				5,874
Mortgage interest	(200)			
	300			
			6,174	
SPA	3,005			
MCA	1,720		(4,725)	
Taxable income			1,449	

Relief against total income – S.380

The relief has two basic principles underlying it:

1. It is a voluntary claim under which the loss can be set against any type of income in two years of assessment. It must be claimed within two years of the end of the year of assessment in which the loss was made.
2. The year of assessment the relief is first given is normally the year of assessment in which the loss making period of account ends.

Example

Lamb, a butcher who has been in business for some years, draws up his accounts to 31st December, and in year ended 31st December, 1989 he makes a trading loss.

That loss could be claimed against the total income of 1989/90 and 1990/91.

Notice, S.380 loss relief is given in the CURRENT YEAR of assessment the lossmaking period of account ends, and the following year of assessment.

Up to 5th April, 1990, the loss could be relieved against the total income (gross income less all annual charges, including covenants to charity) of the relevant tax year of both the lossmaking trader and his or her spouse, but in a particular order:

1. Earned income of the lossmaking spouse.
2. Investment income of the lossmaking spouse.
3. Earned income of the other spouse.
4. Investment income of the other spouse.

However, with the advent of independent taxation from 6th April, 1990 the offset of trading losses against the income of the spouse was abolished for 1990/91 onwards.

Therefore, from 1990/91 and future tax years, the self-employed making trading losses have two alternatives in each of the two years of assessment. The main aim in making a choice is the maximum utilisation of personal allowance. Remember that unrelieved losses can be carried forward, whereas unused personal allowances cannot, and therefore are wasted. Sufficient income should thus be left to absorb the personal allowances as far as possible. It is not possible to claim only part of the loss available. If a claim is made, the loss must be offset up to the maximum of the income or loss available, whichever is the smaller. The choices are:

1. Not to claim S.380 loss relief at all, and carry the unrelieved loss forward to the next tax year.
2. To claim against all the earned and investment income of the self-employed spouse. Remember, from 1990/91 onwards no loss relief can be offset against the income of the other spouse.

S.380 losses can be augmented by capital allowances. It should, however, be remembered the claim in a particular year for capital allowances can be restricted if desired.

No such restricted claim can be made in the case of trading losses.

Example

Carpenter, a joiner for many years, has these results:

	Profit (loss)	Capital allowances claimed
Year ended 30th September, 1989	12,520	(1,800)
Year ended 30th September, 1990	(15,600)	(600)
Year ended 30th September, 1991	5,400	(400)

Other income and payments:

	1990/91	1991/92	1992/93
Rents of Mr. Carpenter	600	700	800
Wages of Mrs. Carpenter	8,000	8,700	9,200
Interest from NSB investment account of Mrs. Carpenter	200	240	270
Mortgage interest paid (mortgage in joint names (gross amounts paid) (tax deducted under MIRAS))	(600)	(640)	(620)
Covenant to charity (covenant solely in name of Mr. Carpenter) (gross amount paid)	(200)	(200)	(200)

Computations and tax liabilities:

1990/91

Mr. Carpenter

Sch.D, Case I		12,520	
Capital allowances		(1,800)	
		10,720	
Sch.A		600	
		11,320	
Mortgage interest (600) × ½ =	(300)*		
Covenant	(200)	(500)	10,820
Loss available (current year)	(15,600)		

Mrs. Carpenter

Sch.E		8,000
Sch.D, Case III		200
		8,200
Mortgage interest (600) × ½ =		(300)
		7,900
SPA	3,005	
MCA (transferred)	1,720	(4,725)
		3,175 × 25% =793.75
Mortgage interest 300 × 25% =		75.00
		868.75

Capital allowances	(600)	(16,200)	
Utilised (S.380)		10,820	(10,820)
Carry forward		5,380	
			NIL

* Tax payable on covenant 200×25% = 50.00.
Note: Tax deducted under MIRAS is not collected if there is insufficient income.

1991/92

Mr. Carpenter			**Mrs. Carpenter**		
Sch.D, Case I		5,400	Sch.E		8,700
Sch.A		(400)	Sch.D, Case III		240
		5,000			8,940
Mortgage interest			Mortgage interest		
(600) × ½ =	(300)		(600) × ½ =		(300)
Covenant	(200)	(500)			8,640
	(5,380)	200	SPA	3,005	
SPA		(200)	MCA	1,720	(4,725)
		NIL			3,915
				3,915×25% =	978.75
			Tax on Mortgage interest		
			300×25% =		75.00
					1,053.75

Tax on covenant 200×25% = 50.00.
Note: It would be disadvantageous for Mr. Carpenter to claim loss relief.

1992/93

Mr. Carpenter			**Mrs. Carpenter**		
Sch.D, Case I		5,400	Sch.E		9,200
Capital allowances		(400)	Sch.D, Case III		270
		5,000			9,470
Loss relief b/f	(5,380)		Mortgage interest		
Utilised	5,000	(5,000)	(600) × ½ =		(300)
					9,170
Loss carried forward	(380)	Nil	SPA	3,005	
Sch.A		800	MCA	1,720	(4,725)
		800			4,445

Mortgage interest				4,445×25%=1,111.25
(600)×½=	(300)		Tax on Mortgage	
Covenant	(200)	(500)	interest (300)×25%=	75.00
		300		1,187.50
SPA		(300)		
		NIL		

Tax on covenant 200×25%=50.00

Note: It may be advantageous if mortgage interest were wholly transferred to Mrs. Carpenter.

Actual loss as basis of a claim

Sometimes instead of taking the loss of the period of account as the basis of the S.380 claim, the actual loss of the year of assessment (from 6th April to 5th April) is used. The occasions are:

1. In the first three years of assessment from commencement of business.
2. In any year of assessment immediately following a year when this "strict" basis of S.380 has been used.
3. In the final year of assessment on cessation of trade (but not in the previous two).
4. Whenever the taxpayer wishes to claim it.

Example

Hayseed, a farmer, has these results:

Year ended 30th June, 1989	Profit	5,400
Year ended 30th June, 1990	Loss	(8,600)
Year ended 30th June, 1991	Profit	4,000

If the "strict" basis of S.380 relief was used the losses available would be:

		S.380 loss
1989–90:		
5,400×3/12=	1,350	
(8,600)×9/12=	(6,450)	(5,100)
1990–91:		
(8,600)×3/12=	(2,150)	
4,000×9/12=	3,000	Nil
Carry forward	850	

Losses in early years of trade

When trade commences and losses are made in the first four years of assessment they can be claimed against the total income (in the same order as a S.380 claim) of the three preceding years of assessment beginning with the earliest year first. Capital allowances can be similarly used.

Example

A trader commences on 1st December, 1990 and makes his accounts up to 5th April. His results were:

1st December, 1990 to 5th April, 1991	Loss	(2,500)	(1990–91)
6th April, 1991 to 5th April, 1992	Loss	(5,600)	(1991–92)

The 1990–91 loss (4 months to 5th April, 1991) can be offset against the total income of:

1987–88
1988–89
1989–90

The 1991–92 loss (year ended 5th April, 1992) can be offset against the total income of:

1988–89
1989–90
1990–91

Terminal loss relief

When trade ceases unrelieved trade losses, capital allowances and annual charges connected with the trade can be offset against the trade profit of the penultimate year and the two previous years of assessment (a sort of S.385 relief but going backwards).

Unrelieved losses, etc. are for the last twelve calendar months of trading and therefore probably mean apportioning periods of account, even some not used as basis periods.

A worked example

A trader finishes on 31st May, 1992 having previously drawn up accounts to 30th June. His relevant results were:

	Profit/(loss)
Year ended 30th June, 1988	3,780
Year ended 30th June, 1989	2,860
Year ended 30th June, 1990	1,500
Year ended 30th June, 1991	420
11 months to 31st May, 1992	(4,930)
Capital allowances were claimed:	
1989/90	1,380
1990/91	1,740
1991/92	1,860
1992/93 Balancing charge	(490)

The computation should be done in three stages:

1. Compute the assessments for the relevant years (not forgetting the Inland Revenue's claims in the penultimate and ante-penultimate years).
2. Compute the qualifying terminal loss.
3. Relieve the terminal loss against the relevant trading profits as computed in 1.

Stage 1: relevant assessments:

1989/90 (y/e 30/6/88):			
	Sch.D, Case I	3,780	
	CA	(1,380)	2,400
1990/91 (y/e 30/6/89):			
	Sch.D, Case I	2,860	
	CA	(1,740)	1,120
1991/92 (y/e 30/6/90):			
	Sch.D, Case I	1,500	
	CA	(1,760)	Nil
	Excess of capital allowances of 360		
1992/93 (6/4/92 to 31/5/92):			
	Sch.D, Case I (4,930)$\times^2/_{11}$=	(896)	
	Balancing charge	490	Nil
	Unrelieved loss	(406)	

Stage 2: qualifying terminal loss

Unrelieved losses:

1/6/91 to 5/4/92			**6/4/92 to 31/5/92**		
1/6/91 to 30/6/91					
420$\times^1/_{12}$=	35		(4,930)$\times^2/_{11}$=	(896)	
1/7/91 to 5/4/92					
(4,930)$\times^9/_{11}$=	(4,034)	(3,999)	Balancing charge	490	(406)

Unrelieved capital allowances:

	1991/92			**1992/93**
The lower of:				
1. Actual unrelieved allowances	360			Nil
OR				
2. Total allowances for year apportioned to period prior to 5th April and within last 12 months of trading. 1,860$\times^{10}/_{12}$=	1,550	(360)	(being lower than 1,550)	
Total of terminal loss		(3,999)		
		(406)		
		(360)		
		Nil		
		(4,765)		

Note that any of the calculations cannot show a profit – they must be a loss or nil.

Stage 3: relieve the qualifying loss

Total loss		Year of relief	
	(4,765)	1991/92	Nil
Relieved	Nil	Assessed	Nil
Carry back	(4,765)		
		1990/91	1,120
Relieved	1,120		(1,120)
Carry back	(3,645)	Assessed	Nil
		1989/90	2,400
Relieved	2,400		(2,400)
Unrelieved and wasted	(1,245)	Assessed	Nil

Relief for investment in corporate trades (business expansion scheme)

This business expansion scheme replaced the original business start up scheme which applied only for 1981/82 and 1982/83, under which relief against income tax at the highest rates paid could be claimed for the investment made.

Under the new scheme, relief can be had against the highest rates of income tax for an investment in any trading company in newly issued share capital.

Certain conditions must be satisfied by the company, the trade it carries on, and the investor.

Company

It must be unquoted, resident in the UK for tax purposes, and exist wholly or mainly for the purposes of carrying on a qualifying trade, or is the parent company of subsidiaries which carry on qualifying trades.

Qualifying trades

All trading activities qualify with certain exceptions. The main exceptions are commodity-dealing, leasing, banking and other financial activities, dealing in goods otherwise than in ordinary wholesale or retail trading.

From the Finance Act, 1988 getting the Royal Assent (which was July, 1988) qualifying companies include those providing qualified assured tenancies over a minimum period of 4 years. Excluded, a house or flat with a capital value in excess of £125,000 in Greater London or £85,000 elsewhere, and assured shorthold tenancies. It used to be required prior to 20th March, 1990, that the valuation of the property should take into account increases in value brought about by infrastructure improvements or better local transport. From 20th March, 1990, houses are not now excluded if they increase in value beyond the limits simply because of improvements in the locality.

The rule limiting companies with more than 50% of their net assets in land and buildings will not apply to such companies.

Relief is, however, not available in respect of wholesaling or retailing trades when the goods (e.g. wine or antiques) are held as investments and the company does not actively attempt to sell them. As from 16th March, 1987, a film production company qualifies if throughout the previous three years it has been engaged either in film production or distribution of films made in the period.

Shares issues after 18th March, 1986 do not qualify if the company issuing them has more than half of its net assets in the form of land and buildings at any time within the three year relevant period. This restriction does not apply to the first £50,000 of share capital raised by a company in any twelve months after 18th March, 1986. The first disposal of qualifying shares issued after 18th March, 1986 are exempt from capital gains tax.

Companies are limited (from 1st May, 1990) to £750,000 of qualifying share capital in any 12 month period (except for ship charter and private rented housing when the limit is £5,000,000). BES relief is not available on ordinary share capital subscribed in excess of the £750,000 limit, issued in a period of 6 months or previous 6th April, whichever is longer.

Individuals

An individual qualifies if he subscribes for shares on his own behalf or through the medium of an approved investment trust. He must be both resident and ordinarily resident in the UK throughout the fiscal year the shares are purchased, and he must not be connected with the company at any time from its incorporation, or if later, two years before the issue to five years after their acquisition.

A person is connected with the company if he alone or with his associates controls more than 30% of the capital or voting power.

"Associates" includes ancestors, spouse and children and business partners. He is also connected with the company if he receives remuneration as an employee, ignoring reasonable expenses and return on investments.

The individual, together with his spouse, can only have relief on a minimum of £500 and a maximum of £40,000 per tax year.

With effect from 6th April, 1987 a person who invests under the scheme in the first half of a tax year can claim up to half of the relief against income for the previous tax year, subject to a maximum carryback of £5,000. The option may only be exercised when the relief is claimed. The rest of the relief is allowed for the tax year in which the investment is actually made.

Capital losses on shares in unquoted companies

Losses made by individuals on disposals of unquoted shares issued on or after 6th April, 1980 can be offset against income for income tax purposes. The share must have been subscribed for on their issue and not bought or inherited. The relief is only available on shares in U.K. resident trading companies which have existed for at least 6 years or traded for a continuous shorter period.

Miscellaneous

Anti-avoidance rules

1. No loss can be relieved under any of the above provisions unless the trade is carried on commercially, and the losses are not deliberately made.
2. In farming, horticulture and market gardening, if losses have been made for five continuous years, S.380 loss relief can be refused in the sixth year unless it is shown the trade is carried on with a view to profit.

Transfer of a business to a company

When a trader converts his business to a limited company and there are unrelieved losses at the end he can (instead of claiming terminal loss) elect to carry them forward and offset them against income he receives from the company (director's remuneration and dividends). The relief does not extend to unused capital allowances.

Chapter Ten

Partnerships

The business profits of partnerships are subject to income tax under the normal rules of Sch.D, Cases I & II. The taxable profit is calculated in the same way as for a sole trader and then divided between the partners in accordance with their agreed split of the profit. Each individual share is then assessed to tax according to the individual partner's circumstances and he is entitled to set his personal allowances against his share, etc. However, as with all partnership matters there is joint and several liability, and if one partner fails to pay his share of tax the others can be made responsible for it.

Profit

When referring to the taxable profit of a partnership, this means the profit before deduction of any partners' salaries, interest on capital or other methods of appropriating the profit. These items are merely methods of appropriating the profit, they do not affect the size of it.

When dividing the profit between the partners this is done according to the agreed profit sharing methods of the relevant year of assessment, not the basis period. If the profit sharing ratio changes part way through the year of assessment, account has to be taken of this.

Example

Abbey, Bailey and Carton are in partnership as architects. Up to 30th June, 1990 they share profits:

	Annual salary	Interest on capital	Split of residue
Abbey	6,000	12%	50%
Bailey	4,000	12%	25%
Carton	3,000	12%	25%
	13,000		

From 1st July, 1990 they decide to share:

	Annual salary	Interest on capital	Split of residue
Abbey	5,000	12%	30%
Bailey	3,000	12%	35%
Carton	3,000	12%	35%
	11,000		

The accounts for the year ended 31st December, 1989 show:

Office salaries and wages	48,000	Gross fees	122,078
Other office expenses	23,152		
Depreciation	5,000		
Entertaining (all disallowable)	2,616		
Partners' salaries	13,000		
Interest on capital	1,200		
Net profit	29,110		
	122,078		122,078

The capital in the business throughout the period was:

Abbey	6,000
Bailey	2,000
Carton	2,000

Capital allowances are claimed for 1990/91:

Jointly owned partnership assets		510
Individual cars:		
Abbey	1,400×80% (business use) =	1,120
Bailey	1,100×75% (business use) =	825
Carton	900×70% (business use) =	630

All three partners are married and have no other income:
Taxable profit for 1990/91:

Accounting profit		29,110
Add:		
Interest on capital	1,200	
Partners' salaries	13,000	
Entertaining	2,616	
Depreciation	5,000	21,816
Taxable profit		50,926
Partnership capital allowances		510
		50,416

Split of profit:

6th April, 1990 to 30th June, 1990:

$50{,}416 \times {}^{3}/_{12} = 12{,}604$

		Abbey		Bailey		Carton	
Salaries							
$13{,}000 \times {}^{3}/_{12} =$	3,250	1,500		1,000		750	
	9,354						
Interest on capital							
$1{,}200 \times {}^{3}/_{12} =$	300	180		60		60	
Net profit	9,054	(50%) 4,527	6,207	(25%) 2,264	3,324	(25%) 2,263	3,073
1st July, 1990 to 5th April 1991:							
$50{,}416 \times {}^{9}/_{12} = 37{,}812$							
Salaries							
$11{,}000 \times {}^{9}/_{12} =$	8,250	3,750		2,250		2,250	
	29,562						
Interest on capital							
$1{,}200 \times {}^{9}/_{12} =$	900	540		180		180	
Net profit	28,662	(30%) 8,598	12,888	(35%) 10,032	12,462	(35%) 10,032	12,462
			19,095		15,786		15,535
Individual capital allowances			1,120		825		630
			17,975		14,961		14,905
Personal allowances (SPA & MCA)			(4,725)		(4,725)		(4,725)
Taxable income			13,250		10,236		10,180

Remember, therefore, that adjustment of the taxable profit is according to the details of the basis period, but the split of the taxable profit between the partners is done according to the apportionment of profit in the year of assessment.

If partners have private, individual income, it is Inland Revenue practice to offset personal allowances against private income first, in preference to partnership income.

Change in membership

When there is a change in the membership of a partnership, the business for tax purposes, is deemed to have finished and commenced with the cessation of the old partnership and the start of the new. However, in certain circumstances, the ordinary cessation and commencement rules do not apply:

1. If at least one individual is a member of both partnerships an election can be made for the "continuation basis" of assessment to apply. This means the two partnerships are treated as one continuing entity and all assessments before,

during and after the change of membership continue on the preceding basis, with an appropriate split of the profit in the actual year of assessment the change takes place. The election has to be in writing, signed by all members of the old and new partnerships (or their personal representatives), and signed within two years of the date of change.

2. If no continuation election is made for any change of partnership after 19th March, 1985, the cessation rules apply to the old partnership as usual, but the new partnership is assessed on the profits for the actual tax year (April to April) for the first and the following three tax years (the first four tax years). In the fifth and sixth tax years the assessment will normally be based on the preceding year basis, but an election can be made to have those two years on the actual basis as well, with preceding year basis from the seventh tax year onwards.

These new rules on commencement do not apply to:

a) Sole traders.
b) Partnerships newly formed.

Example

Darley, Edmondson and Farrimond are in partnership. Darley retires on 30th September, 1990 and is replaced by Guthrie from 1st October, 1990. A continuation basis election is signed by all the partners.

The profits (adjusted for tax) have been:

Year ended 30th September, 1987	20,000
Year ended 30th September, 1988	24,000
Year ended 30th September, 1989	27,000
Year ended 30th September, 1990	28,000
Year ended 30th September, 1991	31,000
Year ended 30th September, 1992	36,000
Year ended 30th September, 1993	40,000
Year ended 30th September, 1994	48,000

The profits are split:

Up to 30th September, 1990:

Darley	50%
Edmondson	30%
Farrimond	20%

From 1st October, 1990:

Edmondson	40%
Farrimond	30%
Guthrie	30%

Without an election the assessments would be:

Darley, Edmondson and Farrimond:			
1990/91 (6/4/90 to 30/9/90)	28,000×6/12=		14,000
1989/90 (revised to 6/4/90 to 5/4/90)	27,000×6/12=	13,500	
	28,000×6/12=	14,000	27,500
1988/89 (revised to 6/4/88 to 5/4/89)	24,000×6/12=	12,000	
	27,000×6/12=	13,500	25,500
Edmondson, Farrimond and Guthrie:			
1990/91 (1/10/90 to 5/4/91)	31,000×6/12=		15,500
1991/92 (6/4/91 to 5/4/92)	31,000×6/12=	15,500	
	36,000×6/12=	18,000	33,500
1992/93 (6/4/92 to 5/4/93)	36,000×6/12=	18,000	
	40,000×6/12=	20,000	38,000
1993/94 (6/4/93 to 5/4/94)	40,000×6/12=	20,000	
	48,000×6/12=	24,000	44,000
1994/95 (Year ended 30/9/93)*			40,000
1995/96 (Year ended 30/9/94)*			48,000

*Note: The partners could elect to have these two assessments on the current tax year basis, with preceding year beginning with 1996/97 (Year ended 30/9/95).

With an appropriate election all assessments would be on preceding year basis.

The 1990/91 (27,000) assessment would be apportioned between the individual partners:

		Darley		Edmondson		Farrimond		Guthrie
Darley, Edmondson & Farrimond:								
13,500	(50%)	6,750	(30%)	4,050	(20%)	2,700		Nil
Edmondson, Farrimond & Guthrie:								
13,500		Nil	(40%)	5,400	(30%)	4,050	(30%)	4,050
		6,750		9,450		6,750		4,050

Losses

Partnership losses are a complicated subject, and their apportionment varies depending on whether there is a claim to:

1. Set them off against general income (S.380) in which case they are divided on the split of profit in the actual year (current year) the loss is made.

Limited partners cannot claim against general income losses in excess of the capital they have at risk. Surplus profits have to be carried forward against future partnership trading profits.

2. Set them off against future trading profits (S.385) in which case they are divided on the split of profit in the basis period (preceding year) the loss is made.

Sometimes a "fictitious" loss arises when the partnership overall makes a profit, but when apportioned to individual partners between salary, etc. one partner appears to have a negative allocation. In that case he is adjusted to "nil" and the profit reallocated amongst the remaining partners. This situation arises when the partners have made too small a profit to fund the salaries, part of which are paid out of capital.

Example

Johnson and Kelly trade as partners. Their accounts show:

Allowable expenditure		60,000	Receipts	73,000
Depreciation		3,000		
Partners' salaries:				
Johnson	20,000			
Kelly	5,000	25,000	Accounting loss	15,000
		88,000		88,000

They share profits/losses equally.

Tax adjustment:

Accounting loss		(15,000)
Partners' salaries	25,000	
Depreciation	3,000	28,000
Taxable profit		13,000

Allocation:

	Total	Johnson	Kelly
Profit	13,000		
Salaries	25,000	20,000	5,000
Fictional loss	(12,000)	(6,000)	(6,000)
		14,000	(1,000)

Kelly is assessed on nothing, Johnson on £13,000.

You should now attempt the "Income Tax" questions: 4, 5, 6, 20, 22 (*see* pages 249–62).

Chapter Eleven

Schedule E – Income from Employment

Employment

Schedule E taxes the earnings from employment. It is not always too clear what is meant by "employment" as opposed to "self-employment" taxable under Schedule D, Cases I & II.

Some employers may prefer hired staff to be treated as self-employed. From an employer's point of view, they would then not have to operate the PAYE system, deducting at source income tax and national insurance contributions and pay them over to the Collector of Taxes. A recipient who was treated as self-employed would receive his money gross, pay his tax a significant time later by assessment, probably pay less national insurance, and may obtain more allowance for expenditure incurred.

What is meant by employment is difficult to define in some cases. "Employment" generally means there is a "contract of services", where the employer exercises significant control over the employee, having the right under the contract to determine such things as the level of pay, the hours of work, the place of work, the duties to be performed, and probably the holiday and sick pay regulations.

On the other hand, "self-employment" means a "contract for services", where the charge for services is negotiable, and the worker largely determines the hours of work, where the work is performed, how it is performed, and probably involves many contracts with different principals at the same time rather than working only for one person.

If there is any doubt regarding the classification then the following factors should be considered.

1. The financial arrangements. Is the rate of remuneration imposed by the principal or directly negotiable; who takes responsibility for losses incurred; and can the worker participate in larger than expected profits?

Who is responsible for expenses such as insurance for negligence, etc?

2. Who provides the equipment and maintains and repairs it?

3. Is the person hired free to work for other principals?

4. Do the duties require attendance at a specified place and times, and are the duties strictly regulated?

5. Who is responsible for administrative arrangements; does the person hired have independent office facilities?

6. Does the person hired have the appearance of self-employment? Is he or she registered for VAT, listed in yellow pages; does he or she advertise regularly and independently of the principal?

The consequences of making the wrong choice can be very serious for the principal. If he is judged to have employees rather than self-employed subcontractors, he can be charged for all the unpaid PAYE income tax and national insurance contributions, and may well, in addition, suffer a heavy penalty.

Emoluments

Emoluments from employment are taxable under Schedule E, the tax being generally paid by deduction at source under the PAYE scheme.

''Emoluments'' mainly consist of three elements:

1. Payment in cash.
2. Benefits-in-kind.
3. Compensation payments and other capital sums.

Payments in cash

Introduction

Schedule E is taxable on a current year basis. Up to 5th April, 1989 this meant being taxed strictly on what was called the ''earnings'' or ''arising'' basis, that is what was earned even though not necessarily received in a particular tax year. However, two other bases were in practice often used to determine the year of assessment for occasional large sums such as annual bonuses or commission.

Example

A salesman earned a basic salary of £1,000 per month plus commission calculated and paid annually after the employer's year end which is 31st December. He earned commission of:

y/e	31st December, 1987	£4,000 paid 1st May, 1988
	31st December, 1988	£6,000 paid 1st May, 1989
	31st December, 1989	£9,000 paid 1st May, 1990

For 1988/89 his earnings were:

Salary	$1{,}000 \times 12 =$	12,000
Commission (earnings basis) for period 6/4/88 to 5/4/89:		
$6{,}000 \times {}^{9}/_{12} =$	4,500	
$9{,}000 \times {}^{3}/_{12} =$	2,250	6,750
Total emoluments		18,750

The "accounts" basis equated the company's year end with the tax year so that on that basis the taxable commission for 1988/89 would have been £9,000 (for the y/e 31/12/88). The "receipts" basis assessed the commission in the tax year it was received. From 6th April, 1989, only the receipts basis is used to assess Sch.E. liability.

Emoluments are treated as "received" for assessment purposes when the *earliest* of the following events occurs:

1. When actual payment is made of, or on accounts of, earnings;
2. When a person becomes entitled to payments of, or on account of, emoluments.

In the case of directors, emoluments will, additionally, be treated as received when:

3. Sums on account of emoluments are credited in the company's accounts or records (irrespective of any restrictions on the director's rights of withdrawal).
4. Emoluments for a period of account are determined before the end of that period.
5. The amount of emoluments for a period of account is determined, if that is after the end of that period.

Example

For the year ended 31st December, 1990 a company votes directors' bonuses at a Board meeting held on 10th December, 1990 but they are only credited to the loan accounts on 1st May, 1991. The bonuses will be taxed in 1990/91.

Calculation of employers' profits: To prevent tax avoidance in family controlled companies, and others, a new provision is introduced for deducting remuneration in calculating trading profit for all accounting periods ending after 5th April, 1989.

If remuneration has not been paid within 9 months after the end of the period of account in which it was earned, and for which it is charged, it is not deductible in calculating the taxable profit of the employer, but is only allowed for the period of account in which it is actually paid. It is treated as "paid" when it is "received" for Schedule E purposes. Thus, there is a direct link between the deduction to the employer and the assessment on the recipient employee.

Example

A company allocates £30,000 to an employee (not a director) as a bonus for y/e 31st December, 1990, but does not pay it to him until 30th June, 1992. The bonus would be treated as a deduction against income of the employer for the y/e 31st December, 1992, not y/e 31st December, 1990.

Benefits in kind

General

Good or services paid instead of cash to an employee are still assessable as earnings. The main difficulty is quantifying the amount assessable, and some benefits are, but only occasionally, free of tax.

There are three main categories of benefit, two of them depending on the level of earnings of the employee, the third consisting of benefits where the rules do not depend on the amount of earnings.

The earnings rule divides employees into "lower paid" and "higher paid" (although these terms are no longer used, officially), the relevant level for 1990/91 being £8,500. In determining this level, all cash earnings and benefits valued as for a higher paid employee are added together, but no deduction at all is allowed for any expenses.

Example

A company accountant has these details for 1990/91:

Salary 600 per month × 12	=	7,200
Yearly bonus	=	700
Value of benefits assuming he is higher paid		800
Gross taxable earnings		8,700
Expenses deductible for tax	=	(300)
Net taxable earnings		8,400

The important figure is the gross taxable earnings, £8,700 and the salesman is therefore deemed to be higher paid.

Also included as earning over £8,500 are directors who, whatever their level of earnings, have a "material interest" in their company (more than 5% of the share capital) unless they work for a non-profit-making organisation.

Employees earning £8,500 or less:

The rule is that benefits are valued according to their "moneysworth" or secondhand value. Thus, an asset which cost the company £400 but is worth only £250 secondhand, is valued as a benefit of £250 when it is given to the employee. This can apply to consumer durables, clothing, etc. Assets loaned to a lower paid employee have no secondhand value to him and thus no benefit arises.

Employees earning over £8,500:

The general rule is that the measure of the benefit is the cost to the employer of providing the benefit whether it be gifted or loaned. Special rules apply to the provision of cars and these are dealt with in appendix 1.

Loaned assets are deemed to have an annual value of 20% of their original cost or, if greater, the cost of providing it (e.g. the employer rents it). Thus, on the loan by the employer of a television set costing £400 would give an annual benefit of £80.

If an asset is first loaned and later given to the employee the benefit on the gift is the original cost less benefits assessed during the period of loan, unless its secondhand value is greater.

Example

An employer provides a colour television costing £500 for the private use of a higher paid employee. It was purchased on 1/10/89 and given to him on 30/6/90, when its secondhand value was £300.

1989/90 (loaned 1/10/89 to 5/4/90) $500 \times 20\% = 100 \times 6/12 = 50$

1990/91 (loaned 6/4/90 to 30/6/90) $500 \times 20\% = 100 \times 3/12 = 25$

Gift	500
Assessed on loan	75
	425

Total benefit for 1990/91 25+425=450

Beneficial loans at less than a rate of interest set by the Treasury (which is varied from time to time) are assessed on the difference of the interest actually paid and the Treasury rate. No benefit arises if the taxpayer could obtain tax relief on the interest (e.g. a loan of up to £30,000 to buy his only or main residence) or the net benefit does not exceed £200 in the year.

Example

In a tax year a director receives a £50,000 loan at 4% from his employer which he uses to buy his only or main residence.

50,000×10% (assumed Treasury rate)	=	5,000 (gross benefit)
Qualifying for relief 30,000@10%	=	(3,000)
		2,000
Interest actually paid (on 20,000 non-qualifying portion of loan) 20,000×4%	=	(800)
Net assessable benefit		1,200

Other benefits specifically taxed on the higher paid but not on the lower paid include:

1. The provision of scholarships (unless awarded before 15th March, 1983) to a member of the employee's family.
2. Private medical insurance premiums.

The provision of child care by an employer for his employees is specifically excluded from being an assessable benefit, provided certain conditions are satisfied. These conditions are that the employer should at least partly be responsible for the financing and management of the child care.

Benefits when level of earnings is irrelevant

Some benefits do not depend on the level of earnings to determine whether or not they are taxable, and if so the amount of the benefit.

Some are free of tax:

1. A payment prior to commencement of employment provided it is not merely advance salary, e.g. a payment to an amateur sportsman to give up his amateur status and play professionally.
2. Reasonable gifts by an employer on occasions when merited, e.g. marriage and retirement, long service awards (£20 value per year of service is deemed "reasonable"). A Christmas or birthday bonus paid every year would be considered taxable.
3. Pension contributions by an employer to a pension scheme which has been approved by the Inland Revenue.
4. Shares allocated under a profit-sharing scheme approved by the Inland Revenue. See appendix 4 for details.
5. Part of earnings under a profit related pay scheme (PRP). (see appendix 5 for details.)
6. Removal expenses when the move is at the instigation of the employer.
7. Subsidised staff canteens if the facilities are available to all the staff.

Items which are taxable include:

1. Luncheon vouchers in excess of 15p per day.
2. Self-contained living accommodation, dealt with in more detail in appendix 2. The provision of free bed and board (e.g. in the hotel trade) is not assessable on the lower paid.
3. Cash vouchers and transport vouchers (e.g. season tickets). The full value is taxable. Lower paid employees of transport undertaking are not assessed on transport vouchers if the scheme was operative on 25th March, 1982.

Costs of training

If an employer incurs the cost of a qualifying training course for employees it is an allowable trading expense for the employer and is not chargeable on the employee as a benefit-in-kind.

A qualifying course has to be designed to teach or to improve an employee's skill or knowledge, and must be relevant to employment or self-employment. The course must not exceed one year and must be held within the U.K. The employee must attend substantially full-time and must have been employed by the employer for at least two years full-time.

The employee must undertake the course whilst still employed or within one year after cessation of employment, and must cease employment with the employer within two years of the end of the course. Re-employment with the same employer within two years is not allowed.

The costs incurred can include attendance and examination fees, books and travel costs.

Administration

Employers have to submit a special return to the Inland Revenue of benefits provided for each higher paid employee, the form known as P11D.

Expenses claims have, at least in theory, to be made separately by the employee.

When expenses are paid by an employer to match expenses incurred by an employee wholly in the performance of his duties, the Inland Revenue will sometimes grant a dispensation, which means the employer does not have to make a return on form P11D of the expenses reimbursed, and the employee need not make a separate expenses claim.

Compensation on termination of employment

Lump sum payments on loss of office or retirement may or may not be taxable:

1. Statutory redundancy payments, compensation for service overseas (when salary was free of U.K. tax), compensation for death of or injury to an employee, and commuted lump sums from approved pension schemes are free of tax.

2. Every pound of a capital sum to which an ex-employee is contractually entitled (e.g. percentage of a transfer fee due to a footballer) is taxable unless the capital sum is no more than would normally be paid.

3. Payments for compensation for loss of office, and ex-gratia (voluntary) payments are treated the same way.

Prior to 6th April, 1988 the first £25,000 was free of tax (although statutory redundancy pay reduced this), the next £25,000 (to £50,000 total) was then taxed at half the relevant rates, the next £25,000 (to £75,000 total) at three-quarters of the relevant rates, and any further payments were fully taxed.

From 6th April, 1988 the first £30,000 of such payments are free of tax (still subject to the reduction for statutory redundancy pay received), but then the balance is fully taxed as though it were the highest part of income received in the relevant tax year.

Example

Dai the Death, a Welshman, is made redundant from his employment as an undertaker on 30th November, 1990. He earned £13,000 from 6th April, 1990 until 30th November, 1990. He obtained further employment on 1st February, 1991 and earned £1,500 up to 5th April, 1991.

His other income for 1990/91 was £2,000, he paid mortgage interest of £1,200 (gross) in the year, under the MIRAS scheme, and was married.

He was paid £3,000 statutory redundancy pay and £50,000 additional compensation on being made redundant.

The tax payable is:

Sch.E	13,000			
	1,500	14,500		
Other income		2,000		
		16,500		
Mortgage interest		(1,200)	tax deducted	300.00
		15,300		
SPA 3,005				
MCA 1,720		(4,725)		
		10,575	×25% =	2,643.75
Tax payable on income				2,943.75

Compensation for loss of office:

Gross receipt		50,000
Exempt	30,000	
Statutory redundancy pay	(3,000)	(27,000)
Taxable		23,000

20,700 − 10,575	=	10,125 × 25%	=	2,531.25
		12,875 × 40%	=	5,150.00
		23,000		
Tax payable on compensation				7,681.25

Deduction of expenses

Expenses "wholly, exclusively and necessarily" paid by the employee can be a deduction from the gross earnings. To be allowed the expenditure must be absolutely essential (not just desirable) and there can be no element of personal choice, each employee in the same situation would have to expend the same (e.g. where you live is a matter of personal choice and therefore the expense of travelling to and from work is not allowable).

The main expenses under Sch.E are:

1. Superannuation contributions to approved schemes.
2. Subscriptions to professional bodies.
3. The cost of essential tools and clothing provided by the employee. For certain trades standard annual deductions have been agreed by the Revenue.
4. Travel costs from the work base to other places of work, unless reimbursed by the employer (but not travel from home to place of work).
5. From 1st October, 1990 there is a new relief for single gifts of cash by individuals to charities for amounts of between £600 and £5,000,000. As with covenants, these gifts will be made under deduction of basic rate tax, but also qualify for higher rate relief.

Charities: payroll deduction scheme
An individual employee may, for 1990–91, elect to contribute to charity, up to £600 (from 6th April, 1990) a year through a payroll deduction scheme, whereby the employer deducts the contributions from gross pay and only applies PAYE to the net pay. The employer must hand over the deductions to an approved agent who will pay the charities.

Overseas earnings

When an individual works outside the UK or a foreigner works in the UK there may be a reduction or exemption from UK tax.

If an employee is outside the UK for a continuous period of 365 days or more he gets complete exemption from UK tax on his earnings. During the period of overseas employment he can return to the UK without prejudice to his exemption provided his return visits do not exceed either 62 continuous days or one-sixth in aggregate of his total period of service abroad.

Example
An employee goes to work abroad on an overseas contract:
He works:

		Days in UK	1/6th calculation
Day 1 to day 200	Overseas		
Day 201 to day 260	In UK	60 (under 62)	
Day 261 to day 400	Overseas		$400 \times \frac{1}{6} = 67$
Day 401 to day 440	In UK	40 (under 62)	
Day 441 to day 460	Abroad		$460 \times \frac{1}{6} = 77$
Day 461	Returns permanently to UK		

To count as a day abroad the employee must be out of the UK at midnight.

Relief for non-UK domiciled individuals

Relief from UK tax granted to non-UK domiciled individuals working in the UK is being phased out. Up to 5th April, 1984 such an individual was entitled to a 50% deduction from emoluments unless he had been resident in the UK in 9 out of the 10 previous tax years in which case the deduction was reduced to 25%. However:

1. If the employee was not entitled to such relief on 13th March, 1984 then no relief is available from 14th March, 1984 unless he took up his duties before 1st April, 1984 under an existing contract.
2. From 6th April, 1984 no relief at all is given to any individual resident in the UK for 9 out of the previous 10 tax years.

3. If the individual was entitled to the 50% relief before 6th April, 1984 and would have continued to be entitled to that relief, then the relief was gradually phased out as folows:

Up to 5th April, 1987	50%
6th April, 1987 to 5th April, 1989	25%
6th April, 1989 onwards	Nil

Overseas travelling expenses

The rules regarding the tax treatment of overseas travelling expenses have been retrospectively amended from 6th April, 1984 as follows:

1. An employee working abroad, but resident and ordinarily resident in the UK is entirely free of tax on any reimbursement by the employer of travel expenses between the UK and the overseas place of employment.
2. Similar reliefs are available to self-employed UK citizens carrying on a business entirely abroad.
3. In the case of an expatriate working in the UK reimbursed travel expenses are free of UK tax for the first 5 years from arrival in the UK.
4. If an employee works abroad for at least 60 days, the cost of travel and accommodation for his family to visit him abroad paid for by the employer is not a taxable benefit.

A UK resident who is in receipt in the UK of emoluments paid from abroad for years when he has been resident in the UK (the so-called ''remittance basis'') is assessable on his remittances to the UK.

Example
An individual who works abroad and is paid a £40,000 annual salary is resident in the UK for 1990–91. He remits £22,000 to the UK to meet his living expenses. He is taxable in the UK on £22,000.

Pay as you earn (PAYE)

This is the method of collecting tax due under Sch.E but the determination of the amount of that tax (and the amount of taxable income) are subject to the rules of Sch.E.

At the beginning of each tax year the Inland Revenue allocate each taxpayer a code number based on his claim for personal allowances, and special tables for special circumstances.

When an employee leaves the employer completes form P45 in triplicate. This shows the total pay received and the total tax deducted. One part of the form goes to the tax office, and the other two are given to the employee who in turn hands them on to his next employer. If there is a gap in employment generally a refund is due when the first payment is made in the next employment.

When allowances are withdrawn, instead of collecting the extra tax due in one amount (which may be considerable) the Revenue spread its collection over the balance of the tax year by using a "Week 1" procedure. If all the underpayment is not collected that year the balance is transferred to the following tax year for collection under PAYE.

For all higher paid employees, the employer has annually to submit to the relevant Tax District a form P11D which is a return of benefits in kind provided for that employee during the year.

PAYE deductions are paid over to the Inland Revenue monthly.

Benefits paid to the unemployed and strikers and many other government benefits are also taxable. The main ones are widows' and old age pensions, maternity pay and job release allowances.

Appendix 1: provision of private cars for higher paid employees

The calculation of the benefit is standardised depending on the particular circumstances.

1. If the employee uses a car for business for 2,500 miles or less per annum the benefit is 1½ times the scale benefit (see below). This is termed "insubstantial" business use.

2. If the employee uses the car more than 2,500 miles but less than 18,000 miles per annum for business his benefit is determined by a table of scale rates which are calculated on the engine size or price of the car. They cover the benefit arising from provision of the car, maintenance and running costs, apart from private petrol and the provision of a chauffeur.

3. If the car is used for business for 18,000 miles or more per annum, the scale charge is halved.

When *any* private petrol is provided by the employer at an advantageous price, an additional fuel benefit is added as a benefit in kind. The amount of the fuel benefit is halved if the annual business mileage (or proportionate equivalent) is 18,000 miles or more. However, it is *not* affected if the business mileage is less than 2,500 miles.

The scale of benefits for 1990/91 are as follows:

Cars costing up to £19,250:

Engine size	Under 4 years old	4 years old or over*
1400 cc or less	1,700	1,150
1401 cc to 2000 cc	2,200	1,500
2001 cc or more	3,550	2,350
Cars costing over £19,250:		
£19,250 to £29,000	4,600	3,100
Over £29,000	7,400	4,900

*Note: The age of a car is measured on the last day of the relevant tax year (1988/89, 5th April, 1989).

If the car is not available to the employee until part way through the year or is withdrawn from availability to him part way through the year, the benefit is proportionately reduced on a daily basis. If the car is unavailable for use for a period of at least 30 consecutive days, the benefit is again reduced.

Any second or subsequent car provided for an employee is taxed at 1½ times the scale benefit, regardless of its business use.

Petrol scale benefit for 1990/91:

Engine size:	
1400 or under	480
1401 to 2000	600
Over 2000	900

4. Cars provided from a ''pool'' are not a taxable benefit. To be a pool they must be provided as part of a fleet for the use of all employees primarily for business purposes. No one car must be regularly reserved for the use of one employee, and the car must not be regularly kept overnight on or near the private residence of an employee.

Example

Henry Robinson joins a new company on 1/7/90. He is paid £40,000 a year and provided with two cars, the company paying for all private and business petrol:

Car 1:	Cost (June, 1988)	£17,000
	Engine size	3,000 cc
	Business mileage 1/7/90 to 5/4/91	15,000 miles (equivalent to 20,000 miles for 12 months)
Car 2:	Cost (August, 1983)	£6,000
	Engine size	1,200 cc
	Business mileage 1/7/90 to 5/4/91	4,000 miles

Sch.E:

Salary 40,000

Car 1: Scale benefit:

$$3{,}550\times\frac{1}{2}^{*} = 1{,}775\times\frac{279\S}{365} = 1{,}356$$

Fuel benefit:

$$900\times\frac{1}{2}^{*} = 450\times\frac{279\S}{365} = \underline{344} \qquad 1{,}700$$

Car 2:	Scale benefit:			
	$1{,}150 \times \frac{1.5^{**}}{1} = 1{,}725 \times \frac{279§}{365} =$	1,318		
	Fuel benefit: $480 \times \frac{279}{365}$	367	1,685	3,385
				43,385

Notes: *Business mileage over 18,000 per annum, leading to only 50% of benefit being chargeable.
**Second car always charged at 1½ times scale benefit (not fuel benefit).
§Cars only available from 1/7/90 to 5/4/91 (279 days).

Appendix 2: self-contained living accommodation

General

Self-contained living accommodation provided by an employer is a taxable benefit on all employees irrespective of earnings if it is "beneficial", that is, merely a perquisite of the job. It can be free of tax if the occupation is "representative" that is the accommodation is provided because of the special nature of the job.

There can also be additional benefits if the employer pays expenses on behalf of the occupying employee such as fuel bills, etc. or provides furniture. The two exceptions are:

1. Rates paid by the employer are not a taxable benefit if the occupation is representative. Payment of community charge is taxable benefit.

2. Furniture provided by the employer on loan to a lower paid employee is not assessable because of the "moneysworth" rule.

Representative occupation

The provision of accommodation is free of tax if provided:

1. For an employee when it is essential for him to occupy the premises to perform the job. Examples are the armed forces, certain security staff and country policemen.

2. It is traditional to provide accommodation for workers, e.g. agricultural labourers, bank managers at isolated branches.

3. There is a security threat to the employee, e.g. security forces in Northern Ireland, some politicians.

If the accommodation itself is not a taxable benefit because of representative occupation, then certain ancillary benefits can be wholly or partly exempt. We have already mentioned that rates paid by the employer are not a taxable benefit in these circumstances. Other payments of running costs or the provision of furnishings or staff are limited to an overall benefit of 10% of net emoluments, provided the recipient does not have a material interest in the company, i.e. they do not have more than 5%, together with their associates, of the company's share capital.

Example

A company provides a house for a senior employee, the Inland Revenue agreeing the occupation is representative.

The company pay:

Rates			700
Heat and light			1,400
Wages and domestic staff			12,000
Furnishing provided cost 35,000×20% =			7,000
			21,100

The employee earns:

Salary			35,000
Bonus			10,000
Car – scale benefit			2,200
fuel benefit			600
			47,800
Expenses:			
	Pension fund	1,750	
	Others allowable	900	(2,650)
			45,150

The taxable benefit on ancillary benefits paid in connection with the accommodation is limited to 45,150×10%=4,515 giving a total taxable Sch.E income of 45,150+4,515=49,665.

Beneficial occupatoin

The accommodation itself leads to one and possibly two taxable benefits:

1. The minimum taxable benefit is the gross annual value of the premises for the old rating purposes (GAV). If the house is new, and has not been valued for rates, the Inland Revenue will issue a deemed value. Plus;

2. If the cost of providing the premises exceeds £75,000, a percentage (the same as the rate of interest on beneficial loans) on the excess. If the property has been owned by the employer (or what is technically known as any relevant person – those connected with the employer) for six years prior to the occupation by an employee, the additional charge is based on the market value of the premises at the date of occupation by the employee.

Both of these are reduced by any rent paid by the employee.

Example

A company gross annual rateable value provides a house for a new director. The house costs £200,000, the GAV of the property is £700. The Treasury rate of interest is, say, 17%. The director pays rent of £500 per annum.

GAV	700
Additional charge 200,000 − 75,000 =	
125,000 × 17% =	21,250
	21,950
Rent paid	(500)
Net assessable benefit	21,450

Ancillary benefits provided by the employer are taxable in full, without any restriction for the 10% rule. These would include payment by the employer of community charge, fuel charges, and the cost of providing furniture (20% rule would apply) and domestic staff.

Appendix 3: profit sharing and share option schemes

Profit sharing

These schemes have little to do with the actual sharing of companies' profits but is merely a method of making shares available to employees so that they are taxable to capital gains and not under Sch.E on disposal.

Such schemes involve a trust being set up which is available to all employees and contributions to the fund are allowable deductions against the company's profit.

The maximum value of shares allocated to any one employee is not to exceed, from 6th April, 1989, the greater of £2,000 or 10% of employee's salary (with an upper limit of £6,000). The shares must be retained for a minimum period of 2 years. If they are disposed of in under 2 years a full income tax charge results, but this is then tapered until at 5 years or over the charge is only to capital gains tax.

Approved share option schemes

Under a new scheme from 6th April, 1984 no income tax is charged on exercise of an option by the employee, on captial gains unless at the time the shares are granted they are provided at less than market value.

Employees who have over 10% of a close company's shares are not eligible, and the maximum which can be held is the greater of £100,000 or 4 times the participator's emoluments.

Share incentive schemes

Disadvantages of the profit sharing schemes outlined above is that they must be open to all employees and maximum amounts are limited. An employer can operate a more general share incentive scheme. However, if shares are acquired at less than market value an income tax charge arises.

Employees in higher paid employment can be assessed to income tax on acquisitions of shares on deferred terms or partly paid shares. Then the employee is deemed to enjoy the benefit of an interest free loan equal to the excess of the market value of the shares over the price paid.

Appendix 4: profit related pay (PRP)

When a profit related pay scheme which has been approved in advance by the Inland Revenue is operated by an employer, half the profit related pay is free of tax. PRP is defined as the lower of:

1. 20% of total pay; or
2. £4,000 per annum.

For income tax assessment purposes, PRP counts as income for the year of assessment in which it is paid rather than the year in which it is earned (the "receipts" basis, not the "earning" basis).

Tax relief is given on PRP by the employer through the operation of PAYE and the employer can claim tax relief on the whole of the PRP payments as a deduction against taxable trading profit, as he can for all ordinary salary payments.

With certain exceptions, such as employers in or under the control of central and local government, any employer can register a scheme for any profitable group, company or firm, or for any profitable sub-unit of these. The scheme has to be approved and registered by the Inland Revenue (by the Profit Related Pay Office) before the start of the first "profit period" (generally the employer's accounting period) the scheme is to cover. Applications for registration and the year-to-year operation of a scheme has to be independently audited.

A scheme's rules have to provide a clear relationship between PRP and profits, and at the start of a scheme, if profits in the first year of operation are unaltered, PRP has to be at least five per cent of the eligible employees' pay.

"Controlling directors", those with a 25 per cent or more interest in the company, must be excluded from PRP schemes, and employees with less than three years service and part-timers working less than 20 hours a week may be excluded, but apart from that at least 80 per cent of the employees at the beginning of each profit period covered by the scheme must be eligible to receive PRP.

Appendix 5: Personal equity plans (PEPs)

This is a scheme to encourage investment in UK incorporated companies. Under such a plan reinvested dividends are free of income tax and reinvested capital profits are free of capital gains tax.

To qualify:

1. The investor must be aged 18 or over, and resident and ordinarily resident in the UK.

2. A maximum of £6,000 can be invested each tax year.

3. The fund must be invested in ordinary shares listed on a UK stock exchange, but if investment is in unit trusts or investment trusts, then the trusts involved must invest at least 50% in UK equities from 6th April, 1990.

4. Cash can be held in the plan, but interest paid on the cash is subject to composite rate tax.

5. It is possible to switch investment in shares to unit and investment trusts provided the value of the holdings in unit or investment trusts does not exceed half the total value of the fund immediately after the switch.

6. The fund must be managed by an approved manager.
7. A PEP fund can invest up to £3,000 in unit or investment trusts.

Appendix 6: employees using their own cars in the course of employment

Up to 5th April, 1990, employees using their own cars in the course of their employment, on their employers' business, could be paid a tax free mileage allowance for business mileage. Only if the payment exceeded these rates was the excess taxed as earnings. The tax free rates were:

Engine size	**Up to 1000 cc**	**1001 to 1500 cc**	**Over 1500 cc**
Tax free rate per mile	24.5p	30p	34p

Capital allowances, as plant and machinery, could not be claimed on the cost of the car.

From 6th April, 1990, the scheme has been altered in two ways:

1. The tax free mileage allowance has been altered, generally to the disadvantage of the employee.
2. Capital allowances can now be claimed on the cost of a private car used om the employer's business, and tax relief can be claimed on interest paid on a loan to buy a car used on business journeys connectd with the employment.

The tax free mileage allowance that can be paid to an employee for journeys undertaken on the employer's business depends on the total business mileage done in the tax year. The tax free rate is different for the first 4,000 business miles in a tax year, and at a lower rate for all business miles in excess of 4,000 miles in a year.

Engine size	**Up to 1000 cc**	**1001 to 1500 cc**	**1501 to 2000 cc**	**Over 2000 cc**
Tax free mileage rates up to 4,000 miles	24.5p	30p	34p	43p
Over 4,000 miles	9.5p	11.5p	13.5p	16.5p

From 6th April, 1990, employees can also claim plant and machinery allowances on a proportion of the cost of the car as is justified by their proportion of business use.

An employee can also, from 6th April, 1990, claim tax relief on an appropriate proportion of the interest on a loan used to purchase the car.

As some employees may be worse off under the new arrangements if they do over 4,000 miles a year on their employer's business, it is provided that any additional taxable amount arising from these new arrangements, that is that they will now be paid a smaller tax free mileage rate, is not to exceed £1,000 per tax year. However, this transitional arrangement is only limited to the same mileage done before 6th April, 1990. If there is any increase in the annual business mileage, any additional taxable mileage payments arising from the increased mileage is taxable in full.

Chapter Twelve

Income from property – Schedule A

General

All rents and other income arising from property is assessable under Sch.A except:

1. Rents from furnished accommodation which come under Sch.D, Case VI unless the taxpayer elects (within 2 years of the end of the relevant year of assessment) to have the rent from the property assessed under Sch.A. The proportion of the rent relating to the furniture is still assessed under Sch.D, Case VI. The advantage for making a Sch.A election would be to allow a loss on the Sch.D, Case VI to be offset against Sch.A income.
2. Mineral rents and royalties.

The basis of assessment is rent due in the actual year of assessment (less allowable expenditure). However, the tax is payable on 1st January in the year of assessment, but the actual rents receivable are not known until the following April. Therefore, a provisional assessment is raised on the rents received in the previous year. This can be amended if the taxpayer can show (before January) that the current year's income will be less than the previous year's. In any event the assessment will be amended to the actual income after the end of the year.

The assessment is based on rent due. If it has not actually been paid over then the landlord can have the assessment reduced provided he can show reasonable attempts have been made to try and obtain payment.

Allowable expenditure

Expenditure of the Landlord is allowable on much the same principles of Sch.D, Case I, revenue expenditure being allowed, capital expenditure not. Therefore the costs of maintenance, repair, insurance, etc. are allowable together with any tenant's expenses (rates, etc.) paid by the landlord and charged for in the rent.

Each source of income (e.g. lease) must be dealt with separately, and except as allowed for below any payment on a lease cannot be allowed against income from another lease. The expense must have been incurred on the same property in the current or a previous year except for expenditure incurred:

1. In a period when the landlord personally occupied the premises.
2. In a period when the property was let at less than a commercial rent.
3. Any period when the property was unoccupied following 1 or 2.
4. A period between purchase and ending with 1 or 2.

When there is allowable excess expenditure on a let property it can be relieved against income from other property on the following basis:

1. Income from a landlord's repairing lease can absorb excess expenditure from any other lease at a full rent.
2. Excess expenditure from a tenant's repairing lease can only be carried forward against future income from the same lease or offset against income from a landlord's repairing lease (not against another tenant's repairing lease).

Example

A landlord has three properties. Nos. 1, 2 and 3, all let at full rent but 1 and 2 are tenant's repairing leases and 3 a landlord's repairing lease.

In year 1 the situation is:

	1	2		3
Rents	600	500		400
Expenditure	850	300		250
	(250)	200		150
Offset against No. 3	150		Offset on No. 1	(150)
Carry forward	(100)			Nil

Net Sch.A assessment for year 1 = 200

In year 2:

		1		2		3
Rents		600		500		400
Expenditure of year	450					
B/F	100	550		570		340
		50		(70)		60
			Offset against No. 3	60	Offset on No. 2	(60)
			Carry forward	(10)		Nil

Net Sch.A assessment = 50

Premiums on short leases

Premiums received on leases exceeding 50 years are not assessable to income tax, but premiums on leases of shorter duration are, subject to a form of tapering relief which is to relieve from income tax 2% of the premium for each year of its duration less the first.

Example
A landlord receives a premium of £30,000 on a lease for 40 years.

Full premium	30,000
Relieved from income tax:	
2% × 39(40 − 1) × 30,000 =	(23,400)
Assessable to income tax	6,600

If the premises on which the premium has been paid are used for business purposes then the tenant can gain tax relief on the proportion of the premium assessed to income tax (£6,600 in the above example). The tenant can treat this part of the premium as rent paid during the duration of the lease and he gets a yearly allowance of the resultant

6,600/40 = 165 per annum for 40 years

Capital allowances

Capital allowance can be claimed on plant and machinery purchased for repair and maintenance of the premises or for the use of tenants.

Under Sch.D, Case VI on furnished lettings the taxpayer cannot claim capital allowances on the furniture he initially provides (but are apparently given on furniture in holiday lettings – see below). He can only claim tax relief on the cost of furniture he replaces. As an alternative, he can claim an annual deduction of 10% of the rents received, excluding any part of the rent which covers tenants' liabilities.

Example
A landlord charges an annual rent of £1,400 on a furnished flat of which £300 is to cover tenants' expenses – fuel costs, etc.

He would get a renewals allowance on the furniture of:

Full rent	1,400
Tenants' outgoings	(300)
	1,100 × 10% = 110

Therefore, assuming allowable expenditure of £350, the assessment would be:

Full rent		1,400
Expenditure	350	
Renewals allowance	110	(460)
Assessable		940

Furnished holiday lettings
Broadly, the income from furnished lettings which satisfy certain conditions is treated virtually as trading income, even if not actually assessed under Sch.D,

Case I. Thus the income is treated as earned, losses can be offset against general income, and the income can be utilised in a retirement annuity premium claim. In capital gains roll-over and retirement reliefs are available.

To be so treated, the following conditions must be satisfied:

1. The accommodation must actually be let on a commercial basis.
2. The letting must be of furnished accommodation.
3. The accommodation must be available for commercial letting to the public generally as holiday accommodation for periods which amount in aggregate to not less than 140 days in a period of 12 months.
4. The accommodation must actually be let for at least 70 days in the 12 months.
5. During 7 of the 12 months, the accommodation must not normally be in the same occupation for a continuous period exceeding 31 days.

It is possible to submit a claim for averaging when determining whether the provision of accommodation satisfies the furnished holiday letting requirements.

Chapter Thirteen

Miscellaneous Sources of Income

Bank and building society interest

Clearing banks, buildings societies, local authorities and other financial institutions paying interest on deposit in the UK to individuals resident in the UK are on interest paid from 6th April, 1985 taxed on the so-called "composite rate" scheme. The actual rate of tax the institutions pay to the Inland Revenue varies from year to year, but normally is less than the basic rate of income tax the individual recipient is deemd to have had paid on his behalf. However, the tax deducted at source cannot be reclaimed in any circumstances either by the institution or the individual. It can only be offset as a credit on tax due. Such interest is assessed on the current year basis.

The main exceptions, where the interest can be paid without deduction of tax (paid gross) are:

1. National savings bank accounts. Interest on the ordinary account is exempt up to £70 per individual (husband and wife get separate £70 exemptions). This exemption does not apply to other accounts, such as monthly income, deposit, etc.
2. Certain government securities especially those purchased at the Post Office through the National Stock Register.
3. Non-resident depositors if the bank holds a valid declaration by the depositor.
4. Solicitors' and estate agents' undesignated client accounts.
5. Non-negotiable bonds and mortgage loans of local authorities if issued or renewed before 19th November, 1984.

Trustee Savings Bank and the National Giro Bank interest are also subject to the composite rate.

When interest is paid gross, it is assessed on the preceding year basis, with special rules in the opening and closing years of interest being paid (see later), under Schedule D, Case III.

The composite rate scheme is due to be abolished from 6th April, 1991, that is from tax year 1991–92. This is to enable people on low incomes (e.g. non-working wives) to invest in UK banks and buildings societies and other financial institutions without incurring a tax penalty.

From 6th April, 1991, basic rate tax will not be deducted from bank and building society interest if the account holder can certify the interest will not be subject to tax. If not, then basic rate tax will be deducted at source, but repayment can be claimed at the end of the tax year if there has been any overpayment. This will bring bank and building society interest into line with the treatment of company dividends assessable under Schedule F.

Example
Davies has the following income for the years ended 5th April, 1990 and 1991. His tax liability for 1990/91 is being computed:

Income for years ended	**5th April, 1990**	**5th April, 1991**
Salary (self)	14,000	25,000
Salary (wife)	6,000	7,000
Deposit account,		
National Midland Bank (self)	600 (net)	639 (net)
Share account,		
Allfax Building Society (wife)	700 (net)	852 (net)
National Savings Bank:		
Ordinary account (self)	80 (gross)	100 (gross)
(wife)	90 (gross)	120 (gross)
Deposit account (self)	300 (gross)	350 (gross)

1990/91 liability:

Husband:			**Wife:**		
Sch.E		25,000	Sch.E		7,000
Composite rate interest:			Composite rate interest:		
Nat. Midland Bank	639		Allfax Bldg Society	852	
Credit 639×⅓ =	213	852	Credit 852×⅓ =	284	1,136
Sch.D, Case III:			Sch.D, Case III:		
NSB Ord. A/c	80		NSB Ord. A/c	90	
Exempt	(70)		Exempt	(70)	20
	10				
Deposit A/c	300	310			
		26,162			8,156
SPA	3,005				
MCA	1,720	(4,725)	SPA		(3,005)
		21,437			5,151
20,700×25%	=	5,175.00	5,151×25%	=	1,287.75
737×40%	=	294.80			
21,437		5,469.80			
Credits:			Credits:		
Composite rate		(213.00)	Composite rate		(284.00)
Net tax payable		5,256.80	Net tax payable		1,003.75

Basis of assessment

When interest is paid gross the basis of assessment is:

1. The first and second tax years when interest is paid (*not* the tax year the account is opened), current year basis.

2. Third tax year and subsequent years, preceding year basis, with the taxpayer having the option to claim current year basis for the third year only.

3. On cessation of interest (e.g. closure of account) the final tax year is current year and the penultimate tax year as well if the interest therefore is higher than preceding year basis.

If a source ceases to yield any income for six consecutive years then a claim can be made for cessation basis to apply from the date interest last arose. If interest is then subsequently paid again, commencing basis arises.

In theory at least each separate deposit and withdrawal is treated as a commencement and cessation on that proportion of the interest, but in practice it is only applied to purchases and sales of blocks of government securities and sometimes to very large deposits and withdrawals from bank accounts.

Example

Gregory opens a National Savings Bank Deposit A/c in February, 1984 and closes it on 30th June, 1991. Interest paid:

31/12/85	105
31/12/86	212
31/12/87	198
31/12/88	224
31/12/89	398
31/12/90	414
30/6/91	82

Liability to tax:

1985/86 (first tax year interest credited)	105 (CY)
1986/87	212 (CY)
1987/88 (third tax year, taxpayer's choice of PY (212) or CY) (198) (PY)	198 (CY)
1988/89	198 (PY)
1989/90	224 (PY)
1990/91 (penultimate year, originally PY, amended to CY on closure of account in 1990/91) 398 (PY)	414 (CY)
1991/92 (final year)	82 (CY)

Company dividends (Schedule F)

Dividends paid by UK resident companies are paid under deduction of basic rate income tax (advance corporation tax to the company deducting it – see Chapter 14

–Corporation Tax) and is assessed on the individual recipient on a current year basis under Schedule F. The credit can be reclaimed in whole or in part if appropriate.

Trusts and settlements

Income from trustees paid to beneficiaries is paid under deduction of tax:

1. At the basic rate of income tax when the recipients are entitled to the income (life tenants having an interest in possession). The life tenants are assessable whether or not the income is actually paid, they are assessable on entitlement to income.

2. At the combined basic rate and additional surcharge (25%+10%=35%) for contingent beneficiaries of a discretionary or accumulation and maintenance settlements. Beneficiaries are only liable to tax on income actually paid, in the tax years it is paid, to them.

In both cases, tax deducted and paid by trustees, at whatever rate, is recoverable as appropriate by beneficiaries.

Example

Tempest is a widower aged 70, who in 1990/91 receives:

Old age pension			2,500
Pension from former employer			5,000
(Tax deducted, PAYE)			(800)
Income from grandfather's trust of which Tempest is life tenant – paid in 1990/91			852 (net)
Tax liability 1990/91:			
Sch.E:			
Old age pension			2,500
Private pension		800	
PAYE		5,000	7,500
Trust income	852		
Credit	284		1,136
			8,636
AA (single person)			(3,670)
			4,966
4,966×25% –			1,241.50
Credits:			
PAYE	800.00		
Trust income	284.00		(1,084.00)
Tax payable direct			157.50

Tax exempt special savings accounts (TESSAs)

Available from 1st January, 1991, are special bank and building society accounts, the interest from which is exempt from income tax. To achieve this exemption certain conditions must be satisfied:

1. The account must be opened by an adult (someone over 18) for a period of five years.
2. Up to £3,000 can be invested in the first year and up to £1,800 in each later year, up to an overall maximum investment of £9,000 in the five year life of the account. Husbands and wives can have separate TESSA accounts.
3. To achieve exemption from income tax over the five years, there must be no withdrawals of capital during the five year life of the account. Any capital withdrawal will lead to all the interest credited to the account throughout the entire period being subject to income tax.
4. Interest credited to the account can be withdrawn at any time, but will be subject to a deduction of basic rate tax, and will be subject to the higher rate by assessment if necessary if withdrawn within the 5 years.

Deep discount bonds

Definition

A deep discount security or bond is one issued at a discount of more than 15% of the redemption figure, but which exceeds ½% per annum for each complete year between the dates of issue and redemption. Excluded are:

1. Shares in a company.
2. Securities where the redemption is index-linked.
3. Redeemable securities which are treated as a distribution, and therefore subject to payment of ACT.

Charge to tax

The accrued income of any period of ownership is assessed as income under either Sch.D, Case II or VI, and is taxed in the year of disposal. For capital gains purposes, the disposal value is reduced by the figure taxed as income, which may give rise to an allowable capital loss.

The accrued income attributable to any period of ownership is calculated by the formula:

$$\frac{(A \times B)}{100} - C$$

Where:

A = adjusted issue price, which is the issue price plus the income elements for all previous income periods.

An income period is generally a twelve monthly anniversary from issue, or the period to redemption.

B = yield to maturity, which is the percentage yield compounded at the end of each income period.

C = amount of interest, if any, attributable to the income period, and has to be shown on the security certificate.

You should now attempt the "Income Tax" questions: 9, 18, 23, 25, 27 (*see* pages 249–62).

Chapter Fourteen

Corporation Tax

Introduction

Corporation tax is payable by all companies and unincorporated associations (sports clubs, etc.) resident in the UK, on all their profits and foreign resident companies on the profits they make in the UK.

Chargeable period

The chargeable period is a "chargeable accounting period" (CAP) which is the equivalent of a basis period in income tax. Corporation tax, however, is always a current year basis of assessment, there is no question of any preceding year basis. A CAP can never exceed 12 months in length, but can be shorter, in that a CAP must end on the earliest of one of the following:

1. The company's accounting date.
2. The commencement of a winding up or the appointment of a liquidator.
3. The company ceasing to be resident in the UK.
4. The company commencing or ceasing to trade.

Example

A company drew up accounts for the fifteen months 1st January, 1989 to 31st March, 1990. Its CAPs for corporation tax purposes would be:

12 months 1st January, 1989 to 31st December, 1989

3 months 1st January, 1990 to 31st March, 1990

Thus, if a company always draws up twelve monthly accounts to the same date, its period of account and the CAP will always coincide.

Rates

The rates of corporation tax are set for financial years which end on 31st March e.g. financial year 1990 runs from 1st April, 1990 to 31st March, 1991.

The actual rates of corporation tax are dependent on the level of "profit" made by the company. Moreover, the rates have been gradually reduced.

If "profit" exceeds £1,000,000 for FY 1990 (£750,000 for FY 1989 and earlier years), the standard rate of corporation tax is:

Financial year	Rates of tax
1986 (1/4/86 to 31/3/87)	35%
1987 (1/4/87 to 31/3/88)	35%
1988 (1/4/88 to 31/3/89)	35%
1989 (1/4/89 to 31/3/90)	35%
1990 (1/4/90 to 31/3/91)	35%

When "profit" is less than £200,000 for FY 1990 (£150,000 for FY 1989 and earlier years) then the small company rate applies which is:

Financial year	Rate of tax
1987	27%
1988	25%
1989	25%
1990	25%

For companies with profits between £200,000 and £1,000,000 the tax is initially calculated at the full standard rate and then a deduction made of the sum of what is known as the taper or marginal relief fraction. This fraction is:

$$\text{Upper limit } (1{,}000{,}000) - \text{profit (see later)} \times \frac{\text{Chargeable profit}}{\text{Profit}} \times \text{a fraction}$$

The fraction varies from financial year to financial year. Relevant ones are:

Financial year	Taper relief fraction
1985	$^1/_{40}$
1986	$^3/_{200}$
1987	$^1/_{50}$
1988	$^1/_{40}$
1989 & 1990	$^1/_{40}$

Profit and chargeable profit

"Profit" consists of all income, chargeable gains (see later) and franked investment income (FII). "Chargeable profit" is the total of all items assessable under the schedules and cases of income tax (corporation tax uses them as well, with some small adaptations) plus capital gains less annual charges and interest payments. "Franked investment income" is dividends received from other UK resident companies and is not chargeable to corporation tax, but is included in the total of profit which determines the rate of tax on income. Dividends from foreign resident companies are taxable as income under Sch.D, Case V.

Example

A company draws up its accounts to 31st March, 1991. It has these results (all figures adjusted for tax):

Trading profit	220,000
Bank interest (gross)	690
Chargeable gains	700
Franked investment income	284 (net)
The company paid loan interest of	1,000 (gross)

The liability to corporation tax is:

Income		Chargeable gains	Franked investment income (including tax credit)	
Sch.D, Case I	220,000		Net	284
Sch.D, Case III	690	700	Credit 284×⅓	95
	220,690			379
Loan interest	(1,000)			

219,690+700+379=220,769 (Profit)
219,690+700=220,390 (Chargeable profit)

Corporation tax:

On income 220,390×35%	=	77,136
Reduced by taper relief:		
$(1{,}000{,}000-220{,}769)\times\frac{220{,}390}{220{,}769}\times\frac{1}{40}$	=	(19,447)
Gross corporation tax		57,689

The effective marginal rate of tax on profits over £200,000 and less than £1 million for FY 1990 is 37.5%. For earlier years the rates were:

Financial year	Marginal rate
1985	42.5%
1986	36.5%
1987	37%
1988 to 1990	37.5%

This marginal rate represents the percentage of additional tax payable on profit over £200,000.

Example

A company draws up its accounts to 31st March, 1991 making a trading profit of 210,000.

Corporation tax situation:

210,000×35%	=	73,500

Taper relief:

$$(1{,}000{,}000-210{,}000)\times\frac{210{,}000}{210{,}000}\times\frac{1}{40} \quad = \quad (19{,}750)$$

Tax payable		53,750
Tax on 200,000 of profit at 25%	=	(50,000)
Additional tax on profit over 150,000		3,750

Percentage of additional tax (3,750) to additional profit (10,000) is:

$$\frac{100}{10{,}000}\times 3{,}750=37.5\%.$$

To prevent abuse of the lower rates, the profit limits are divided equally between "assoicated companies", which are companies under common control, e.g. companies under the control of the same parent company or same group of individual shareholders. Thus, if there are four companies in the group, the limits per company would be:

1. Small company rate on profits up to 200,000 × ¼ = 50,000.
2. Marginal relief on profits up to 1,000,000 × ¼ = 250,000.

Example

B Ltd. is a wholly owned subsidiary of A Ltd. For the year ended 31st March, 1990 they have these results:

A Ltd.		B Ltd.	
Trading profit	27,000	Trading profit	120,000
Chargeable gain	200	Bank interest	600
		Chargeable gain	420
		Franked inv. income	500 (gross)

A Ltd:

Sch.D, Case I 27,000 Chargeable gain 200 = 27,200 (Profit)

27,200 × 25% = 6,800

B Ltd:

Sch.D, Case I	120,000	Chargeable gain 420		FII 500
Sch.D, Case III	600			
	120,600	(Income) + 420		= 121,020 + 500
				= 121,520 (Profit)

121,020 × 35% = 42,357

Taper relief:

$$(500{,}000^{*}-121{,}520)\times\frac{121{,}020}{121{,}520}\times\frac{1}{40} \quad = \quad (9{,}423)$$

Gross corporation tax 32,934

*Note: 1,000,000 limit divided between two companies means 500,000 per company.

Chargeable gains

Companies do not actually pay capital gains tax on their disposals of capital assets. Whilst the capital gains/losses are calculated according to the rules of capital gains tax, they incorporate the chargeable gains into the figure of "profit" and pay corporation tax. No annual exemption can be claimed by a company against its capital gains as can be claimed by an individual.

Gains made up to 16th March, 1987 differed in two ways from gains on disposals made from 17th March, 1987 onwards:

1. The rate of tax was effectively 30%. This was achieved by reducing the net gains (gross capital gains in the accounting period reduced by capital losses brought forward and made in the period) by a fraction and taxing the reduced amount to the standard rate of corporation tax.

2. Advance corporation tax could not be offset against the corporation tax due on capital gains.

Example

A company has these results for year ended 31st March, 1987:

Trading profit	20,000
Capital gain (made on 1/2/87)	700
Dividend paid	18,000 (net)

Tax chargeable:

Sch.D, Case I: 20,000×29%=5,800; Capital gain 700×6/7=600×35%=210*

ACT:

$18{,}000\times\frac{29}{71}$ =	7,352
Maximum offset:	
20,000×29% =	(5,800)
Surplus ACT	1,552
MCT payable	Nil+210=210

*Note: 700×30% = 210

Gains arising from disposals after 17th March, 1987

For gains arising from disposals on or after 17th March, 1987 these two rules have been removed, and now:

1. Capital gains are taxed to corporation tax at the same rate that applies to income. That is:
   a) Small company rate if profits are £200,000 or less.
   b) Marginal relief if profits are between £200,000 and £1,000,000.
   c) Standard rate if profits exceed £1,000,000.

Capital gains will now be included as part of "income" in calculating the marginal relief deduction.

2. ACT can now be offset against the tax arising from capital gains.

Example

A company has these results for y/e 31st March, 1991:

Trading profit	210,000	
Capital gain	10,000	
Dividends received	7,200	(net of tax credit)
Dividends paid	200,000	(net)
Franked investment income =	7,200	
Credit 7,200 × ⅓ =	2,400	
	9,600	

Tax chargeable:

Sch.D, Case I: 210,000; Capital gain: 10,000

Profit is therefore	210,000+10,000+9,600 =		229,600
Sch.D, Case I:	210,000		
Capital gain:	10,000		
	220,000×35% =		77,000
Marginal relief:			
(1,000,000−229,600) ×	$\frac{220,000}{229,600} \times \frac{1}{40}$ =		(18,455)
			58,545
ACT offset:			
Dividend paid	200,000 × ⅓ =	66,667	
FII credit		(2,400)	
		64,267	
Maximum 220,000×25% =		(55,000)	(55,000)
Surplus ACT		9,267	
MCT payable			3,545

Allowing for capital losses

Capital losses can only be offset against capital gains of the same or future accounting periods, but can never be offset against income. Thus, in the calculation it is recommended capital gains be separated from the income if capital losses are involved.

Example

A company has an accounting period to 31st March, 1991 and makes a trading profit of 30,000. It also has disposals of capital assets as follows:

1/11/90	Gain	4,000
2/2/91	Loss	(6,000)
19/3/91	Loss	(5,000)

Tax chargeable:

Sch.D, Case I	30,000	Capital gain: =	4,000
		Capital losses:	(4,000)
			Nil

Tax payable:

30,000×25% = 7,500

Excess capital losses carried forward: (6,000)+(5,000) =	(11,000)
Offset in y/e 31/3/91	4,000
Carried forward	(7,000)

Payment of corporation tax

Corporation tax is payable in two ways:

1. Advance corporation tax (ACT) becomes due whenever a "qualifying distribution" is paid DURING the actual chargeable accounting period.

"Qualifying distribution" in practice means dividends but other payments are also included.

The rate of ACT is always based on the basic rate of income tax for any fiscal year.

2. Nine months after the end of the chargeable accounting period, the balance of the corporation tax called mainstream corporation tax (MCT) becomes payable. Companies trading prior to 6th April, 1965 had up to then a longer period of payment (potentially up to 21 months) and were allowed to retain this longer period into the payment of corporation tax. However this longer period is now being phased out; in three equal steps over three years commencing with the first accounting period beginning on or after 17th March, 1987. When complete all companies will pay MCT nine months after the end of the accounting period.

Example

A company has a 30th June accounting date. The intervals of payment will be:

Accounting period	**Payment due by**
1/7/86 to 30/6/87	18 months (1/1/89)
1/7/87 to 30/6/88	15 months (1/19/89)
1/7/88 to 30/6/89	12 months (1/7/90)
1/7/89 to 30/6/90	9 months (1/4/91)

A new scheme for the payment of corporation tax, described as the Pay and File scheme, is to be introduced as from 1st April, 1993.

Under the new scheme, corporation tax will be payable nine months after the end of the accounting period, but there will be no prior assessment. Any estimate of the tax due in advance of accounts and tax computations being produced will be the responsibility of the company itself, not the inspector of taxes.

In making their estimates of tax due, companies will be able to claim relief for capital allowances, and groups of companies will be able to allow for group relief. These reliefs can be claimed at will by filing appropriately amended returns up to the later of two years after the end of their accounting period and the date of final determination of tax liability or losses. There is to be, however, an overriding time limit of six years from the end of the appropriate accounting period.

Payment of advance corporation tax

ACT is paid under a quarterly accounting system. For the periods ended 31st March, 30th June, 30th September, 31st December and the company's accounting date (if different to the preceding days) the company has to report (on a form CT61) and pay to the Inland Revenue any ACT due for the quarter. The form and payment must be sent to the Inland Revenue within fourteen days of the end of the quarter, e.g. for the quarter ended 30th June the last day for payment of the tax is 14th July.

Credits on dividends from other UK companies (franked investment income) can be offset against ACT due on dividends paid, but no more can be claimed back than has been paid in that accounting period. Surplus FII credits have to be carried forward to future accounting periods.

Income tax deducted from annual charges is paid to the Inland Revenue and the offset of income credits on income received (unfranked investment income) are also accounted for under the quarterly system. Again, income tax credits cannot be reclaimed in excess of income tax payments. Any excess of credit at the end of the accounting period is offset against corporation tax due.

Advance corporation tax and income tax are always kept completely separated.

Example

A company draws up its accounts for the twelve months to 31st March, 1991. It made a trading profit of £39,216. The following were also paid and received:

1st May, 1990 – Dividend paid of £4,900 (net)

11th July, 1990 – £2,100 (net) dividend received from another UK company.

15th September, 1990 – £700 (net) interest on 7% Treasury Stock received.

3rd February, 1991 – £280 (net) loan interest paid.

Quarterly accounting:

Period to 30th June, 1988:

1/5/90 Dividend paid 4,900 × ⅓ = 1,633 ACT paid by 14th July, 1990.

Period to 30th September, 1990:

11/7/90 FII received 2,100×⅓=700 ACT credit recovered (leaving 933 still held by Inland Revenue).

15/9/90 Unfranked investment income (UFII) received. Income tax credit 700×⅓=233 not yet recoverable as no income tax deducted and paid in the accounting period.

Period to 31st December, 1990:

No transactions, no return needed.

Period to 31st March, 1991:

3/2/91 Annual charge (loan interest) paid 280×⅓=93 income tax, but 233 to be recovered from 15/9/90 so nothing paid, leaving 140 still to be recovered.

Summary:

ACT	– 933 paid to Revenue
Income tax	– 140 still to be recovered from Inland Revenue.

Annual corporation tax assessment:

Sch.D, Case I		39,216			FII	2,100
UFII	700				Credit	700
Credit	233	933				2,800
		40,149				
Annual charge (loan interest)	280					
Tax deducted	93	(373)				
		39,776	+	2,800	=	42,576 (Profit)

Gross corporation tax:

Corporation tax 39,776×25%	9,944
ACT already paid	(933)
	9,011
Excess income tax credit to be recovered	(140)
MCT payable by 1st January 1991	8,871

If too much ACT is paid in an accounting period the amount which can be offset against the gross corporation tax is restricted to a maximum equivalent to net income times the current basic rate of income tax. Also ACT can be offset against corporation tax on capital gains.

Example

For the year ended 31st March, 1991 a company has these results:

Trading	1,200,000
Capital gain	6,000
Dividend paid 1st June, 1990	990,000

Corporation tax payable:		
Sch.D, Case I	1,200,000	
CG	6,000	
	1,206,000	
Gross CT 1,206,000×35% =		422,100
ACT on dividend:		
990,000×⅓ =	330,000	
Maximum offset:		
1,206,000×25% =	(301,500)	(301,500)
Surplus ACT	28,500	
MCT payable		120,600

Surplus ACT

Surplus ACT can be utilised by:

1. Carrying it back to accounting periods beginning within six years of the start of the relevant period.
2. A parent company can surrender ACT to its subsidiaries.
3. It can be carried forward, without time limit, to future accounting periods.

Surplus franked investment income can be:

1. Offset against trading losses.
2. Carried forward and offset against dividends paid in future accounting periods.

Example

A company has these results:

Accounting period: 12 months ended:	**31/3/88**	**31/3/89**	**31/3/90**	**31/3/91**
Trading profit	20,000	10,000	14,000	5,000
Capital gains	500	Nil	6,000	Nil
Dividends paid in period (net)	900	6,300	12,600	15,000

Y/E 31/3/91:

Sch.D, Case I 5,000×25% =		1,250	
Maximum ACT offset 5,000×25% =	1,250	(1,250)	
ACT 15,900×⅓ =	5,300		
Surplus ACT	4,050		4,050
MCT		Nil	

Y/E 31/3/90:			
14,000+6,000=20,000×25%=		5,000	
Maximum ACT 20,000×25%=	5,000		
ACT for year 12,600×⅓=	(4,200)	(4,200)	
	800	800	
Surplus ACT from y/e 31/3/91	(800)	(800)	(800)
	Nil	Nil	3,250
Y/E 31/3/89:			
Sch.D, Case I 10,000×25%=		2,500	
Maximum ACT 10,000×25%=	2,500		
ACT for year 6,300×⅓=	(2,100)	(2,100)	
	400	400	
Surplus ACT from y/e 31/3/90	(400)	(400)	(400)
	Nil	Nil	2,850
Y/E 31/3/88:			
20,000+500=20,500×27%=		5,535	
Max ACT 20,500×25%=	5,535		
ACT for year $900\times{}^{27}/_{73}$=	(333)	(333)	
	5,202	5,202	
Surplus ACT from y/e 31/3/89	(2,850)	(2,850)	(2,850)
	1,975		Nil
MCT payable		2,352	

Notes:

1. Any further surplus ACT could have been carried back to Y/E 31/3/87, 31/3/86 and finally 31/3/85.

2. Any further surplus ACT could be carried forward to Y/E 31/3/92, onwards.

ACT cannot generally be carried forward if there is, in a three-year period, both a change of ownership of the company and also a major change in the nature of the trade.

Changes in rates

The limits of profit for the various rates of corporation tax constantly vary as do the rates of ACT. If an accounting period straddles two financial/fiscal years, then apportionments need to be done for all the rates.

Example

A company draws up accounts for year ended 30th June, 1986 with these results:

Trading profit	600,000

Dividends were paid:

July, 1985	35,000
May, 1986	195,000

The basic rates of income tax were:

1985/86	30%
1986/87	29%

Gross corporation tax:

FY 1985	$600{,}000 \times \frac{9}{12}$ =	$450{,}000 \times 40\%$ =	180,000
FY 1986	$600{,}000 \times \frac{3}{12}$ =	$150{,}000 \times 35\%$ =	52,500
			232,500
ACT offset:			
	$35{,}000 \times \frac{3}{7}$ =	15,000	
	$195{,}000 \times \frac{29}{71}$ =	79,647	94,647
MCT payable			137,853

The maximum ACT offset for the accounting period would be:

$450{,}000 \times 30\%$ =	135,000
$150{,}000 \times 29\%$ =	43,500
	178,500

Computation of profit

It has already been said that "profit" consists of income, capital gains and franked investment income.

"Income" consists of the same schedules and cases as income tax, with a few adaptations, and all are on current year basis. There is no preceding year basis period in corporation tax. The components of "income" are:

1. Sch.D, Case I, trading profit. Points to note:
   a) Current year basis is used.
   b) Capital allowances are treated as an allowable expense, and not treated separately as in income tax.
   c) There can be no adjustment for "private use" by a limited company. Any such use by the directors is a Sch.E matter for them personally, but the company will be allowed the expense as a deduction if it is commercially justifiable as remuneration of an employee. Generally there will be assessable on the individual a Sch.E benefit in kind.
2. Sch.D, Case III. Bank interest, and other interest received gross.
3. Sch.D, Cases IV and V. Overseas income. Points to note:
   a) The GROSS income (before deducting any foreign tax paid) is assessed.
   b) Double taxation credit relief (normally the foreign tax paid) is a deduction from MCT before any ACT offset.
4. Sch.A. Income from property.
5. Unfranked investment income (UFII). Receipts of interest, etc. from which INCOME TAX (not ACT) has been deducted at source, e.g. loan and debenture interest, interest on certain government securities. Points to note:
   a) The GROSS amount is assessable.
   b) The tax credit can be offset against income tax deducted by the company

from annual charges paid, under the quarterly acounting procedure (CT61). Any excess credit on UFII is deducted from the MCT for the accounting period.

Annual charges are deducted from the income, and excess annual charges are then deducted from net capital gains. As there is no equivalent of the higher rate (of income tax) in corporation tax, there are no special restrictions on the deductibility of annual charges. Virtually all annual charges and payments of interest (if not a deduction against trading profit) are allowable.

Capital gains are firstly offset against capital losses then against trade losses (but not if brought forward) and then annual charges. The tax charged can then be offset against ACT.

Franked investment income (FII) is dividends received from other UK resident companies. They are not subject to corporation tax but:

1. The ACT credit is offset against ACT due on dividends paid.

2. Gross FII is a component of the figure of profit (which in turn determines the rate of gross corporation tax on income).

3. Surplus FII can either be offset against trade losses or carried forward to future accounting periods.

4. Dividends from overseas companies are not FII, and are subject to corporation tax under Sch.D, Case V.

Example

A company has these results in a twelve month accounting period:

Trading profit 42,966 before deducting capital allowances of 8,967. Rents received 925.

Dividends received:		
From UK resident companies	714	(net)
From overseas resident companies	510	(net)
	200	(foreign tax paid)
	710	(gross)
Building society interest received	129	(net)
Interest received on 7% Treasury Stock	360	(net)
Capital gains	509	
Capital losses brought forward	(109)	
Payments in the accounting period:		
Debenture interest	1,029	(after deduction of income tax)
Covenant to charity	70	(after deduction of income tax)
Dividend	3,572	(net)

The liability to corporation tax would be (figures are taken to the nearest pound):

Income				Capital gains		FII (gross)	
Trading profit		42,966					
Capital allowances		(8,967)		Gains	509	Net	714
Sch.D, Case I			33,999	Losses	(109)	Credit	
Sch.A			925		400	714×⅓=	238
Sch.D, Case V		510					
		200	710				952
Building society interest		129					
Credit 129×⅓=		43	172				
UFII		360					
Credit 360×⅓=		120	480				
			36,286				
Debenture interest	1,029						
Tax deducted 1,029×⅓=	343	1,372					
Covenant to charity	70						
Tax deducted 70×⅓=	24	94	(1,466)				
			34,820	+ 400 + 952 = 36,172 (Profit)			

Gross corporation tax:		
34,820+400 = 35,220×25% =		8,805
Credit relief on foreign income		(200)
		8,605
ACT offset:		
ACT on dividend 3,572×⅓ =	1,191	
FII credit	(238)	(953)
MCT payable		7,652

Losses

Corporation tax losses can in practice be divided into two types:

1. Non-trade losses such as capital losses and losses on rental income (Sch.A1).
2. Trade losses.

Non-trade losses

All non-trade losses follow the same general rules:

1. Losses of a particular type can only be offset against income of the same type (like against like).

2. Surplus losses can only be carried forward and set off against income of the same type in future accounting periods.

3. Losses cannot be carried back to previous accounting periods or offset against any other form of profit, or transferred under group relief provisions (see later).

Example

Images Ltd. has these results:

Y/e 31/3/90		**Y/e 31/3/91**	
Trading profit	10,000	Trading profit	12,000
Chargeable gains	500	Chargeable gains	1,000
Capital losses	(800)	Capital losses	(100)
Rental income	600	Rental losses (expenditure exceeding income)	(950)

Y/e 31/3/90

Sch.D, Case I	10,000	Chargeable gain	500
Sch.A	600	Capital loss	(500)
	10,600		Nil

10,600×25% = 2,650

Capital loss

	(800)
	500
C/F	(300)

Y/e 31/3/91

Sch.D, Case I	12,000	Chargeable gain		1,000
Sch.A	Nil	Losses B/F	((300)	
		Loss in year	(100)	(400)
	12,000			600

12,600×25% = 3,150

Losses:

Capital loss		**Sch.A losses**	
B/F	(300)	Current year	(950)
Current year	(100)	Relief	Nil
	(400)	C/F	(950)
Relieved	400		
	Nil		

Trade losses

Trade losses are more versatile than the non-trade variety, in that in the current and previous accounting periods they can be offset against other types of profit, such as investment income and chargeable gains.

The order of relief is:

1. In the accounting period a loss is incurred, it can be relieved against other income and chargeable gains of the same period.

2. Any unrelieved loss can then be carried back to the previous accounting period and relieved against income, either trading or investment, or chargeable gains.

3. If there are still any unrelieved trading losses, they are then carried forward but only against future trade profits, not other income or gains.

Note that, unlike income tax, corporation tax losses are relieved before annual charges and interest. Any annual charges and interest thus going unrelieved can be carried forward (never backwards) and offset against future trade profits, provided they are connected with the trade (loan interest, royalties, etc.).

Example

The Calamity Mining Co. Ltd. has these results:

	Y/e 31/3/90	**Y/e 31/3/91**	**Y/e 31/3/92**
Trading profit/(loss)	10,000	(25,000)	6,000
Rents received	1,000	1,000	1,000
Capital gains	2,500	2,000	1,200
Loan interest paid	(1,500)	(1,500)	(1,500)

Y/e 31/3/91

		Trade loss	**Loan interest**
Sch.D, Case I	Nil	(25,000)	
Sch.A	1,000		
Capital gain	2,000	3,000	(1,500)
	3,000		
Loss relief	(3,000)	(22,000)	
	Nil		

Y/e 31/3/90

Sch.D, Case I	10,000		
Sch.A	1,000		
Capital gain	2,500		
	13,500		
Loss relief	(13,500)	13,500	(1,500)
	Nil	(8,500)	(3,000)

Carry forward (11,500)

Y/e 31/3/92

Sch.D, Case I	6,000		
Loss relief	(6,000)		6,000
	Nil	Carry forward to	
Sch.A	1,000	Y/E 31/3/91	(5,500)
Capital gain	1,200		
	2,200		
Loan interest	(1,500)		
	700 × 25% = 175.00		

Note: As an examination technique, when answering loss relief questions, start with the period of loss, go back to the previous period, then go forward. Do *not* work chronologically.

If the accounting period in which the loss is made is less than 12 months in length, any surplus loss can only be carried back the same length of time.

Example

The Smith Vegetarian Meat Co. Ltd. has these results, after having changed its accounting reference date from 31st December to 30th June.

	Y/e 31/12/89	6 months to 30/6/90	Y/e 30/6/91
Trading profit/(loss)	3,000	(15,000)	4,000
Rents received	1,500	750	1,500
Loan interest paid	(2,000)	(1,000)	(2,000)

6 months to 30/6/90

		Trade loss	Loan interest
Sch.D, Case I	Nil	(15,000)	
Sch.A	750		
Loss relief	(750)	(750)	
	Nil	(14,250)	(1,000)

Y/e 31/12/89

Sch.D, Case I	3,000	Loss can *only* be carried back for	
Sch.A	1,500	6 months	
	4,500		
Loss relief			
$4{,}500 \times {}^{6}/_{12} =$	(2,250)	2,250	
	2,250	(12,000)	
Loan interest	(2,000)		
	250		(13,000)

MCT payable 250×25%=62

Y/e 30/6/91			
Sch.D, Case I	4,000		
Loss relief	(4,000)		4,000
	Nil		(9,000)
Sch.A	1,500		
Loan interest	(1,500)	2,000 − 1,500 =	(500)
	Nil	Carry forward to Y/E 30/6/91	(9,500)

When carrying back a trade loss to a previous accounting period, it takes priority in being relieved not only against interest and annual charges, but ACT relief as well. It may thus disturb relief for annual charges and ACT previously given.

Example
The Finkelstein Catering Corporation exports bacon butties to Israel. Not surprisingly it finds trading rather difficult. It has these results:

	Y/e 31/3/88	**Y/e 31/3/89**	**Y/e 31/3/90**
Trading profit/(loss)	6,000	(20,000)	5,000
Rents received	1,000	1,000	1,000
Capital gains	2,000	600	1,700
It pays:			
Loan interest (gross)	(2,500)	(2,500)	(2,500)
Charitable covenant (gross)	(500)	(500)	(500)
Dividend (net)	3,000	Nil	2,100

Y/e 31/3/89		**Trade loss**	**Loan interest**
Sch.D, Case I	Nil	(20,000)	
Sch.A	1,000		
Capital tain	600		
	1,600		
Loss relief	(1,600)	1,600	(2,500)*
	Nil	(18,400)	

*Note: The charitable covenant is not a trade charge (paid in connection with the trade) and therefore cannot be carried forward.

Y/e 31/3/88

Sch.D, Case I	6,000		
Sch.A	1,000		
Capital gain	2,000		
	9,000		
Loss relief	(9,000)	9,000	(2,500)*
	Nil	(9,400)	5,000
		(14,400)	

*Notes: Again, the charitable covenant cannot be carried forward. Before bringing loss relief backwards, it would have been relieved on the original assessment.

Similarly, ACT of $3,000 \times \frac{27}{73} = 1,110$

would have been relieved in the original assessment. Now it has been displaced by bringing loss relief backwards. Surplus ACT can be carried back up to 6 years, or forward as long as is necessary.

Y/e 31/3/90

		B/F	(14,400)
Sch.D, Case I	5,000		
Loss relief	(5,000)		5,000
	Nil		(9,400)
Sch.A	1,000		
Capital gain	1,700		
	2,700		
Covenant	(500)		
	2,200		
Loan interest	(2,200)		(300)
	Nil	Carry forward	(9,700)

Surplus ACT of 2,100 × ⅓ = 700 has been created on the dividend paid.

Alternative current period reliefs

In the current year the loss is made, as an alternative or in addition to the reliefs mentioned above, two other reliefs are available.

1. In a group of companies (the parent company must have over 75% of the ordinary shares of the subsidiaries) any company with a trading loss can transfer it in the accounting period it was made to another company in the same group. The recipient company can then use the loss against its own income and capital

gains of the same accounting period. It cannot carry any surplus loss forwards or backwards (see "Groups" for a more detailed explanation).

2. If there is any surplus franked investment income of the same or previous accounting period, the loss can be used to recover the ACT credit. The loss can then be carried forward and offset against future trade profit if certain conditions are satisfied.

Relief on termination of trade

When a company ceases trading and there are:

1. Trade losses which cannot be relieved in any other way,
2. Annual charges connected with the trade which cannot be relieved for the last twelve months of trading.

They can be set against trade profits of the same trade for the thirty-six months preceding the final twelve months.

Example

A company ceased trading on 31st December, 1991, drew up its accounts to 31st March and had these results:

	Trade profit (loss)	Rental income
31st March, 1988	2,450	100
31st March, 1989	870	100
31st March, 1990	1,100	100
31st March, 1991	(4,400)	100
9 months to 31st December, 1991	(2,900)	Nil

First of all, the loss has to be relieved in every other way before terminal loss can be claimed.

CAP to 31st March, 1991:		**Loss**
Sch.D, Case I	Nil	(4,400)
Sch.A	100	
	100	
Loss relief	(100)	100
	Nil	(4,300)

CAP to 31st March, 1990:		
Sch.D, Case I	1,100	
Sch.A	100	
	1,200	
Loss relief	(1,200)	1,200
	Nil	(3,100)

Then the terminal loss can be computed for the last twelve months of trading 1st January, 1991 to 31st December, 1991:

1st January, 1991 to 31st March, 1991 (3,100) × $^3/_{12}$ =	(775)
1st April, 1991 to 31st December, 1991	(2,900)
	(3,675)

This is then relieved against the trading profits of the thirty-six months working back from 31st December, 1990 – back to 1st January, 1988.

Back to 1st April, 1989 the profit is already nil.

1st April, 1988 to 31st March, 1989:

Sch.A	100	**Loss**
Sch.D, Case I	870	(3,675)
Loss relief	(870)	870
	Nil	(2,805)
Sch.A	100	
	100×25%=25	

1st January, 1988 to 31st March, 1988 (in accounting period ended 31st March, 1988):

Sch.D, Case I	2,450		
Loss relief:		B/F	(2,805)
2,450 × $^3/_{12}$ =	(613)		613
	1,837		(2,192)*
Sch.A	100		
	1,937×25%=484		

*Note: The remaining loss of (2,192) is wasted, as it cannot be relieved in any other way.

Close companies

Introduction and definitions

Close companies are, in the main, unquoted family-owned companies. Special rules (all disadvantageous to the company and its members) apply which are intended to prevent the use of such companies for tax-avoidance purposes.

The detailed definition of a close company is one which:

1. Is under the control (by ownership of over 50% of voting power or ordinary share capital) of five or fewer participators and their associates.

OR

2. Is under the control (by ownership of over 50% of voting power or ordinary share capital) of any number of directors and their associates.

OR

3. Assuming that the company is close:

From 1st April, 1989, if more than half the assets in a winding up would accrue to the above number of participators or directors.

A "participator" is a person with a financial interest in the company apart from trade creditors and UK resident banks.

The term "director" includes anyone concerned in the company's management and who, together with his associates, controls more than 20% of the ordinary share capital.

"Associates" are ancestors, brothers and sisters, spouse, descendants and business partners. The settlor (and members of the settlor's family) and trustees of a settlement are associated, as are the beneficiaries of the same settlement or estate, and the beneficiaries and trustees of a settlement.

Certain companies are not treated as associates:

1. Subsidiaries of companies which are not themselves close.
2. Companies under the control of the Crown and not otherwise a close company.
3. Companies resident abroad.
4. Companies where 35% of the voting power is owned by the "public" and the shares have been quoted and dealt in on the Stock Exchange in the prevous twelve months. In deciding the shareholding held by the public, those held by a "principal member" (generally the five largest shareholders) are not included.

The consequences of being a close company (which are discussed item by item in more detail below) are:

1. The definition of "distribution" is extended.
2. Loans made by the company to its members are treated as distributions.
3. The company must distribute a certain level of its income. If it does not, income tax is assessed as though that level had been distributed – the apportionment of relevant income.

Extended meaning of distribution

The definition is extended so that benefits in kind given to participators and their associates who are not employees are treated as distributions.

Loans to participators and associates

Such loans are treated as distributions and corporation tax assessed accordingly, but it cannot be treated as ACT. It can be reclaimed proportionately to the repayment of the loan.

Loans up to £15,000 to full-time employees of the company who have 5% or less of the ordinary shares are exempt from this treatment.

If such a loan is ever written off it is treated as income of the recipient at that time.

The tax can be assessed by the Inland Revenue even if the loan has been repaid before the assessment has been raised.

Example
A close company with a trading profit of 80,000 in an accounting period has these transactions

1. Provides a benefit in kind for a director, loan of a car, scale benefit (say) 1,050.
2. Loans a car to a shareholder, scale benefit rate 1,050.
3. Provides an interest free loan to a director of 3,600 (say Treasury rate 10%).

The company would claim capital allowances on the car provided for the director, but the Inspector may challenge allowances on the car provided for a shareholder as not being "wholly and exclusively" for the purposes of the trade.

The tax treatment of the benefits would be:

1. Scale benefit 1,050 assessed Sch.E as benefit in kind on director.
2. Scale benefit on shareholder: 1,050

ACT generated 1,050 × ⅓ =	350
Gross distribution (franked payment) assessed Sch.F on shareholder	1,400

3. a) Loan to director 3,600 would involve company in paying 3,600 × ⅓ = 1,200 additional corporation tax only recoverable when loan repaid.

b) Also an assessable benefit on recipient director under Sch.E as a "beneficial loan" – annual benefit 3,600 × 10% = 360 unless it was a qualifying loan and/or less any interest actually paid.

Company:	80,000 × 25% =	20,000
	Less: ACT	(350)
	MCT payable	19,650

Close investment holding companies

Introduction

Before April, 1989, the investment income of a close company could be specially taxed by way of a theoretical dividend being "apportioned" to shareholders if insufficient dividend was declared. The apportionment could then be charged to higher rate income tax payable by either the company or shareholders.

From April, 1989, this system has been replaced by a system where a "close investment holding company" is taxed at the full rate of corporation tax, and cannot claim the small company rate or marginal relief.

Definition

A "close investment holding company" (CIC) is any close company which is not a trading company or member of a trading group.

Companies dealing in land, shares or securities, can be treated as trading companies.

A property investment company which conducts its activities on a commercial basis is not defined as a CIC. The same treatment is given to a company which invests in property and also trades, and subsidiaries in a group which are property investment companies. This means that the parent company of a property investment group, or a mixed property investment and trading group, are not treated as a CIC.

Trading company: A company is a trading company for an accounting period if its business consists wholly or mainly of trading. It is sufficient that the company exists wholly or mainly for the purpose of trading, it does not necessarily have to trade in an accounting period.

The trade must be conducted on a commercial basis.

Member of a trading group: A simple holding company or one which simply makes loans to subsidiaries are treated as members of a trading group, as are companies which hold property for subsidiaries, or provide other services.

If a parent company merely holds shares in a subsidiary that does not trade, but itself has shareholdings in trading subsidiaries, the top company will be deemed a member of a trading group.

Consequences of being a close investment holding company

A CIC is assessed on its profits in the normal way; there are no restrictions on deductions, et.

The CIC, however, is taxed only at the full corporation tax rate; the small company and marginal rates are not available.

In certain circumstances the recipients of dividends cannot claim a repayment of tax credits.

There is a restriction of credit relief on dividends paid to non-residents.

If a life policy is held by a CIC, the policy proceeds come within the apportionment rules, but there is no charge on the company itself. There can be corporation tax charge on policies taken out after Budget Day, 1989.

Groups

Definitions

There are two relevant definitions in the taxation of groups:

1. "51% group" where the parent company owns more than 50% of the ordinary share capital of bhe subsidiaries.
2. "75% group" where the parent company owns at least 75% of the ordinary share capital of the subsidiaries.

A 75% group is automatically, by definition, also a 51% group, and companies in any group are, by definition, "associated" companies.

Group elections

Members of a 51% group can elect that ACT be ignored, if they wish, on payments of dividends from subsidiaries to parents. The dividend is then paid net, and no ACT is paid to the Revenue to be reclaimed by the parent company. Such payments are called "group income" and are never treated as FII in the hands of the parent, whether or not ACT is paid.

They can also elect to pay annual charges from subsidiaries to parent without reference to basic rate income tax. If so, the annual charge is paid gross. Whether or not income tax is deducted, the gross payment is still an allowable deduction for the subsidiary and charged as UFII on the parent.

Surrender of ACT

A parent can surrender ACT to a subsidiary company. It can surrender any amount of ACT, not necessarily just a surplus.

The subsidiary can carry forward the surrendered ACT if it is surplus to its requirements, but not generally beyond the time when the subsidiary leaves the group.

Group transfers

In a 75% group chargeable assets (chargeable to capital gains) can be transferred from one group member to another without it being an occasion of charge. The new owner simply takes over the original cost price. Again the asset only becomes liable when the asset is disposed of outside the group.

Example

A and B are members of the same group. A buys a factory for £60,000, later transfers it to B when it is £85,000 and in turn B sells it outside the group for £100,000. The assessable gain on B is £40,000 (ignoring indexation).

Group relief

Members of a 75% group can transfer, one to the other, trade losses and annual charges.

The transfer can only be on a current year basis, and group relief in the hand of the recipient company cannot be transferred backwards or forwards in time. A transfer can be offset against the claimant company's income and capital gains.

Example

A Ltd. is the parent company of B Ltd. which is a wholly owned subsidiary. In three successive accounting periods they have these results:

		Accounting Period 1	*Accounting Period 2*	*Accounting Period 3*
A Ltd.	Trading profit (loss)	1,000	(3,560)	1,800
	Rent received	50	160	120
B Ltd.	Trading profit	200	1,800	2,000
	Loan interest paid (gross)	300	300	300

Assessments would be:

Accounting period 1

A Ltd.	Sch.D, Case I		1,000	B Ltd.	Sch.D, Case I		200
	Sch.A		50		Loan interest	300	
					relieved	(200)	(200)
			1,050				
	Group relief					100	Nil
	from B Ltd.		(100)		Transferred as		
					group relief	(100)	
	Assessed to corporation tax		950			Nil	

Accounting period 2

A Ltd.	Sch.D, Case I		Nil	B Ltd.	Sch.D, Case I		1,800
	Sch.A		160		Loan interest		(300)
			160				1,500
	Loss	(3,560)					
	Relieved	160	(160)				
		(3,400)	Nil				
Transferred as group relief		1,500			Group relief from A Ltd.		(1,500)
Carry forward		(1,900)					Nil

Accounting period 3

A Ltd.	Sch. D, Case I		1,800	B Ltd.	Sch.D, Case I		2,000
	Loss brought forward	(1,900)			Loan interest		(300)
	Relieved	1,800	(1,800)				1,700
Carry forward		(100)	Nil				
	Sch.A		120				
			120				

Consortium relief

A consortium, for tax purposes, exists when at least 75% of the ordinary share capital of the consortium company is owned by UK resident companies which each own at least 5% or more of the ordinary share capital.

A consortium can:

1. Make group income elections on dividends and interest payments from the consortium company to its parents.

2. Claim relief for trade losses, etc. from either the consortium company to its parents or from a parent to the subsidiary, restricted to the proportionate shareholding of the parent.

Example

Four UK companies have these shareholdings of XYZ (the consortium company):

A 35% B 30% C 25% D 10%

In an accounting period XYZ makes a trading loss of (200,000). The claims would be:

A	(200,000)×35%	=	(70,000)
B	(200,000)×30%	=	(60,000)
C	(200,000)×25%	=	(50,000)
D	(200,000)×10%	=	(20,000)

If, say, XYZ made a profit of 100,000 the maximum loss any of the parents could transfer to it would be:

A	100,000×35%	=	35,000
B	100,000×30%	=	30,000
C	100,000×25%	=	25,000
D	100,000×10%	=	10,000

A company which has received losses under consortium relief but cannot absorb the loss itself, can transfer it to another company (not a member of the consortium) which is in a 75% group relationship with the company which has received the loss. The loss must be relieved first in all other possible ways by the recipient company before being transferred to another group member.

Example

A Ltd. is a member of a consortium but also has a separate wholly owned subsidiary company X Ltd. R Ltd. is the company owned by the consortium.

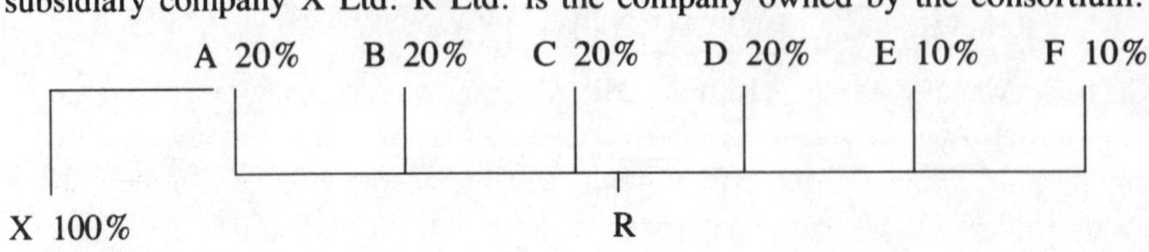

A loss could be transferred R to A. If A could not utilise all the loss, the balance could be transferred to X.

A loss can also be transferred in the reverse direction. If a company, which is a subsidiary of another company, which is a member of a consortium, makes a trading loss, it can of course surrender that loss, or part of it, to its parent company under group relief provisions. However, any loss which the parent company could not absorb could be passed on to the company owned by the consortium, limited as always by the proportionate shareholding in the consortium company.

Example
X Ltd. is a wholly owned subsidiary of A Ltd.
A Ltd. is also a member of a consortium which owns R Ltd.
A Ltd. owns 20% of the share capital of R Ltd.

In a twelve month accounting period, X Ltd. makes a trading loss of (60,000), A Ltd. a trading profit of 35,000, and R Ltd. makes a trading profit of 80,000.

A Ltd. could absorb 35,000 of X Ltd.'s trading loss, reducing it to (25,000). Of this, (16,000) could be passed on by A Ltd. to R Ltd. and be offset against R Ltd.'s profits, reducing them to 80,000 − (16,000) to 64,000. The loss of (16,000) is 20% of R Ltd.'s profit of 80,000, the same as A Ltd.'s shareholding in R Ltd.

Of the original loss of (60,000) 25,000 has gone to A Ltd., 16,000 to R Ltd. making a total offset of 41,000. The remaining unrelieved loss is therefore (19,000). This can only be carried forward and relieved against the trading profit of R Ltd. for future accounting periods.

Again, it is a prerequisite of consortium relief that R Ltd.'s loss be absorbed as much as possible by A Ltd. under group relief provisions before consortium relief can be utilised.

Planning considerations for groups

There are no tax advantages to be had by being a group of companies. All the status provides is some of the benefits not otherwise available to a single company carrying on different activities, possibly in different trading divisions.

To be associated companies is only to have the disadvantages of dividing the profits limits between the companies. The most advantageous situation is that of a 75% group structure. With this arrangement all the tax reliefs available to a group of companies can be claimed.

The major relief not available to a group is the right to transfer capital losses from one company to another. Therefore to take advantage of offsetting group capital losses against group capital gains, all the chargeable assets of the group should be placed in one asset-owning group company, possibly a special subsidiary which owns, say, all the property in the group. Then capital losses can be matched with capital gains as and when they arise.

A company in a group that only exists to own assets, or own shares in other companies, should not, as a general rule, be classified as non-trading if it is a member of a trading group, and exists mainly to provide some service to a trading group as a whole.

You should now attempt the "Corporation Tax" questions beginning on page 283.

Chapter Fifteen

Capital Gains Tax

Introduction

Capital gains tax was introduced to tax any profit made on the disposal of capital assets from 6th April, 1965 by any person resident and ordinarily resident in the UK. It is irrelevant if the asset disposed of is situated in the UK or abroad providing the owner is resident, etc. in the UK at the time of disposal.

Persons not resident in the UK are not liable to tax on the disposal of assets, even those situated in the UK, unless they are business assets in use at the time of disposal.

A capital loss can be offset against gains of the same year, or unrelieved losses carried forward and offset against capital gains of future years.

Rates of tax and payment (individuals)

Up to 6th April, 1988 the tax payable by individuals and trustees was calculated as follows:

1. Gross gains for the tax year (using the current year basis) were offset against capital losses of the year and unused losses brought forward.

2. An annual exemption was then deducted from the remaining capital gains, the amount of which was increased each year.

3. The remaining taxable gains were then assessed to capital gains tax at a flat rate of 30%, payable on or by 1st December following the tax year.

Example

A. Gayne had these results for 1987/88:

Gross gains of £12,000, capital losses for the year of (£1,500), and unused losses brought forward from earlier years of (£1,000).

Gross gains		12,000
Losses of current year	(1,500)	
Losses brought forward	(1,000)	(2,500)
Net gains		9,500
Annual exemption for 1987/88		(6,600)
Taxable gains		2,900

Tax payable: 2,900×30%=870.00 (payable on or by 1st December, 1988)

However, from 6th April, 1988 the method of charging the tax has been changed, so that instead of charging a flat rate, the taxable gains are treated as the highest part of taxable income and charged at income tax rates. An annual exemption is still allowed, which for 1989/90 and 1990/91 is £5,000.

Example

For 1990/91 A.C. Rule had these results:

Gross gains of £14,000.
Losses of the year (£1,200).
Unused losses from previous years (£800).
He had an income of £22,000 and was married.

Gross gains		14,000
Total losses	(1,200)	
	(800)	(2,000)
		12,000
Annual exemption (1990/91)		(5,000)
Taxable gains		7,000

Gross income		22,000
SPA	3,005	
MCA	1,720	(4,725)
		17,275×25%=4,318.75

Capital gains tax payable:

Taxable gains	7,000		
25% rate of income tax (20,700−17,275)=	(3,425)×25%	=	856.25
Balance taxable at 40%	3,575 ×40%	=	1,430.00
Total capital gains tax payable			2,286.25

Payable on or by 1st December, 1991.

Rates of tax and payment (trustees)

Trustees of settlements qualify for an annual exemption half that given to individuals. Therefore for 1989/90 it is £2,500. The taxable gains are then subject to income tax rates which are:

1. For trustees of a settlement with an interest in possession just the basic rate (25% for 1990/91).

2. For trustees of discretionary or accumulation and maintenance settlements, the basic rate plus the additional rate of surcharge (25% + 10% = 35% for 1990/91).

For trusts which are set up by the same settlor the £2,500 exemption is apportioned equally between them.

Example

The Set-em Up Joe Trust is discretionary and for 1990–91 has gains of £6,000.

Gross gains	6,000	
Annual exemption	(2,500)	
Taxable gains	3,500 × 35%	= £1,225.00
Payable on or by 1st December, 1991.		

Rates of tax and payment (companies)

Companies do not actually pay capital gains tax, but instead are liable on chargeable gains as part of their corporation tax profit. Up to 16th March, 1987 this used to be at a rate equivalent to 30%, but as from 17th March, 1987, chargeable gains have been taxed at the same rate of corporation tax as income.

Companies do not have any annual exemption to offset against chargeable gains.

Therefore, for capital gains made by companies:

1. They are added to income and taxed at the same rate of corporation tax (see the "Corporation Tax" chapter for more detail on this). And

2. Advance corporation tax can be offset on the corporation tax charged on the capital gains.

Example

For the year ending 31st March, 1991 the Opaque Optical Co. plc had these results:

Trading profit	240,000
Capital gains	10,000
Dividend paid	210,000 (net)

Tax payable:

Sch.D, Case I	240,000	
Chargeable gain	10,000	
	250,000	
$250{,}000 \times 35\% =$		87,500
Marginal relief:		
$(1{,}000{,}000-250{,}000)\times\frac{250{,}000}{250{,}000}\times\frac{1}{40}=$		(18,750)
Gross corporation tax		68,750
Advance corporation tax offset:		
Dividend paid $210{,}000 \times ⅓ =$	70,000	
Maximum ACT offset:		
$250{,}000 \times 25\% =$	(62,500)	(62,500)
Surplus ACT	7,500	
MCT payable		6,250

Husband and wife

Up to 6th April, 1990 a husband and wife living together were taxed as one unit:

1. The capital losses of one spouse were set off against the gains of the other spouse.
2. They only qualified for one annual exemption between them.
3. The chargeable gains were assessed at income tax rates as the highest part of the combined income.

With the advent of independent taxation from 6th April, 1990, the system has changed:

1. The capital losses of one spouse can no longer be offset against the gains of the other spouse, including capital losses brought forward from before 6th April, 1990.
2. Each spouse qualifies for an individual and separate annual exemption.
3. Chargeable gains are taxable at the highest income tax rates on each individual spouse's income, treating the chargeable gains as the deemed highest part of the income.

Example

In 1990/91 Alexander and June Winterbottom have these results:

Alexander, losses brought forward (3,000), gains in 1990/91 £1,600.

June, losses made in 1990/91 (1,200), gains in 1990/91 £9,700.

Income in 1990/91: Alexander £28,000 and June £22,000, and they pay mortgage interest of £600 (gross), all allocated to Alexander for tax purposes.

Assessment 1990/91:

Alexander			**June**	
Income tax:			Income tax:	
Income		28,000	Income	22,000
Mortgage interest		(600)		
		27,400		
SPA	3,005		SPA	(3,005)
MCA	1,720	(4,725)		
		22,675		18,995
	20,700×25% =	5,175.00	18,995×25% =	4,748.75
	1,975×40% =	790.00		
		5,965.00		

Capital gains tax:

Losses b/f	(3,000)	Gains	9,700		
Gains 1990/91	1,600	Losses	(1,200)		
Losses to c/f			8,500		
to 1991/92	(1,400)	Annual exemption	(5,000)		
		Taxable gains	3,500		
		Tax payable:			
		25%×(20,700−18,995)	1,705	=	426.50
		40%×	1,795	=	718.00
					1,144.50

Transfers of chargeable assets from one spouse to the other, are not an occasion of charge, provided the spouses are living together as man and wife at the time of transfer.

Definitions

A ''disposal'' is not necessarily just a sale. It also includes gifts and the receipt of a capital sum by way of compensation for damage, loss or exploitation of an asset. Some occasions are specifically exempted from being occasions of chargeable disposal. These include:

1. Death.
2. Transfers of assets between spouses.
3. Gifts to charities and certain national bodies.
4. Intra-group transfers between companies.

If no price is paid on a disposal, or the price is not commercial, the market value of the asset is used instead of the actual price paid in computing the gain. This is especially so in disposals between connected persons.

Exemptions and reliefs

All forms of property including intangible property (shares, leases, rights over property) are chargeable to capital gains tax unless specifically exempt. The main exemptions are:

1. Private motor cars.
2. Currency for a person's own use.
3. Decorations for valour if won or inherited by the owner.
4. Betting and lottery wins.
5. Chattels (defined as tangible, movable objects) if either:

a) They are wasting assets (they have an estimated useful life of less than 50 years).

b) They are sold for less than £6,000 (£3,000 up to 5th April, 1989) (see later).

However, legal currency (such as gold sovereigns) does not qualify for this exemption.

6. Bonuses, etc. on life assurance policies.

7. From 1st July, 1986, gains or losses from disposals of gilt-edged stock, qualifying corporate bonds and transactions in futures and options in these securities.

8. The principal private residence of the taxpayer if he has lived in it throughout the period of ownership (this is dealt with in more detail later).

Calculation of gains

General

The ordinary computation is that from the total sale price (or market value) is deducted:

1. The cost of acquisition.

2. The cost of additions and improvements since acquisition, but not the cost of repairs and maintenance.

3. Any incidental costs included in the above such as legal and estate agents' fees, valuation and survey fees.

4. All the above can, since April, 1982, be increased because of inflation by an amount based on the increase in the Retail Price Index.

5. The incidental costs of sale.

Example
A man bought a house for his son to live in in 1983. It cost £12,000 with legal, etc. costs of £700. In 1987 he built an extension at a cost of £5,000 and sold it in 1990 for £90,000 with legal, etc. costs of £900.

The gain is:

Sale price			90,000
Original cost	12,000		
Legal costs of acquisition	700		
	12,700		
Indexation allowance (say) (see below)	1,000	13,700	
Cost of extension	5,000		
Indexation allowance (say)	300	5,300	
Legal costs of sale		900	(19,900)
Gain			70,100

Computation of capital gain

There are four basic calculations used in the calculation of capital gains and losses:

1. The indexation principle.
2. The "rollover" principle.
3. The calculation of gains on a part disposal of an asset.
4. Special rules that may apply to assets acquired on or before 31st March, 1982.

Indexation allowance

To compensate for the effects of inflation on the cost of acquisition of an asset, or expenditure on improvements, an addition is made to the expenditure to allow for inflation since the expenditure was made to the date of disposal of the asset.

This addition to the cost is known as the "indexation allowance", because its calculation is based on movements in the Retail Price Index. The earliest that it can apply is 31st March, 1982, and it has been amended over three phases:

1. For disposals from 6th April, 1982 to 5th April, 1985, an asset had to be owned for twelve months before indexation applied, and then never for the first twelve months' ownership.

2. For disposals from 6th April, 1985 to 5th April, 1988, this twelve month rule was abolished, and for assets purchased prior to 31st March, 1982, the indexation added to expenditure before that date was based on the value of the asset at 31st March, 1982 if it was of advantage to the taxpayer.

3. For disposals from 6th April, 1988 the rules have been amended yet again on expenditure incurred on or before 31st March, 1982. Now, for assets owned on that date, the value at 31st March, 1982 can be substituted for the original expenditure if of advantage to the taxpayer, as well as calculating indexation on that value.

From now onwards, the Retail Price Index will be referred to as the "RPI". To calculate the index figure to be added to expenditure on a disposal:

1. Take the RPI figure for the month of disposal.
2. Deduct the RPI for the month of expenditure (or March, 1982 if later).
3. Divide by the RPI for the month of expenditure (or March, 1982 if later).

The resultant decimal figure is taken to three places of decimals, rounding up or down as necessary.

Tables of indexation factors are available, but all the examples in this book are worked using the formula and the RPI.

Example

Selham Ltd. bought a property for £55,000 in August, 1981, its value at 31st March, 1982 was £90,000. It was extended at a cost of £40,000 in July, 1985, and sold for £280,000 in August, 1990.

RPI figures are:

March, 1982	79.44
July, 1985	95.20
August, 1990 (say)	125.00

Sale price			280,000
Value at 31/3/1982 (larger than cost)	90,000		
Indexation:			
$90{,}000 \times \frac{125-79.44}{79.44}$ (0.574) =	51,660	141,660	
Cost of improvement	40,000		
Indexation:			
$40{,}000 \times \frac{125-95.2}{95.2}$ (0.313) =	12,520	52,520	(194,180)
Gain			85,820

The figures for the RPI or the indexation factors will always be given on an examination paper.

Indexation cannot only reduce a gain but can also increase or even create a loss.

Example

An asset was purchased for £60,000 and indexation adds 10% to the original cost up to the date of disposal. It was sold for:

1. £50,000.
2. £63,000.
3. £70,000.

Sale price		50,000	63,000	70,000
Cost	60,000			
Indexation	6,000	(66,000)	(66,000)	(66,000)
Gain/(loss)		(16,000)	(3,000)	4,000

Some occasions of disposal are specifically designated as not giving rise to a gain or a loss, what is popularly known as a no gain/no loss situation. Examples are transfers of assets between husband and wife, or transfers of assets between members of the same group of companies when the parent has at least a 75% shareholding in the subsidiaries (a 75% group). In spite of there being no chargeable gain or allowable loss on such occasions, indexation is still applied to uplift the expenditure on the asset.

Example
Jim Green bought a property in March, 1984 for £40,000, and gave it to his wife in November, 1986. She sold it in January, 1990 for £86,000.

RPI figures are:

March, 1984	87.5
November, 1986	99.3
January, 1990	119.5

Gift to wife in November, 1986:		
Cost	40,000	
Indexation:		
$40{,}000 \times \frac{99.3-87.5}{87.5}$ (0.135) =	5,400	
Indexed cost to wife	45,400	
Sale by wife in January, 1990:		
Sale price		86,000
Cost	45,400	
Indexation:		
$45{,}400 \times \frac{119.5-99.3}{99.3}$ (0.203) =	9,216	(54,616)
Gain		31,384

If an asset was purchased on or before 31st March, 1982, and the original expenditure exceeded the value at 31st March, 1982, then the original expenditure can be the deductible amount, and also the amount to which indexation from March, 1982 is applied (see later).

The rollover principle
This is a rule whereby the assessment of a gain can be postponed by offsetting the gain against either:

1. The cost of a replacement, or
2. The cost to the person who becomes the new owner.

The gain is only assessed when in 1. the replacement is sold or in 2. the new owner disposes of the asset.

Example

A man acquired a building for £20,000 (index-linked) and disposed of it to his son when it was worth £50,000, leaving a gain of £30,000.

1. If the building was used as a business asset by the father and was followed by the purchase of a replacement building for £85,000, the deemed cost of the replacement for capital gains purposes would be reduced to £55,000 (85,000 − 30,000). If the deemed cost of £55,000 had increased to £70,000 with indexation, the gain on a sale of the replacement at £130,000 would be £60,000 (130,000 − 70,000).

2. If the disposal was the occasion of a gift to his son, the gain of £30,000 would be postponed by the son taking over his father's cost price of £20,000. If the son later sold the biulding for £65,000 and the 20,000 had increased to 28,000 with indexation the gain would be 37,000 (65,000 − 28,000).

On a deemed disposal in a rollover situation, the cost, etc. has to be index-linked in the ordinary way and only the net gain is rolled over.

Example

A trader bought a business asset (A) in July, 1984 at a cost of £40,000. He sold it for £60,000 on 9th August, 1985, replacing it with another business asset (B) on 10th September, 1986 for £70,000 and sold that for £85,000 in August, 1990.

Assume RPI:

July, 1984	89.1	September, 1986	98.3
August, 1985	95.5	August, 1990 (say)	125.0

Sale of (A):

Sale price		60,000
Cost	40,000	
Indexation allowance		
$40{,}000 \times \frac{95.5 - 89.1}{89.1}$ (0.072) =	2,880	(42,880)
Gain		17,120

Sale of (B):

Sale price		85,000
Cost price	70,000	
Rollover relief on (A)	(17,120)	
	52,880	
Indexation allowance		
$52{,}880 \times \frac{125 - 98.3}{98.3}$ (0.272) =	14,383	(67,263)
Gain		17,737

Part disposals

On a part disposal only part of the original cost, etc. can be deducted from the sale price or market value, and that part is calculated by the formula:

$$\text{Total cost of whole} \times \frac{\text{Sale price of part}}{\text{Sale price of part} + \text{Market value of part retained}}$$

In addition, there can be deducted any expenditure wholly attributable to the part sold.

Example

A block of flats was purchased for £20,000 in 1983 and two of the six were sold for £24,000 in 1990. £5,000 had been spent in 1987 on modernising the two flats sold. The market value of the flats retained was £42,000.

Sale price			24,000
Cost of part sold $\frac{20{,}000 \times 24{,}000}{42{,}000 + 24{,}000}$ =	7,272		
Indexation (say)	300	7,572	
Cost of modernising the flats sold	5,000		
Indexation (say)	50	5,050	12,622
Assessable gain			11,378

On a part disposal the deductible expenditure in respect of the whole asset has to be apportioned before calculation of the indexation allowance. The indexation is then applied only to the expenditure which is relevant to the part disposal.

Example

XYZ acquired an asset in June, 1982 for £25,000 and sold part of it in August, 1990 for £15,000 when the portion retained had a market value of £27,000.

Assume RPI:

June, 1982	81.9
August, 1990 (say)	125.0

Sale price of part		15,000
Apportioned cost $25{,}000 \times \frac{15{,}000}{15{,}000 + 27{,}000}$ =	8,929	
Indexation allowance $8{,}929 \times \frac{125 - 81.9}{81.9}$ (0.526) =	4,697	(13,626)
Gain		1,374

Carry forward a remaining cost of 25,000
− 8,929
16,071

When the asset involved is land and a part of it is sold, then the assessment of the gain can be postponed if:

1. The sale price is 20% (5% prior to 6th April, 1986) or less of the total value of the land owned; and

2. The sale price is £20,000 or less. This rule does not apply if the land was compulsorily purchased by a public or local authority.

The gain is postponed by deducting the sale price from the cost of the remaining land.

Example
A landowner purchased his property in 1983 for £150,000. A small piece is sold in 1990 for £16,000 when the remaining land has a value of £310,000.

Sale price		16,000
Cost $150{,}000 \times \dfrac{16{,}000}{326{,}000\ (310{,}000+16{,}000)} =$	7,362	
Indexation (say)	1,000	(8,362)
Gain		7,638

As the sale price is less than 65,200 (326,000×20%) the gain could be avoided by offsetting the sale price against the total cost of the land carried forward:

Original cost	150,000
Sale price	(16,000)
Remaining cost carried forward	134,000

Assets purchased prior to 6th April, 1982

For disposals from 6th April, 1988, the taxpayer has a choice of how to calculate the gain on disposal of assets acquired on or before 31st March, 1982.

1. If he makes an irrevocable written election (before 6th April, 1990 or, if later, up to two years after the accounting period or tax year in which the first disposal of a pre-March 1982 asset takes place) then only the value at 31st March, 1982 is used as the deemed cost, irrespective of result, and this rule is then applied to all assets acquired pre-March, 1982.

2. If no such election is made, then the assets owned at 31st March, 1982 are deemed to be sold and reacquired at their value on that date, and that value used in substitution for the actual cost. However:

(a) If the original cost would give a lower gain or smaller loss, the restricted amount is used.

(b) If the original cost gave a gain instead of loss or vice versa, it is written off as no gain/no loss.

Example
Birch purchased an asset for £100,000 in June, 1980. Its value in March, 1982 was £180,000. It was sold for £800,000 in August, 1990.

RPI:	March, 1982	79.44	
	August, 1990	125.00	
Sale price			800,000
Value at 31st March, 1982		180,000	
Indexation:			
$180{,}000 \times \frac{125-79.44}{79.44}$ (0.574) =		103,320	(283,320)
Gain			516,680

However, this use of the value at 31st March, 1982 cannot work to the disadvantage of the taxpayer. If original cost would have given a more advantageous result, original cost is still used, if no election has been made.

Example
Collins purchased an asset for £15,000 in June, 1981. It was worth £10,000 in March, 1982. It was sold for £25,000 in August, 1990.

RPI figures are as in the previous example.

Sale price		25,000
Original cost	15,000	
Indexation:		
$15{,}000 \times \frac{125-79.44}{79.44}$ (0.574) =	8,610	(23,610)
Gain		1,390

On the same principle of March, 1982 value not increasing a gain, neither can it increase a loss unless an irrevocable election has been made to use March, 1982 value.

Example
Daniels purchased an asset for £60,000 in June, 1981. It was worth £80,000 in March, 1982. It was sold for £40,000 in August, 1990.

RPI figures as in previous examples.

Using cost			**Using March, 1982 value**		
Sale price		40,000	Sale price		40,000
Cost	60,000		Value	80,000	
Indexation:			Indexation:		
60,000×0.574 =	45,920	(105,920)	80,000×0.574 =	(45,920)	(125,920)
Loss		(65,920)	Loss		(85,920)

The allowable loss is (65,920).

When the use of cost gives a gain or loss and the use of March, 1982 the opposite result, this is written off as nil, a no gain/no loss situation, if no election has been made.

The indexation allowance is always calculated using the higher of the two values.

Example

Edwards bought an asset for £40,000 in June, 1981; it was worth £80,000 in March, 1982 and sold for £90,000 in August, 1990.

RPI as in previous examples.

Use of cost			**Using March, 1982 value**		
Sale price		90,000	Sale price		90,000
Cost	40,000		Value	80,000	
Indexation:			Indexation:		
40,000×0.574 =	45,920	(85,920)	80,000×0.574 =	45,920	(125,920)
Gain		4,080	Loss		(35,920)

The result is no gain/no loss.

Assets owned at 6th April, 1965 (the date capital gains tax was introduced) could be written off as no gain/no loss if use of original cost gave one result and use of value at 6th April, 1965 a different result. This conclusion cannot be upset by use of value in March, 1982.

The use of value at March, 1982 excludes not only the original cost of the asset, but also any expenditure on improvements before April, 1982.

Example

An asset was purchased for £70,000 in 1980, and improved at a cost of £30,000 in 1981. It was valued at £150,000 on 31st March, 1982.

Sale price		250,000
Value at March, 1982	150,000	
Indexation 150,000×0.574 (say) =	86,100	(236,100)
Gain		14,000

If an asset was purchased before April, 1982 and improved after that date, the costs of improvements are only indexed from the date they were incurred.

Example

Gough purchased an asset for £20,000 in June, 1981. It was worth £30,000 in March, 1982. It was improved at a cost of £15,000 in June, 1984, and sold for £90,000 in August, 1990.

RPI as before, but June, 1984 89.2

Sale price			90,000
Value at March, 1982	30,000		
Indexation 30,000×0.574 =	17,220	47,220	
Improvements	15,000		
Indexation (from June, 1984)			
$15{,}000 \times \frac{125-89.2}{89.2}$ (0.401) =	6,015	21,015	(68,235)
Gain			21,765

Some reliefs involve calculating a gain according to what happened in certain periods of time. If March, 1982 value is used then any happenings before April, 1982 which may reduce a gain are ignored.

Example

Harcourt purchased a house for £40,000 in April, 1980. Its value in March, 1982 was £80,000. It was sold for £160,000 on 5th August, 1990.

He lived in it as his private house up to April, 1984 and then rented it out up to the sale in August, 1990.

RPI: March, 1982	79.44	
August, 1990 (say)	125.00	
Sale price		160,000
Value at March, 1982	80,000	
Indexation		
$80{,}000 \times \frac{125-79.44}{79.44}$ (0.574)=	45,920	(125,920)
Gross gain		34,080

Exempt for time used(deemed for private purposes:

6/4/82 to 6/4/84	2
Last 2 years of ownership	2
(See section of private houses)	
	4 years
6/4/82 to 5/8/90	8.33 years

Subject to capital gains tax $34{,}080 \times \frac{4.33}{8.33} = 17{,}715$

It is possible for a taxpayer to elect to have all his assets valued at 31st March, 1982 irrrespective of whether this would be to his advantage or not in calculating gains and losses.

Such an election would mean the taxpayer did not have to maintain records and details of purchases, etc. which happened before April, 1982.

An election can be made, whether a disposal has been made or not, at any time up to 5th April, 1990. After that time, if an election is not already in force, one can be made within two years of the end of the first year or accounting period in which the disposal of an asset held at 31st March, 1982 takes place.

Relief for gifts

Relief from capital gains tax on making gifts depends on whether the gift was made before 14th March, 1989, or on or after that date.

Gifts made before 14th March, 1989

When an individual or trustee made a gift to another individual or body of trustees, provided a written election was made to the Inspector of Taxes, the gain arising to the donor, based on the market value of the asset at the time of gift, could be held over by reducing the acquisition cost to the recipient.

Certain conditions had to be satisfied such as the recipient had to be resident and ordinarily resident in the UK for the tax year of receipt and the next five tax years. If they became non-resident the gain became taxable at that date.

If any inheritance/capital transfer tax was payable on the occasion of the gift, it became a deductible expense in calculating any gain on disposal by the recipient.

Example

Don Orr purchased a holiday home for £20,000 in 1984. He gave it to his son in 1985, when it had a market value of £100,000. Inheritance tax of £2,000 was paid on the gift.

The son sold the property for £180,000 in 1990.

Gain on original gift in 1985/86:

Market value on gift		100,000
Cost	20,000	
Indexation (say)	14,000	(34,000)
Gain		66,000

Assuming a gifts relief election had been made the cost to the son would be:

Value	100,000
Gain to Don Orr	(66,000)
	34,000

This can be indexed on the ultimate disposal by the son.

The inheritance tax paid of £2,000 can also be added to the cost, but cannot be indexed.

The son sold the home for £180,000 in 1990.

Capital gain to son in 1990/91:

Sale price			180,000
Deemed acquisition value	34,000		
Indexation (say)	30,000	64,000	
Inheritance tax paid		2,000	(66,000)
Chargeable gain			114,000

Gifts made on or after 14th March, 1989

The general gifts relief ceased to be available from 14th March, 1989. It is now restricted to gifts of certain classes of assets:

1. Business assets, which include:
   (a) Assets used in a trade, profession or vocation by the donor, by his family trading company, or if the donor is a trustee, provided the asset is used in business by the trustee of a beneficiary who has an interest in possession. The deferral can be restricted if the asset has not always been used for business throughout the period of ownership.
   (b) Agricultural property which attracts 50% agricultural property relief for inheritance tax. This generally means land or buildings used by the freeholder in farming.
   (c) Shares and securities in trading companies or holding companies of trading groups where either:
   (i) The shares are unquoted, nor dealt in on the USM, provided the individual owner has the appropriate shareholding which qualifies for retirement relief, basically a minimum of 25% owned personally, or 5% owned personally, but the family holding amounts to over 50%.
   (ii) The owner is a trustee, and he can exercise 25% or more of the voting rights.

The relief can be restricted if the company owns assets not used in a trade.

2. Heritage property and maintenance funds, which include works of art, historic buildings, and land of scenic, historic or scientific interest.
3. Gifts to political parties, that are exempt for inheritance tax.
4. Gifts when there is an immediate charge to inheritance tax, e.g. a gift to trustees of a discretionary settlement, or a gift to a company.

Example
A father gives his shares in the family trading company to his son when they had a market value of £240,000. The shares were originally acquired in 1983 at a value of £20,000.

Market value		240,000
Cost	20,000	
Indexation (say)	(8,000)	(28,000)
Gross gain		212,000
Market value actually received by son		240,000
Gain held over		(212,000)
Son's acquisition value for capital gains		28,000

If the asset is gifted for no consideration, in effect the recipient takes over the asset at the indexed cost of the donor.

It is possible to hold over part of a gain in spite of some consideration being paid by the recipient. However, part of the capital gain may be chargeable, the difference between the donor's acquisition value and the consideration actually paid. Note, however, that indexation is not used in calculating this taxable portion of the gain.

Example
A man sells shares in the family trading company to his son. The father acquired his shares at £40,000 in 1986 and sells them to his son in 1990 for £50,000 when their full market value was £135,000.

Market value on sale		135,000
Cost	40,000	
Indexation (say)	12,000	(52,000)
Gross gain		83,000

However, the gain chargeable to tax is computed without reference to indexation, even though this would more than cover the chargeable gain:

Consideration by son	50,000
Unindexed cost	(40,000)
Assessable capital gain	10,000

Note: the indexation is 12,000 which, if used, would eliminate the capital gain.
Holdover relief:

Gross gain	83,000
Gain assessed to tax on father	(10,000)
To be heldover	73,000
Market value received by son	135,000
Heldover gain	(73,000)
Son's deemed acquisition value for capital gains tax	58,000

If inheritance tax is payable on a gift, then the tax paid can reduce the heldover gain, but cannot be increased by indexation.

Example
A father gives his son shares in the family trading company in 1990 when the shares were worth £80,000. The father had originally acquired them in 1985 for £30,000. The father died in 1991 and the son had to pay £27,000 inheritance tax.

Market value at time of gift		80,000
Cost	30,000	
Indexation (say)	9,000	(39,000)
		41,000
Inheritance tax paid		(27,000)
Gross gain		14,000
Market value received by son		80,000
Heldover gain		(14,000)
Son's acquisition value for capital gains tax		66,000

Payment of tax by instalments
When there is a gift of property giving rise to a payment of tax, it may be paid by instalments if the gift is of certain types of property:

1. Land.
2. A controlling shareholding in a company.
3. A minority holding of shares or securities in a company that is not dealt in on a recognised stock exchange, or the USM.

The payments of tax can be spread over ten equal annual instalments, and are subject to interest even if paid on time. The first instalment is due on the normal due date for payment of capital gains tax.

The remaining tax may be paid in full at any time.

If the gift is to a connected person (relative, etc.) and the asset is subsequently sold within the ten years, any outstanding tax is payable immediately.

Miscellaneous

Gifts to charities are already exempt under different legislation, and thus do not need to be covered by this legislation.

Shares and securities

Introduction

Prior to the introduction of indexation in April, 1983, holdings of shares and securities were dealt with on a "pooling" basis. That is, purchases of the same class of share in the same company on different occasions were not treated as separate assets, but one composite asset. They were "pooled", and on a disposal of some or all of the shares, an average or "pool" price was taken to calculate the original cost.

The introduction of indexation in April, 1982 made pooling no longer a practical proposition for individuals, and a scheme for matching disposals with acquisitions on a last in, first out basis (LIFO) was introduced. However, there was a pool of all purchases of the same share between 6th April, 1965 and 5th April, 1982.

With the revision of pooling as from April, 1985 a form of pooling was reintroduced, with sales being matched on a LIFO basis with three classes of purchases:

1. The "new pool", consisting of all purchases from April, 1982 to the present time. An average purchase price of shares is calculated, and is reindexed every time there is a purchase or disposal.
2. The "1982 pool", consisting of all purchases between 6th April, 1965 and 5th April, 1982. The average purchase price was calculated, but indexed from the March, 1982 value.
3. Pre-April, 1965 purchases were dealt with separately, using the original cost or April, 1965 value, but indexed from the value in March, 1982.

However, with the revision of capital gains tax from April, 1988, the pre-April, 1965 purchases are added to the 1982 pool, and all of them have a base cost of 31st March, 1982 value as their deemed cost, as well as being indexed on the same value. If, however, the original cost is more advantageous, this can still be used.

Example

Pluto Kratt, a mid-European financier, has these dealings in Rusky Risqué Magazines, plc:

Transaction	**Date**	**Shares**	**Price**
Buy	1/4/64	1,000	2,000
Value	6/4/65	Per share	3.00
Buy	1/8/80	700	2,800
Buy	1/9/81	500	2,500
Value	31/3/82	Per share	6.00
Buy	1/3/85	600	4,200
Buy	1/6/86	200	1,600
Sell	9/8/90	1,200	12,000

RPI:		
	March, 1982	79.44
	March, 1985	92.80
	June, 1986	97.80
	August, 1990 (say)	125.00

New Pool:				
Sale (800 shares)			8,000	
Cost				
1/3/85	**Shares:**	**Price:**		
	600	4,200		
Index to June, 1986:				
$4{,}200 \times \dfrac{97.8-92.8}{92.8}$ (0.054)=		227		
		4,427		
1/6/86	200	1,600		
	800	6,027		
Index to August, 1990:				
$6{,}027 \times \dfrac{125-97.8}{97.8}$ (0.278)		1,676	(7,703)	297
1982 Pool:				
Sale (400 shares)			4,000	
Cost:	Shares:	Price:		
31/3/82	2,200 Value at 31/3/82	13,200		
Index to August, 1990				
$13{,}200 \times \dfrac{125-79.44}{79.44}$ (0.574)		7,577		
		$\dfrac{20{,}777 \times 400}{2{,}200}$	(3,778)	222
Total gain				519

As has been said, if the original cost of a share purchased before March, 1982 is higher than 31st March, 1982 value, this can be used as an alternative provided no election has been made for March 1982 value.

Example

A man has the following transactions in the shares of ABC plc:

Transaction	Date	Shares	Price
Buy	1/4/80	300	1,500
Buy	1/2/82	200	1,400
Value	31/3/82	Per share	6.00
Buy	1/4/86	400	4,000
Sale	9/8/90	700	16,800

RPI:		
	March, 1982	79.44
	April, 1986	97.70
	August, 1990 (say)	125.0

New Pool:

Sale Price (400 shares)		9,600	
Cost: 400 shares	4,000		
Index to August, 1990:			
$4{,}000 \times \frac{125-97.7}{97.7}$ (0.279)	1,116	(5,116)	4,484

1982 Pool:

Sale price (300 shares) 7,200

Cost			Price
1/4/80	300	31/3/82 Value	1,800 (300×6)
1/2/82	200	Cost	1,400
	500		3,200

Index to August, 1990:

$$3.200 \times \frac{125-79.44}{79.44} (0.574) = 1{,}837 \qquad 5{,}037 \times \frac{300}{500} = (3{,}022) \qquad 4{,}178$$

8,662

Short-term transactions

When there is an acquisition and disposal of the same share or security within 10 days they are not to form part of the new pool, but are matched for the purpose of calculating the gain or loss.

Example

Mr Gornall has these transactions in the ordinary shares of Goodlife plc:

Transaction		Shares	Price
1/8/87	Buy	500	2,000
3/1/90	Buy	200	2,400
9/1/90	Sell	200	3,400

The 200 shares are purchased and sold with 10 days of each other, so the shares are matched, ignoring the ordinary pooling rules.

As both the purchase and sale are within the same month, there is no indexation.

Sale price	3,400
Cost (3/1/90)	2,400
Gain	1,000

Carry forward 500 shares at a cost of 2,000, plus indexation:

Indexation

	2,000
$2{,}000 \times \dfrac{119.5 - 102.1}{102.1}$ (0.170) =	340
	2,340

RPI:	August, 1987	102.1
	January, 1990	119.5

Bonus and rights issues

Bonus and rights issues are not treated as separate acquisitions of shares, but as extensions of the original purchases, and therefore have to be apportioned between the various pools.

Example

Bobo Nuss holds shares in Sahara Heating plc having done the following deals:

Transaction	Date	No.of shares	Price
Buy	1/4/81	400	800
Value	31/3/82	Per share	3.00
Buy	1/4/86	300	1,200
Bonus issue	1/6/86	1 new share for every 2 held	Nil
Sell	8/1/89	600	6,000

RPI:	March, 1982	79.44
	April, 1986	97.70
	June, 1986	97.80
	August, 1990 (say)	125.00

New pool:

Sale price (450 shares)		4,500
Cost 450 shares (300 original + 150 bonus) =	1,200	
Index to August, 1990:		
$1{,}200 \times \frac{125-97.7}{97.7}$ (0.279) =	335	(1,535)
		2,965

1982 pool:

Sale price (150 shares)			1,500
Valued at 31/3/82 600 shares (400 original + 200 bonus)			
$400 \times 3 =$	1,200		
Index on 31/3/82 value:			
$400 \times 3 = 1{,}200 \times \frac{125-79.44}{79.44}$ (0.574) =	689		
	$1{,}889 \times \frac{150}{400}$		(709)
			791

Total gain 2,965 + 791 = 3,756.

If, however, any additional cost is paid for the new shares, such as on a rights issue, then the addtional cost is only indexed from the date it was incurred, the date of the rights issue. Thus, if we have a new pool and a 1982 pool, the rights issue has to be apportioned between them and:

1. In the new pool, the rights issue can just be treated as a new purchase for indexation purposes.

2. In the 1982 pool, the shares sold have to be apportioned between the original shares sold, and those sold from the rights issue. The original shares are indexed from March, 1982 and the rights issue from the date of the acquisition of the rights.

Example

Ahmed Munni deals in the shares of Connoisseur Holidays (Blackpool) plc. He has these transactions:

Transaction	**Date**	**No. of shares**	**Price**
Buy	1/4/80	300	2,000
Value	31/3/82	Per share	9.00
Buy	1/7/86	600	6,600
Rights issue	1/6/87	1 new share for 2 held	3.00 per new share
Sell	8/8/90	1,200	15,600 (13.00 per share)

RPI:	March, 1982	79.44
	July, 1986	97.50
	June, 1987	101.90
	August, 1990 (say)	125.0

New pool:				
Sale price (900 shares)				11,700
	Shares		**Price**	
1/7/86	600		6,600	
Index to June. 1987:				
$6,600\times\frac{101.9-97.5}{97.5}$ (0.045)			297	
			6,897	
1/6/87	300	300×3.00	900	
	900		7,797	
Index to August, 1990:				
$7,797\times\frac{125-101.9}{101.9}$ (0.227)			1,770	(9,567)
				2,133
1982 pool:				
Sale price (300 shares)				3,900
200 original shares				
100 rights issues				
Value of originals	300×9.00=	2,700		
Index				
$2,700\times\frac{125-79.44}{79.44}$ (0.574)		1,550		
		$4,250\times\frac{200}{300}=$	2,833	
Rights issue	150×3.00=	450		
Index to August, 1990 (trans. June, 1987):				
$450\times\frac{125-101.9}{101.9}$ (0.227)=		102		
		$552\times\frac{100}{150}=$	368	(3,201)
Total gain 2,133+699=2,832				699

Sale of rights issue

If a rights issue is made, and instead of taking it up the shareholder sells the entitlement, then:

1. The cash received is treated as a part-disposal.
2. If the cash received is 5% or less than the total value of the holding after the making of the rights issue, the taxpayer can claim what is known as the "small disposal rule", and have the cash received deducted from the cost carried forward, rather than have a capital gain calculated. This is a form of rollover relief. However, it may not always be an advantage, such as when the capital gain would not be taxed but be covererd by losses or the annual exemption.

Example

Abseiling Grannies plc, a company specialising in holidays for senior citizens, makes a rights issue of 1 new share for 5 held in August, 1988. Doubting their long-term viability, Brown, who bought 1,000 shares for £2,000 in June, 1986, does not take up the rights but sells the entitlement for £700 in August, 1990. After the rights issue the shares have a value of £15.00 each.

RPI:	June, 1986	97.8
	August, 1990	125.0

Sale price		700
Apportioned cost		
$2{,}000 \times \dfrac{700}{700 + 15{,}000^{*}} =$	90	

* 15,000 is the value of 1,000 shares retained after the rights issue.

Index		
$90 \times \dfrac{125 - 97.8}{97.8}\ (0.278) =$	25	(115)
Gain		585

However, the cash received is less than 5% of the total value of the shares after the rights issue:

$$15{,}000 + 700 = 15{,}700 \times 5\% = £785.$$

Therefore, if it was to his advantage, Brown could have the price received deducted from the indexed cost carried forward:

Cost	2,000
Indexed to August, 1990:	
$2{,}000 \times 0.278 =$	556
Indexed cost	2,556
Less: cash received	(700)
Adjusted cost carried forward	1,856

Takeovers

If, on a takeover bid, the people making the bid acquire more than 25% of the ordinary share capital of the target company, there need be no capital gain assessed if the takeover was the offer of shares in the new company for shares in the target company. A form of rollover relief applies, and the indexed cost of the old shares is rolled over against the issue price of the new shares in the company making the takeover bid. However, this treatment needs the permission of the Inland Revenue Special Division, who need to be convinced the takeover is for bona fide commercial reasons, and tax avoidance is not involved. A written application for clearance has to be made to the Inland Revenue.

Example

Goss owns 1,000 shares in ABC plc which he acquired in May, 1986 for £3,000. In July, 1987 XYZ plc makes a takeover bid, offering 2 XYZ shares (value £4.00 each) per ABC share. He sells the 2,000 XYZ shares in August, 1990 for £20,000.

Acquisition of 2,000 XYZ shares in July, 1987:		
Value $2{,}000 \times £4.00 =$		8,000
But:		
Rolled over value of shares at July, 1987:		
Original cost of 1,000 ABC shares		3,000
Indexation from May, 1986 to July, 1987:		
$3{,}000 \times \frac{101.8 - 97.8}{97.8}$ (0.041) =		123
Deemed acquisition value of 2,000 XYZ		3,123
Sale of XYZ in August, 1990		20,000
Acquisition value	3,123	
Indexation from July, 1987 to August, 1989:		
$3.123 \times \frac{125 - 101.8}{101.8}$ (0.228) =	712	(3,835)
Gain		16,165

If the takeover is not entirely for shares, but partly in cash, the cash element is taxable as a part disposal. However, like the sale of a rights entitlement, the small disposal rule, allowing rollover relief, may be claimed as long as the cash received is not more than 5% of the total value of the takeover offer.

Example

Batsblood Pharmaceuticals plc makes a takeover bid for Newtsleg Ltd, a private company producing some rather doubtful patent remedies. The offer, made in August, 1990, is 3 Batsblood shares, valued at £6.00 each, and £2.00 in cash for each Newtsleg share. Miss Hegerty had acquired 4,000 Newtsleg shares for £5,000 in June, 1986.

RPI:	
June, 1986	97.8
August, 1990 (say)	125.0

Sale price (cash element) 4,000 Newtsleg × 2.00 = 8,000

Cost $5{,}000 \times \frac{8{,}000}{8{,}000 + 72{,}000^*} =$ 500

* 72,000 is 3 Batsblood shares at 6.00 each for each Newtsleg = 12,000 × 6.00 = 72,000.

Index $500 \times \frac{125 - 97.8}{97.8}$ (0.278) =	139	(639)
Gain		7,361

The total takeover value was £80,000, of which 5% is £4,000. Therefore the small disposal rule is not available to Miss Hegerty.

Shares owned at 6th April, 1965

Prior to April, 1988 shares acquired before 6th April, 1965, that is, before capital gains tax was introduced, were treated separately to all others on a disposal. The special rules applied to them were:

1. They were the last deemed to be disposed of under the last in, first out rule.
2. Unquoted shares could have the gain calculated according to original cost and then the gain arising before 6th April, 1965 exempted. This portion of the gain was calculated by taking a straight arithmetical apportionment between the gain arising before and after 6th April, 1965.

Alternatively, the taxpayer could elect for the value at 6th April, 1965 to be used instead of cost, but with no time-apportionment.

3. Quoted shares did not have time-apportionment applied to them. The gain was calculated using the most advantageous value of cost or value on 6th April, 1965.

Alternatively, the taxpayer could elect to include shares acquired before 6th April, 1965 in the 1982 pool, deeming them to have been purchased on that date, at their value on that date.

For disposals on or after 6th April, 1988, as 31st March, 1982 value can be used these former rules have largely been made obsolete. But if the gain or loss using the former rules would give a smaller gain or loss, then they are used instead of the 31st March, 1982 value. If the old rules give a gain or loss, and 31st March, 1982 value the opposite result (e.g. a gain instead of a loss), then the result is nil, no gain/no loss.

Valuation of shares

The valuation of unquoted shares is highly specialised and not dealt with here. The Inland Revenue have a special division which deals with this subject, the Shares Valuation Division.

The valuation of quoted shares, if there is no sale price, is the lower of two alternatives:

1. The "quarter up" rule, under which you add to the lower of the quoted daily prices a quarter of the difference between the two quoted prices.
2. The "half up" rule, which is the half way price between the actual lowest and highest bargains struck on the day. This figure is always used in valuing shares on 6th April, 1965.

Example

A man gives 2,000 shares in a quoted company to his own son when:

1. The closing prices were 90p and 94p.
2. Bargains struck were 88p and 98p.

The alternatives are:

1. Quarter up 90p+1p (¼×94−90)=91p.
2. Half up 88p+5p (½×98−88) =93p.

Therefore the disposal price of the shares would be:

2,000×91p=£1,820

Gilt-edged securities and corporate bonds

There is no chargeable gain or allowable loss for disposals on or after 2nd July, 1986 for gilt-edged securities or corporate bonds (e.g. debenture or loan stock).

A corporate bond qualifies if it fulfils the following conditions:

1. It was issued after 13th March, 1984.
2. It was issued by a company whose shares are listed on the Stock Exchange or dealt in on the USM.
3. It is a normal commercial loan (e.g. not convertible into shares).
4. It is capable of being marketed and is not an issue by a company to another company in the same group.

Dealings in futures and options in these securities are similarly exempt from the same date.

As qualifying corporate bonds are not subject to capital gains tax, indexation is not available to create or enhance losses, as losses on such bonds do not attract tax relief, and thus actual losses incurred, do not get relieved. To allow for relief when such a bond becomes irrecoverable the actual loss can be offset against capital gains. This is only available for bonds actually held on 14th March, 1989 or purchased after that date.

Authorised unit and investment trusts

When an individual sells his unit trusts and makes a gain he used to be given a credit of 10% of the gain to offset against his liability to tax. This credit, if not fully utilised against gains on unit trusts, could not be used against any capital gains liability on other assets and was not available for repayment. This was withdrawn from 6th April, 1980. SInce then no credit has been available.

Business assets

Business assets are specially favoured in capital gains tax in that they often qualify for reliefs and application of the rollover principles when other types do not. The more important occasions are described below.

Retirement relief

The amount of relief

Retirement relief is an exemption from tax on certain qualifying gains (called ''material disposal of business assets'') for individuals and trustees who dispose of business assets either:

1. On or after the age of 60. Then the relief is mandatory, and does not have to be applied for.

2. If below age 60, when they dispose of assets, they are forced to retire because of ill health which has made them permanently incapable of performing their former type of work. This type of relief has to be applied for and satisfactory evidence produced to the Inland Revenue.

In the first case it is not necessary to retire, just to dispose of assets above age 60. In the second case actual retirement is needed.

Up to 5th April, 1988 the maximum relief was £125,000 of gains. From 6th April, 1988 the relief has been extended to:

1. £125,000 of gains, and
2. Up to half the additional gains between £125,000 and £500,000.

Example

Mr S. Driver retires at the age of 62, sells his business and makes capital gains of £350,000 on the assets.

Gross gains	350,000
Full relief	(125,000)
	225,000
Half relief 225,000×50%=	(112,500)
Taxable	112,500

The individual must have been in business for a minimum of 1 year and a maximum of 10 years to qualify for relief. It is then granted at 10% of the figures mentioned above for each year of service, so that after 10 years he qualifies for 100% of relief.

Example

Hardman retires at 61. He has been in business for 7 years, making gains on disposal of his assets of £220,000.

Gross gains	220,000
Full relief 125,000×70%=	(87,500)
	132,500
Half relief 132,500×50%×70%=	(46,375)
Taxable gains	86,125

If he disposed of further assets when he was 64 (and thus had completed his 10 year maximum qualifying period) the balance of the relief would be available:

Gross gains on the second disposal		140,000
Full relief: 125,000−87,500	=	(37,500)
		102,500

Half relief: Total qualifying gains to date	220,000	
	140,000	
	360,000	
Full relief	(125,000)	
	235,000	
Half relief already given	(46,375)	
	188,625	
Half relief now available 102,500×50% =		(51,250)
Taxable gains		51,250

The 10 year rule need not all be with the same business or company. Successive periods of business can be added together for this purpose, provided there is never a break of more than 2 years.

Example
Haynes started in business on 1st April, 1982. He sold out his first business on 31st March, 1987. He bought another business on 1st October, 1987 and sold that on 31st March, 1991 when he was aged 62.

Gains on sale of second business		110,000
Qualifying period 1/4/82 to 31/3/87	5 years	
1/10/87 to 30/3/91	3½ years	
Total	8½ years	
Full relief 125,000×85% =		(106,250)
Taxable gains		3,750

Types of qualifying disposals

Five types of disposal qualify for the relief:

1. A disposal of business assets used in a sole tradership, or disposal of a share in a partnership.
2. A disposal of shares in an unquoted family trading company, of which the individual owns:

a) At least 25% of the ordinary share capital, OR

b) At least 5% and together with his family owns over 50% of the ordinary share capital. "Family" means spouse, descendants, ancestors, and brothers and sisters.

If disposing of shares in a family company he also needs to be a full-time working director (FTWD). If he has retired from full-time work, he should have worked for the company at least 10 hours a week since retirement. Note that only directors of companies need be in a full-time occupation, not the self-employed or partners.

There is one other difficulty regarding companies which will be mentioned later.

3. "Associated disposals" of business assets. This can include several things, but mainly the ownership of an asset by an individual but used by the partnership of which he is a member, or a family company of which he is a FTWD. The asset has to be used rent free (e.g. the trading premises) and must be disposed of in connection with retirement from the business.

4. Assets owned by trustees, but used in a business by a beneficiary with a life interest in the trust, qualify for retirement relief.

5. Assets owned by an employee for use in his employment may also qualify for relief.

Miscellaneous points

If shares in a family company are sold, the relief is restricted to the proportion of the "chargeable business assets" to the "chargeable assets" of the company. "Chargeable business assets" are those which on disposal are liable to capital gains and are directly used in the business. "Chargeable assets" are any assets owned by the company liable to capital gains, but not used directly in the business.

Example

A full-time working director of a family company retires and sells his shares, making a gain of £300,000. The value of the company's chargeable assets at that time are:

Land and buildings	600,000	Chargeable business assets
Goodwill	200,000	
Plant and machinery*	100,000	
Investments	200,000	

Note: Non-chargeable assets such as stock, cash, debtors, etc. are irrelevant, as are liabilities. Shares in subsidiary trading companies are a "chargeable business asset".

* Plant and machinery may not be chargeable assets, if valued at less than £6,000 per item. They would then be exempt chattels.

The gain qualifying for relief would be:

$300{,}000 \times \dfrac{900{,}000}{1{,}100{,}000} =$	245,455
Full relief	(125,000)
Half Relief	120,455
$120{,}455 \times 50\% =$	(60,228)
	60,227
Plus: $300{,}000 - 245{,}455 =$	54,545
Taxable gains	114,772

For the self-employed to gain relief, they must dispose of "business assets", meaning those which are vital to the operation of the business and whose disposal would have a material effect on the size or scale of the business. Thus, a farmer who sold a marginal piece of land which would not affect his yields may find retirement relief was not granted on any gain made on that disposal.

Replacement of business assets (rollover relief)

When a taxpayer disposes of an asset used in a trade and replaces it with another asset used in the trade in a period beginning 12 months before the disposal, and up to 36 months afterwards, the gain can be rolled over against the cost of the replacement.

Example
Glencoe Ltd. sells its bagpipe factory for £250,000 in 1992 and buys a whisky distillery for £300,000 in 1991. It originally bought the bagpipe factory for £80,000 in 1983.

Sale price		250,000
Cost	80,000	
Indexation (say)	30,000	(110,000)
Gain		140,000
Cost of whisky distillery		300,000
Gain rolled over		(140,000)
Deemed cost of whisky distillery		160,000

Note: Any gain on the whisky distillery could be rolled over as well, if more capital assets were purchased in the qualifying time period (4 years, as above).

The new asset does not have to be used in the same line of trade.

The main condition is that the assets disposed of and acquired must fall within certain classes. These are:
Land, buildings and fixed plant and machinery.
Goodwill.
Ships, aircraft and hovercraft.
Satellites, space stations and spacecraft (including launch vehicles).
Milk and potato quotas.

Note: Rollover relief (on business assets) cannot be claimed on a disposal or acquisition of company shares.

If the asset is sold for a certain sum and the cost of replacements in the requisite period (4 years) is not equivalent to or more than the sale price, the money retained becomes assessable.

Example

McHaggis sells his distillery for £300,000 and replaces it with a plant producing spring water for £270,000. The distillery originally cost £150,000.

Sale price of distillery		300,000
Cost	150,000	
Indexation (say)	60,000	(210,000)
Gross gain		90,000
Cash retained (and assessed to tax)		
	300,000−270,000=	(30,000)
Gain rolled over		60,000

Deemed cost of water plant 270,000−60,000=210,000

If the replacement asset is a "depreciating asset" (one which will have a life of 50 years within 10 years of purchase, i.e. useful life of 60 years on purchase) then "holdover relief" is given, not rollover relief. Holdover relief involves calculating the gain on the disposal of the original asset and then postponing calculating the tax payable (and the date of payment) until the earliest of:

1. Disposal of the new asset.
2. Cessation of trade.
3. 10 years from acquisition of new asset.

Example

William Fort sells his bottling plant for £200,000 (cost £120,000) and buys instead £250,000 of machinery for plucking and canning dead haggis for the English market. The machinery is a "depreciating asset".

Sale price		200,000
Cost	120,000	
Indexation (say)	30,000	(150,000)
Gain		50,000

The gain will be calculated and becomes taxable when the machinery is sold, if he ceases to trade (e.g. when the English get fed up with plucked haggis), or 10 years from acquisition of the machinery.

Rollover relief and March, 1982 rebasing

Any person who acquired an asset prior to April, 1982, and then disposed of it between April, 1982 and April, 1988, claiming rollover or holdover relief on the gain, and then had the gain crystallised after April, 1988 is at a disadvantage regarding 1982 rebasing. They cannot use the value at 31st March, 1982 in calculating the gain as the asset they are disposing of was not owned by them at 31st March, 1982. The solution, in rollover relief, is to halve the gain rolled over.

Example
Mulligan Ltd. purchased a factory (Factory A) in 1980 for £200,000. Its value on 31st March, 1982 was £350,000. It was sold for £450,000 in 1986. This was replaced by purchase of another factory (Factory B) in 1987 at a cost of £600,000. Factory B was sold (and not replaced) for £850,000 in January, 1991.

Factory A:		
Sale price in 1986		450,000
Original cost	200,000	
Indexation (based on March, 1982 350,000) (say)	35,000	(235,000)
Gain		215,000
Factory B:		
Cost		600,000
Rollover relief (gain on A 50%)=215,000×50%=		(107,500)
Deemed cost		(492,500)
Sale of B (in 1991)		850,000
Deemed cost	492,500	
Indexation (say)	49,250	(541,750)
Gain		308,250

If holdover relief is involved, the gain held over is halved.

For various technical reasons, other possible solutions were considered unworkable.

To sum up, this relief operates when:

1. An asset was acquired before April, 1982.
2. It was disposed of in circumstances where the gain was held over or rolled over between April, 1982 and April, 1988.
3. The chargeable disposal occurred after April, 1988.

The exact occasions to which this treatment can be applied are:

1. A replacement of business assets (rollover relief) (S.115, CGTA, 1979).
2. Gifts relief election is made (S.79, FA, 1980).
3. A replacement asset is acquired after receiving compensation or insurance money (S.21, CGTA, 1979).
4. Land is acquired to replace land compulsorily purchased (S.111A, CGTA, 1979).
5. A self-employed or partnership business is incorporated (S.123, CGTA, 1979).
6. A gift of a business asset to a company (S.126, CGTA, 1979).

There is a second list of circumstances when this relief can also apply. These tend to be less numerous in practice:

1. A trade and associated assets have been transferred to a non-resident company in exchange for shares or securities (S.268A, ICTA, 1970).

2. A company ceases to be a member of a group (S.278, ICTA, 1970).

3. Gifts have been acquired on a compulsory acquisition of shares (S.84, CGTA, 1979).

4. Land is compulsorily purchased, replacement land is acquired and the replacement land is a depreciating asset (S.111B(3), CGTA, 1979).

5. A business asset is replaced by a depreciating asset (S.117(2), CGTA, 1979).

6. Gifts relief is claimed, and the donee emigrates (S.79, FA, 1981).

7. Securities, on a reorganisation, have been exchanged for qualifying corporate bonds (para.10, Sch.13, FA, 1984).

Transfer of a business to a company

When a sole trader or a partnership transfers the business to the ownership of a limited company, any change in ownership of the chargeable assets (particularly land, buildings and goodwill) is a chargeable occasion.

However, any resultant gain can be rolled over wholly or partly against the base cost of any shares issued in exchange for the transfer of the business and the business assets. To qualify for full rollover relief only shares should be issued. If any cash is paid by the company in addition it is treated as a part disposal.

To qualify for this form of rollover relief the entire business should be transferred as a going concern together with all the assets of the business.

Private houses

A gain made on the sale of a house which has been the owner's only or main residence is exempt from capital gains tax on the house and garden, provided the entire site does not exceed one acre. The gain on any additional garden can also be exempt provided the additional garden is appropriate to the style and character of the house.

To qualify for relief, the house should be:

1. The only or main residence of the owner.

2. Up to 5th April, 1988, a property occupied by a dependent relative who does not pay rent. The relief continues to operate for disposals after 5th April, 1988 if the relative was then in occupation, and continues in occupation until the disposal. If, however, they leave and are then replaced by another dependent relative, the relief is no longer available.

3. Occupied by the beneficiary of a trust as their main residence.

4. The property of an individual who has to live in a property provided by their employer or property tied to the work is self-employed (e.g. public house tenant), where the property purchased is intended as the only or main residence on vacation of the job-related accommodation.

To qualify for full relief the house should be occupied as the only or main residence throughout the period of ownership. Thus, periods of absence can lead to a proportionate charge to tax. However, certain periods of absence do qualify for relief:

1. The last twenty-four months of ownership.

Other periods of absence qualify for relief provided the house is occupied before and after the period of absence.

2. Up to a maximum of three years' absence for any reason, in one continuous period or aggregated broken periods.

3. Up to a maximum additional four years if living away from home because of employment in the UK.

4. An unlimited period of time if employed overseas. In 3 and 4, if it is impossible to live in the house after a period of absence, because of the terms of employment, this condition is waived by concession.

If there is any business use of the premises the proportionate gain on the part of the property used exclusively for business purposes is assessable. However, there can be exemption on a gain made on a let part of the house within certain limits. These limits are that the exemption is not to exceed the smaller of the exemption on the owner's residential part or £20,000.

Example

Mrs Lucy Borgia (who is widowed after her husband drank some wine) inherited her house on her husband's death when it was valued at £35,000. She split the property into two flats (of equal value), let one and lived in the other. After the death of her male tenant (another wine lover!) the house was sold for £80,000 (after the jury returned a unanimous verdict of guilty).

Sale price		80,000
Value on inheritance 35,000 + 1,000 (indexation)		(36,000)
Gross gain		44,000
Exemption on own flat 44,000 × ½ =	22,000	
Exemption on let portion	20,000	(42,000)
Assessable		2,000

Chattels which are not wasting assets

Chattels (tangible, movable objects) which are not wasting assets are still not assessable unless the sale price is more than £6,000 (£3,000 up to 5th April, 1989). If the sale price is just over £6,000 a form of marginal relief is available by limiting the gain (if beneficial) to the excess of the sale price over 6,000 times $\frac{5}{3}$.

Example

A man bought a picture for £1,000 and some years later sold it for £6,600.

Sale price		6,600
Cost	1,000	
Indexation	200	1,200
Gross gain		5,400
		but limited to:
$6{,}600-6{,}000=600\times {}^5/_3=$		1,000

If a chattel is sold for less than £6,000 but at a loss the loss is limited by substituting a sale price of £6,000.

Example

A man brought a painting for £6,400 and sold it later for £1,700. The loss is restricted to:

$$6{,}400-6{,}000=(400)$$

Short leases

A lease of land for 50 years or less is, for capital gains, a wasting asset and any expenditure on its acquisition is deemed to waste away over its life and thus not wholly available as a deductible cost on its disposal. The "wasting" is calculated according to an actuarial table in the Schedule 3 Capital Gains Tax Act, 1979.

Example

Extract from actuarial table:

Years	Percentage	Years	Percentage	Years	Percentage
17	66.470	12	53.191	7	35.414
16	64.116	11	50.038	6	31.195
15	61.617	10	46.695	5	26.772
14	58.971	9	43.154	4	21.983
13	56.167	8	39.399	3	16.959

Bassett acquired a 15 year lease at a cost of £6,000 premium and 6 years later assigned the remainder of the lease for £4,500 (for the remaining 9 years).

Sale price 4,500

$$-\text{Wasted cost } 6{,}000\times\frac{61.617\%\ (15\text{ years})-43.154\%\ (9\text{ years})}{61.617\%\ (15\text{ years})}$$

$=1{,}798.\ 6{,}000-1{,}798=4{,}202+200$ (indexation) $=$ (4,402)

98

If, instead of assigning the whole lease he granted a sublease then the calculation is different. A premium paid for a lease can be subject to Schedule A as well as capital gains and the assessable amount has to be divided between them.

Example (ignoring Schedule A)

Gough acquired a 17 year lease at a cost of £13,000. 4 years later (13 years still to run on lease) he granted a 10 year sublease for £8,000 (headlease still has 3 years' life at the end of sublease):

Sale price	8,000
$-$Wasted cost $13{,}000 \times \dfrac{56.167 \text{ (13 years)} - 16.959 \text{ (3 years)}}{66.470 \text{ (17 years)}}$	
$= 7{,}668 + 300$ (indexation)	(7,968)
	32

This is subject to a deduction of any part of the premium assessed to income or corporation tax under Schedule A.

Retail prices index

1982	*RPI*	**1983**	*RPI*	**1984**	*RPI*	**1985**	*RPI*	**1986**	*RPI*
Jan	78.7	Jan	82.6	Jan	86.8	Jan	91.2	Jan	96.2
Feb	78.8	Feb	83.0	Feb	87.2	Feb	91.9	Feb	96.6
Mar	79.4	Mar	83.1	Mar	87.5	Mar	92.8	Mar	96.7
Apr	81.0	Apr	84.3	Apr	88.6	Apr	94.8	Apr	97.7
May	81.6	May	84.6	May	89.0	May	95.2	May	97.8
June	81.9	June	84.8	June	89.2	June	95.4	June	97.8
July	81.9	July	85.3	July	89.1	July	95.2	July	97.5
Aug	81.9	Aug	85.7	Aug	89.9	Aug	95.5	Aug	97.8
Sept	81.9	Sept	86.1	Sept	90.1	Sept	95.4	Sept	98.3
Oct	82.3	Oct	86.4	Oct	90.7	Oct	95.6	Oct	98.5
Nov	82.7	Nov	86.7	Nov	91.0	Nov	95.9	Nov	99.3
Dec	82.5	Dec	86.9	Dec	90.9	Dec	96.0	Dec	99.6

1987	*RPI*	**1988**	*RPI*	**1989**	*RPI*	**1990**	*RPI*
Jan	100.0	Jan	103.3	Jan	111.0	Jan	119.5
Feb	100.4	Feb	103.7	Feb	111.8	Feb	120.2
Mar	100.6	Mar	104.1	Mar	112.3	Mar	121.4
Apr	101.8	Apr	105.8	Apr	114.3		
May	101.9	May	106.2	May	115.0		
June	101.9	June	106.6	June	115.4		
July	101.8	July	106.7	July	115.5		
Aug	102.1	Aug	107.9	Aug	115.8		
Sept	102.4	Sept	108.4	Sept	116.6		
Oct	102.9	Oct	109.5	Oct	117.5		
Nov	103.4	Nov	110.0	Nov	118.5		
Dec	103.3	Dec	110.3	Dec	118.8		

You should now attempt the "Capital Gains Tax" questions beginning on page 300).

Chapter Sixteen

Overseas Income and Residence

Introduction

In general terms persons (individuals, companies and trustees) resident in the United Kingdom are taxable in this country on income arising to them from anywhere in the world. The amount and method of assessment can be complicated in the case of individuals by their status of RESIDENCE, ORDINARY RESIDENCE AND DOMICILE.

RESIDENCE is defined as:

1. In the case of an individual the country where he is temporarily living. In the case of a UK citizen he is deemed to be resident unless absent from the UK for a full fiscal year if working abroad, or two fiscal years if abroad for any other reason. A foreign citizen is deemed to be resident in the UK for a fiscal year if he is in the UK for more than 182 days (6 months) in that year.

2. A company is resident where its central management and control is carried on. This is generally where the directors regularly hold meetings and take decisions.

ORDINARY RESIDENCE is a more permanent thing, the country of habitual residence. An individual acquires ordinary resident in the UK by visitng the UK on average for three months a year over a four year period.

DOMICILE is the country an individual regards as his natural home. He normally has a domicile of origin determined at birth, but can change it to a domicile of choice by undertaking a permanent change in place of abode, habits of life, work place, etc.

Overseas income

Individuals

An individual resident in the United Kingdom is assessable on income arising abroad under the following categories:

1. Income earned from overseas employment is assessable under Schedule E but may qualify for a percentage reduction. This topic is dealt with in the chapter on Schedule E.

2. Income from the carrying on of a trade abroad is assessable on the income arising under Schedule D, Cases I & II if the control of the trade is exercised in the UK.

If the trade is controlled abroad (which in practice is rare) then the taxpayer is assessable on the profits actually brought into the UK (the "remittance" basis), and assessment is under Schedule D, Case V.

3. Foreign pensions received by a UK resident are assessed under Schedule D, Case V and subject to a 10% reduction unless the recipient is not ordinarily resident or domiciled in the UK when the remittance basis applies.

4. Investment income arising abroad (rents, bank interest, foreign company dividends, interest on securities, loans, etc.) is assessable under Cases IV and V on the arising basis unless the recipient is not ordinarily resident or domiciled in the UK when the remittance basis again applies.

Example
Mel Bourne, an Australian by birth, but now resident, ordinarily resident and domiciled in the UK has the following income for 1990/91:

Year ended	**5/4/90**	**5/4/91**
Australian pension	1,500	2,000
UK pension	2,200	3,000
Australian dividends (gross)	800	1,000
UK dividends (net)	600	720
Profits of trade carried on from UK	22,000	32,000

1990/91 assessable income:

Sch.D, Case V:			Sch.D, Case I:	
Australian pension	1,500		Gross profit	22,000
$10\% \times 1{,}500$ =	(150)	1,350		
Australian dividends		800	Sch.E	3,000
Sch.F:				
UK dividends	720			
$720 \times \frac{1}{3}$ =	240	960		
		3,110		25,000
Assessable income			28,110	

Companies

If a company is resident in the UK:

1. Trading profits, whether from the UK or abroad, are assessable under Schedule D, Case I on the gross profit arising.

2. Overseas investment income is assessable under Schedule D, Cases IV and V on the gross profits arising. Dividends from foreign resident companies are assessable under Case V and are not franked investment income.

Note that if the company is resident in the UK all foreign income is assessable on the gross amount arising and remittances to the UK are irrelevant.

If a company is resident overseas:

1. Trading profits arising from within the UK are assessable to corporation tax if made from a permanent branch or agency within the UK, the definition of which is complicated. However it does not include just warehousing of imported goods and assessability in the UK generally depends on trading contracts being concluded in the UK and not abroad.

Investment income arising within the UK is also subject to corporation tax if paid to a non-resident company trading within the UK.

2. A non-resident property or investment company pays income tax (usually by deduction at source) on its UK investment income, although in practice certain forms of UK investment income are not taxed by the UK authorities e.g. bank interest, interest on certain UK government securities.

Relief for foreign tax paid

So that a person does not pay tax twice on the same income (in the country of origin of the income and in the country of residence of the recipient) relief is given in one of the two countries. This can be done in one of several ways:

1. By exemption from taxation in the country of origin.
2. By the granting of credit relief in the country of residence.
3. By assessing the net overseas income (net of foreign tax paid) in the country of residence. However, this form of relief is generally given only to companies.

The form of the relief is often arranged by means of a double taxation treaty between the two countries. Relief then granted is called "treaty" relief. Sometimes, if no treaty exists, the country of residence grants relief itself in much the same way. This is called "unilateral" relief, and there is no difference between the general principles underlying the two forms of relief.

Exemption

Complete exemption of tax, if granted at all, is normally given in the country of the income's origin. In practice it is confined generally to international transport concerns (which therefore only pay tax in their country of residence), temporary visitors such as visiting lecturers, teachers and students, and visiting diplomats and workers of international organisations such as the United Nations, EEC and NATO.

Credit relief

Credit relief is usually a deduction from the tax payable in the country of residence in respect of foreign income which would otherwise be doubly taxed, and is normally limited to the lower of the foreign tax or residential country tax on the same income.

The general principle is that the total tax paid worldwide is not to exceed the higher of the two countries' rate of tax. The lower rate is therefore deducted from the country of residence's liability.

Example (illustrating a company situation)
English Ltd trades in Ruritania and makes £1,000 (gross) profit. The Ruritanian rate of tax is:

a) 55%
b) 25%

The UK rate is assumed to be 35%.

a) UK tax on Ruritanian profit:			b) UK tax on Ruritanian profit:		
1,000×35%	=	350	1,000×35%	=	350
−Credit relief (UK tax paid)		(350)	−Credit relief (Ruritanian tax paid)		(250)
Net UK tax		Nil	Net UK tax		100

The same principles operate in income tax, although there are additional difficulties with the higher rate:

1. The UK tax applicable is assumed to be at the highest rate of income tax.
2. If there is more than one source of foreign income involved with two or more foreign rates of tax, relief is given in the order which accords the taxpayer the greatest advantage.

Example
For 1990/91 a UK resident has a UK salary of £23,525 and UK dividends of £720 (net). He pays allowable bank interest of £200 and is married.

He also receives the following foreign income:

	Gross	Foreign tax withheld
Ruritanian rents	500	250 (50%)
Bessarabian dividends	3,700	1,295 (35%)

UK income

Sch.F	720		Sch.E		23,525
Credit 720×⅓ =	240	960	SPA	3,005	
Bank interest		(200)	MCA	1,720	(4,725)
		760			18,800
			19,760		

19,760×25% = 4,940.00

Foreign income

Sch.D, Case V:

Bessarabian dividends	940 ×25% =	235.00	
	2,760×40% =	1,104.00	
	3,700	1,339.00	
Credit relief (Bessarabian tax paid)	=	(1,295.00)	44.00
Ruritanian rents	500×40% =	200.00	
Credit relief (limited to UK tax)	=	(200.00)	Nil
Net UK tax payable			4,984.00

Note that credit relief can only be claimed in the year the foreign income is received. It can only be offset against UK tax liability. Surplus credit cannot be repaid or transferred against another year's liability.

Companies

The rate of foreign tax (and resultantly the gross overseas income) can vary in the case of dividends from overseas companies. The foreign tax included is only the withholding tax if the UK company owns less than 10% of the foreign company's voting power. The underlying tax is available if the ownership of voting power in the foreign company is 10% or more. "Withholding tax" is the tax deducted from the dividend paid, and "underlying tax" is the tax paid on the gross profit out of which the dividend is paid.

Example

A UK resident company owns 25% of the share capital of a Ruritanian company. The Ruritanian company makes a gross profit of £50,000 (paying Ruritanian tax at 15%) and pays a gross dividend of £20,000 (deducting Ruritanian withholding tax of 12%).

The UK company receives:

Gross dividend	20,000×25% =	5,000
Withholding tax	5,000×12% =	(600)
Dividend received		4,400

Assuming a UK rate of tax of 35% this would give an assessment of:

Sch.D, Case V	5,000×35% =	1,750.00
Credit relief		(600.00)
Net UK tax payable		1,150.00

With the underlying tax involved the assessment would be:

Net dividend		4,400	
Withholding tax		600	1,412 total of foreign tax paid
Underlying tax $\frac{5,000 \times 15\%}{85\%}$ =		882	
		5,882	
Sch.D, Case V	5,882×35% =		2,059
Credit relief (600+882)	=		(1,482)
Net UK tax payable			577

Position of credit relief in corporation tax

Credit relief is very similar to the credit on building society interest:

1. It is only a deduction from tax payable in the current year. There can be no repayment of excess credit.
2. Excess credit cannot be carried to any other accounting period back or forward.
3. It cannot be surrendered under group relief provisions.
4. It is given before ACT has been deducted. Prior to April, 1984 credit relief was given after ACT, which was disadvantageous to companies.
5. The credit relief is restricted to the UK corporation tax on the foreign income. It cannot be offset against the corporation tax on any other income.

Example

Albion plc makes trading profits in a twelve month accounting period:

From UK		1,050,000
From abroad:		
Gross profit	100,000	
Foreign tax paid	40,000	60,000

The company paid a dividend in the accounting period of 180,000. The rate of corporation tax is assumed to be 35%.

	UK profit	Foreign profit	Total
Gross income	1,050,000	100,000	1,150,000
Gross CT (35%)	367,500	35,000	402,500
Credit relief (limited to UK CT rate)*		(35,000)	
	367,500	Nil	367,500
ACT offset:			
180,000×⅓ =	(60,000)		(60,000)
MCT payable	307,500	Nil	307,500

*Note: Foreign tax paid 40,000−35,000 (relieved)=5,000 credit relief not utilised.

It is possible by relinquishing credit relief to be assessed on the net foreign income (after deduction of foreign tax paid). This may be preferable when credit relief would otherwise by wasted, e.g. when trading losses have been offset against foreign income.

Example
A UK resident company has:

Trading loss		(10,000)	
Foreign rents received		8,000	(foreign tax paid 2,000)
No dividend has been paid			
Claiming credit relief:			
Sch.D, Case V		8,000	
Loss relief	(10,000)		
Utilised	8,000		
Carry forward	(2,000)		
Net income		Nil	
Claiming net income method of assessment:			
Sch.D, Case V		8,000	
–Foreign tax paid		(2,000)	6,000
Loss relief	(10,000)		
Utilised	6,000		(6,000)
Carry forward	(4,000)		
Net income			Nil

Income tax
A foreign dividend paid to a UK resident may pass through the hands of a UK paying agent which handles the dividend payments in the UK for the foreign company. If so the paying agent may deduct basic rate income tax at source. He may be authorised to deduct less than 25% to allow for the credit relief on the foreign tax paid.

Example
A married UK resident for 1990/91 has a salary of £20,350 and receives a dividend from a foreign company:

Gross dividend	1,000
Foreign tax paid (10%)	100
	900
UK tax deducted by paying agent at a rate authorised by the Inland Revenue of 15% (25% – 10%)	(150)
Dividend received	750

Tax liability:				
Sch.D, Case V	1,000	Sch.E		20,350
		SPA	3,005	
		MCA	1,720	(4,725)
				15,625
		16,625		

16,625×25% =	4,156.25
Credit relief	(100.00)
	4,056.25
UK tax deducted	(150.00)
Net UK tax payable	3,906.25

Tax considerations in overseas trading

Should a UK resident company trade abroad as an overseas branch enterprise or as a subsidiary company resident abroad?

A branch operation would simply be treated in exactly the same way as if it operated in the UK.

1. Profits would be assessed under Schedule D, Case I, but on the other hand trading losses could be offset in exactly the same way as losses incurred in the UK.

2. Capital allowances could be claimed on plant and machinery and individual buildings used in the branch.

However, if the branch started with trading losses and heavy expenditure was incurred on capital expenditure in the early years and corporation tax relief obtained ownership of the branch could then be transferred to an overseas resident subsidiary when the branch moved into profit. Treasury permission used to be needed, but this is no longer necessary.

If operating as an overseas resident subsidiary from the start, no UK tax relief could be obtained on trading losses, and capital allowances would not bc granted in the UK.

Controlled foreign companies

To try and prevent UK resident companies avoiding UK tax by diverting profit into a foreign resident company controlled directly or indirectly by the UK company, from 6th April, 1984 there has been introduced the concept of the "controlled foreign company" (CFC). In simple terms the Inland Revenue will be able to charge a UK resident company corporation tax on a proportion of the CFC's profit if certain tests are not satisfied, which broadly means the Inland

Revenue consider a disproportionate amount of the CFC's profits is being retained in low tax haven primarily to avoid UK corporation tax.

The Inland Revenue have power to make a direction that an assessment to corporation tax be raised on a UK resident company on a proportion of a CFC's profits if:

1. The overseas company is under the overall control of UK residents (including the shareholdings of both companies and individuals); and

2. The tax paid by the overseas company in its country of residence is less than 50% of the amount which it would have paid had the company been resident in the UK. The Inland Revenue issue a list of what they consider low tax havens; and

3. The UK resident company, together with connected or associated persons, has at least a 10% stake in the overseas company.

Even if the above rules apply, a direction and assessment can still be avoided if any of the following tests is satisfied:

1. There is an acceptable distribution paid by the overseas company. This broadly involves a distribution of dividends representing at least 50% of available profits for a trading company and 90% for any other company.

2. Certain foreign activities are exempt if the Inland Revenue approve them.

3. A motive test. Unless the Inland Revenue regard the interest in the foreign resident company as primarily a tax saving exercise, there will be no direction or assessment.

4. A de minimus test. This applies when the overseas company's profits for a twelve month period are less than £20,000.

Any direction and assessment the Inland Revenue make on a company can be appealed against.

Chapter Seventeen

Value Added Tax

Value added tax is a tax on consumers, and is levied on the supplies of goods or services made by a taxable person in the course or furtherance of a business carried on by him.

Generally speaking any transactions done for a consideration in the course or furtherance of a business will be subject to VAT, with the exception of certain services which are specifically exempted under the legislation.

The VAT legislation was originally enacted in the Finance Act, 1972 to be effected from 1st April, 1973 and amendments to the legislation are carried out through the subsequent Finance Acts. It has now been consolidated in the Value Added Tax Act, 1983.

The Customs and Excise also publish guidance booklets on all aspects of VAT. However, these do not have any statutory authority, with the exception of those booklets relating to special schemes for retailers and those dealing with the schemes for sale of secondhand goods.

Administration

VAT is administered by the Board of Commissioners of Customs and Excise who are responsible for policy decisions, controlling the collection of the tax and the general management and overseeing of the collection and control structure of not only VAT but all forms of taxation and duties which the Customs and Excise are responsible for. The control structure is as follows in the tree diagram on p. 202.

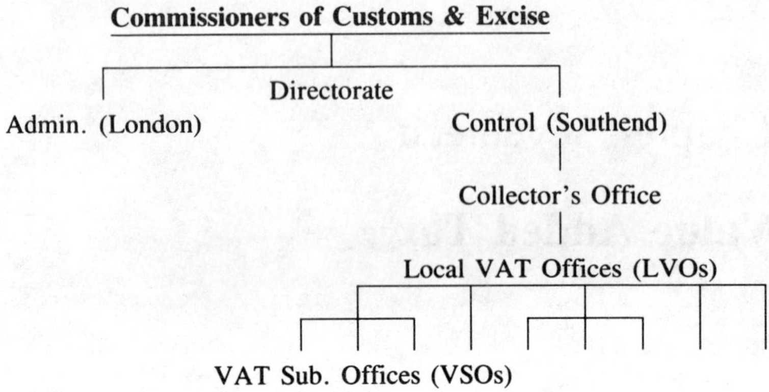

Administration directorate
This is responsible for policy aspects of the VAT system. It contains divisions concerned with liability matters, partial exemption, retail schemes, tax points, secondhand schemes and the application of VAT to imports and exports; all are discussed later.

Collection directorate
This is responsible for issuing registration certificates, sending out VAT returns, collecting monies due and making payments where necessary.

Also, through a network of local VAT offices, some of which have sub-offices attached to them, it deals with the issue of registration forms, and de-registration forms, the examination of a registered person's books (this is known as a control visit and takes place once every 2 or 3 years), the collection of overdue monies or returns, and the issue of assessments.

Taxable person and registration

From 21st March, 1990 the system of registration has been significantly amended and simplified. If a trader has an annual taxable turnover exceeding £25,400 he is obliged to be registered for VAT.

He has to register if either:

1. At the end of any month the value of his taxable supplies in the past 12 months has exceeded £25,400; or
2. At any time there are reasonable grounds for believing that the value of the taxable supplies he will make in the next 30 days will exceed £25,400.

A business must notify the Customs & Excise on form VAT1 within 30 days after the end of the relevant month or within 30 days after the date on which the reasonable grounds first existed.

Voluntary registration

A person whose taxable supplies do not exceed £25,400 in a year may wish to register for VAT in order to reclaim the input tax he suffers and can apply to the Commissioners for discretionary registration and if they agree he will become registered for VAT. Examples of this are:

a) A person who makes only zero-rated supplies, e.g. an exporter, but suffers input tax on his purchases, then it would be to his advantage to reclaim tax he has paid.

b) A person who only makes supplies to other registered persons, i.e. an accountant, and it would then be to his advantage to be able to offset the input tax he suffers, and customers can offset the VAT he charges.

Exemption from registration

Where a taxable person (i.e. one whose turnover is over £25,400) makes only zero-rated supplies and the amount of input credit they are entitled to is nominal, it may not be worth their while to go to the trouble and expense of keeping proper VAT accounts and making VAT returns. They can then apply to the Commissioners for exemption from registration.

De-registration

Where a person ceases to make taxable supplies, he must notify the Commissioners of that fact within 10 days of the date he does so and the Commissioners must then cancel his registration.

A person ceases to be liable to be registered if:

a) At the end of a quarter or prescribed accounting period (if he has then been registered for two years) and the value of his taxable supplies has been £24,400 or less.

AND

b) At any time the Commissioners are satisfied that the value of his taxable supplies in the year then beginning will be £24,400 or less.

Group registration

Where a group of companies are under common control they may all, or such numbers as they choose, elect for group registration. By this, instead of being registered individually, they will have a joint registration and in effect be treated as one company charging output tax on their joint sales and claiming a credit for the input tax they jointly suffer. They do however have the great advantage of not having to charge each other VAT on inter-company transactions.

Divisional registration

This is in effect the reverse of group registration; it applies where one company carries on its business in divisions. It can if it wishes apply to have each of the divisions registered as a separate entity, i.e. as though they were companies in their own right.

Partnership registration

Since a partnership in English law is not a legal entity in its own right, a partnership seeking registration must make a joint application signed by all partners to be registered.

Disaggregation

The Commissioners of Customs and Excise are empowered to direct that in certain circumstances where two or more persons are purporting to trade separately but in reality are trading as a single business, they can be treated as a single business for VAT purposes. The taxpayers have a right of appeal to a VAT tribunal.

Calculation of VAT

Every taxable person is required to account for VAT on the goods or services (known as taxable supplies) that they supply to the extent that the goods or services have increased in value, i.e. the value added to them, e.g. a carpenter buys wood for £20 and makes a bookcase he sells for £30, he is responsible for the VAT on the increase in value of £10.

However, for calculation and collection purposes, he is required to calculate the VAT with regard to his selling price, e.g. the carpenter sells for £30 and at a 15% VAT rate will charge £4.50 VAT, known as OUTPUT TAX.

In order that he is only liable for the VAT on the value he has added to the goods, he is able to deduct from the tax collected any tax he has paid on the purchase of the goods, i.e. the carpenter bought wood for £20 on which he would have paid £3 (VAT at 15%). This is known as INPUT TAX.

Therefore, the net amount he is responsible for is £4.50−£3.00=£1.50, i.e. VAT at 15% on £10.

In this way he is also able to obtain relief for VAT paid on indirect costs, i.e. costs which cannot be directly allocated to a particular item, e.g. telephone, petrol, machinery and office equipment.

For example, a cork manufacturer sells 3,000 corks for £300. His costs (net of VAT) are raw material £100, petrol for van £30, telephone £15 and new typewriter for office £50. All are subject to 15% VAT.

	OUTPUT VAT (i.e. on sales) £300×15%			45.00
Less:	INPUT TAX (i.e. on purchases)			
	Materials	£100×15%	15.00	
	Petrol	£ 30×15%	4.50	
	Telephone	£ 15×15%	2.25	
	Typewriter	£ 50×15%	7.50	
	Total Input		29.25	(29.25)
	VAT liability			15.75

However, should he purchase goods/services from a non-registered person or at a different rate to that charged on his sales, the system of offset automatically accounts for the correct VAT figure, e.g. if in the above example the materials had been purchased from a non-registered person, then the position would be as follows:

Output tax	45.00
Input tax (29.25 − 15.00)	14.25
VAT liability	30.75

On a gross amount (including VAT), the VAT is calculated by applying the fraction $^3/_{23}$ i.e. £115 × $^3/_{23}$ = £15 VAT.

In this way VAT is still collected on the value of the goods at the time of sale.

Similarly where a different rate of VAT applies, e.g.

	Butcher sells meat for £20		(VAT rate zero)
	Buys for £10		(VAT rate zero)
	Telephone costs £5		(VAT rate 15%)
	Petrol £3		(VAT rate 15%)
	Output tax		Nil
Less:	Input tax		
	Meat	Nil	
	Telephone £5 × 15%	0.75	
	Petrol £3 × 15%	0.45	
	Total inputs	1.20	1.20
	VAT repayable to butcher		1.20

Since the good sold are subject to a nil rate of VAT, there is no tax due on the sale and the butcher is able to reclaim any tax he has paid with regard to his expenses incurred in making that sale.

For a registered person to claim relief for the VAT he pays (i.e. input tax) he must possess a VAT INVOICE, and likewise he must supply his customers with a VAT INVOICE on his sales, in order that they may claim relief on the VAT they pay if they are registered persons. In this way VAT is charged and offset all along the line from manufacturer to wholesaler to retailer until the taxable supplies end up with the consumer who is not registered, or if registered is using them for his private purposes and therefore is not allowed to offset the input tax against his sales, e.g.

Mr. X sells tins of paint Sales are £100
Purchase cost £50
Telephone cost £20 of which ½ is for private use.
All are subject to 15% VAT.

Output VAT			15.00
Less: Input			
Purchases	=	7.50	
Administration 10×15%	=	1.50	
Total deductible inputs		9.00	9.00
VAT liability			6.00

From 6th April, 1987 the car fuel benefit scale is used to assess VAT due on petrol provided from business sources at below cost for private journeys by registered traders or their employees. The figures are halved when business mileage exceeds the quarterly or monthly equivalent of 18,000 business miles a year.

Input tax cannot be offset if it has been paid on certain items. The main items are:

1. Cars capable of private use.
2. Business entertaining.

Input tax on services supplied before registration
All registered persons can claim relief for input tax suffered prior to registration on services supplied for the purpose of the business carried on after registration.

VAT invoice

As stated previously, to obtain relief for INPUT TAX suffered, a registered person must have a VAT invoice and is thus required to give an invoice for all supplies he makes on which the following details are to be shown:

a) Invoice number.
b) Time of supply, i.e. tax point (see below).
c) Supplier's name, address and VAT registration number.
d) Customer's name (or trading name) and address.
e) Type of supply (see below).
f) Description sufficient to identify the goods or services supplied.
g) For each description the quantity of the goods or extent of the service, the rate of VAT, and the amount payable excluding VAT.
h) Total amount payable (excluding VAT).
i) Rate of any cash discount offered.
(NB – where cash discount is offered VAT is calculated on the net payable whether the discount is claimed or not.)
j) The total tax chargeable at each rate, with the rate of tax to which it relates.
k) The total amount of tax chargeable.

l) A copy must be retained for production to Customs & Excise.

A VAT invoice must be issued for all positive rated supplies, but in the case of zero-rated supplies or supplies where the customer is not a taxable person, the issuing is optional.

Tax point

This is the point that goods or services are said to be supplied for purposes of calculating the tax. This is usually the date of issue of the VAT invoice. If however the invoice is not issued within fourteen days of dispatch of the goods (or any longer period that has been arranged with the Commissioners) then the tax point is the date the goods are dispatched.

When the goods are actually produced (e.g. assembled) on the recipient's property, the date of supply is when they are made available to the recipient.

In the case of services the tax point is a lot simpler in that it is when the service is performed. Except in the case of continuous supplies of services, e.g. like those provided by an accountant, then the tax point is the earlier of the date payment is received or of the issue of a tax invoice.

Payment of VAT

VAT returns are generally issued for a three month period, and tax payable one month after the end of the quarterly period.

Repayments of input tax can be claimed monthly. When the claimant has not submitted all previous returns, the Commissioners can withhold repayment until all returns have been submitted.

Any business with a turnover of less than £250,000 a year can elect for a scheme whereby it can account for VAT on a cash basis. The liability is the different between output tax on sales for which cash has been received and input tax on debts actually paid. It thus eliminates the problems of having to account for VAT when the customer has not yet paid, and automatically gives bad debt relief.

A business wishing to operate the scheme has to apply to its local VAT office, and once accepted has to operate the scheme for at least two years.

Again, businesses with an annual turnover of less than £250,000 have the option from the second half of 1988 to make a single annual VAT return and pay tax by nine advance payments, normally based on the previous year's liability, with a settlement at the year end.

Supply

The type of supply must be identified between:

a) Sales.

b) Hire purchase, credit sale, conditional sale or similar transaction.

c) Loan.
d) Exchange.
e) Hire, lease or rental.
f) Process (making goods from customers' materials).
g) Sale or commission (e.g. by an auctioneer).

If zero-rated or exempt supplies are shown on a VAT invoice they must be shown separately and each supply at positive rates totalled separately.

Supplies by retailers

A retailer or other taxable person supplying goods or services to the general public need not issue a tax invoice unless asked for one, and if so asked may issue a less detailed tax invoice where the individual supplies cost not more than £50 including VAT, as follows:

a) Supplier's name, address and VAT registration number.
b) Tax point.
c) Description sufficient to identify the goods or services supplied.
d) Amount payable including VAT.
e) Rate of VAT in force at the time of supply.

The invoices must only include goods or services chargeable at one rate of VAT (with the exception of zero-rated oils on petrol invoices).

Rates of VAT

At present there are two rates of VAT:

a) Standard rate which is 15%.
b) Lower rate which is zero.

Standard rate (15%)

This rate applies to the supply of all goods and services by a taxable person, that are not specifically lower rated or exempted.

Zero-rated supplies

It is more advantageous to be zero-rated than exempt, as then input tax can be recovered. Sometimes the definitions overlap, and if a supply falls into both, then it is treated as zero-rated.

The definitions are organised in Groups, zero-rating as follows:

Group 1 – Food

Food is zero-rated if it is:

1. For human consumption.
2. Animal feeding stuffs.
3. Seeds or other means of propagation of plants comprised in 1 or 2 above.
4. Live animals of a kind generally used as, or yielding or producing food for, human consumption.

There are a number of exceptions which are standard rated:

1. Ice cream and frozen yoghurt and similar products.
2. Confectionery, but not cake and biscuits unless wholly or partly covered with chocolate.
3. Beers, wines and spirits, and any other alcoholic drink.
4. Fruit juices and other bottled waters.
5. Potato crisps and similar products.
6. Pet foods.
7. Goods used in homebrewing.

Group 2 – Sewerage services and water
From 1st July, 1990 only services to domestic premises are zero-rated. Supplies to industry, etc. are standard rated from that date. Domestic use includes such places as residential hostels for students and old people's homes.

Group 3 – Books, etc.
This includes newspapers, leaflets, sheet music and others. Excluded are plans for commercial use, and also stationery.

Group 4 – Talking books for the blind and handicapped and wireless sets for the blind.

Group 5 – This was repealed in 1985, and concerned newspaper advertisements.

Group 6 – News services. This was repealed from 1st April, 1989.

Group 7 – Fuel and power
Included in this is coal, coke, most oils and gases and also electricity.

From 1st July, 1990 supplies to non-domestic users are excluded and therefore standard rated. Domestic use is defined in much the same way as for sewerage services.

Group 8 – Construction of buildings
This is an important group, often affecting people not registered for VAT. From 1st April, 1989 excluded from zero-rating are:

1. The construction of most non-domestic buildings and civil engineering works.
2. Demolition services.

Also standard rated are alterations to buildings, the erection of sheds and greenhouses in private gardens, and the installation of certain fixtures in new buildings.

Group 8A – Protected buildings
This zero-rates the substantial reconstruction in an approved form of listed

buildings which are to be used for domestic living purposes. It does not apply to buildings which are not used as domestic accommodation.

Group 9 – International services
This zero-rates certain services which are exported.

Group 10 – Transport
This covers the supply, repair and maintenance of:

1. Ships and aircraft other than those used for pleasure.
2. Vehicles used for transport and carrying twelve or more passengers.
3. Lifeboats.
4. Transport of freight outside the UK.

Group 11 – Caravans and houseboats
These are zero-rated provided they are used as domestic dwellings.

Group 12 – Gold
The supply of gold bullion between central banks and authorised dealers.

Group 13 – Bank notes
The issue by banks of bank notes.

Group 14 – Drugs, medicines, etc.
Within this group are:

1. Goods dispensed on the prescription of a doctor, dentist or pharmacist.
2. The supply to handicapped people of various medical and surgical appliances and other goods for their specific use.

Group 15 – Imports, exports, etc.
This covers the export by a person carrying on a business both inside and outside the UK of goods and services from one place of business to the other, so that he can reclaim input tax.

Group 16 – Charities, etc.
This zero-rates goods donated to charities, the sale of goods by charities, and the supply of medical research equipment.

Also covered is advertising by a charity for educational or fund raising purposes.

Group 17 – Clothing and footwear
This group zero-rates clothing in the following categories:

1. Clothing designed for use by young people and not suitable for older persons.
2. Protective boots and helmets conforming to British Standards but not if supplied by an employer to his employees.
3. Crash helmets for motors cyclists which conform to British Standards.

Exemptions

Exempt supplies do not attract the offset of input tax, but VAT is not added to the cost of the supplies.

Group 1 – Land

A large number of transactions connected with land are exempted. With exceptions, the granting of any interest or right over land is exempted.

The main exceptions are the provision of hotel accommodation (except rooms let for functions), car parking, and such things as fishing and sporting rights.

Traders can make an irrevocable election to standard rate the selling or letting of most non-domestic property or land which would otherwise be exempt.

Group 2 – Insurance

The provision of insurance, etc., by authorised insurers.

Group 3 – Postal services

The provision of postal services by the Post Office.

Group 4 – Betting, gaming and lotteries

These are exempt as they are already subject to gaming licence duty.

Admission charges to premises are standard rated.

Group 5 – Finance

Certain financial services are exempt including:

1. The making of advances and granting credit.
2. The provision of hire purchase.
3. The operation of bank accounts, and dealings in securities.

Foreign exchange dealings, changing of money and most interest payments are exempt.

Group 6 – Education

Exempt are the provision of education except for profit by schools and colleges, and training or retraining for trades and professions.

Group 7 – Health and welfare

This exempts the services of doctors, dentists, etc. It also covers services provided by hospitals.

Health farms, beauty clinics, etc., are standard rated.

Group 8 – Burial and cremation

Services in connection with funerals are exempted.

Group 9 – Trade unions and professional bodies

The supply by such bodies of services to their members.

Group 10 – Sports competitions
This exempts rights granted to enter competitions in sport or physical recreation, where all the entry fees are returned as prizes, or it is organised by a non-profit making body.

Group 11 – Works of art, etc.
The disposal of works of art, etc., which are donated for the public benefit to museums, etc.

Group 12 – Fund raising events
This exempts goods and services supplied in connection with fund raising events by charities and non-profit making bodies which will use the proceeds for their activities.

Partial exemption
Since a person who makes exempt supplies is not liable to charge VAT and has no right to claim a deduction of any INPUT TAX, he suffers. A problem arises where the person makes both taxable and exempt supplies, e.g. an accountant who provides taxable accountancy services, but also has an insurance agency which is an exempt service. These people are classed as PARTIALLY EXEMPT and special rules apply to them as follows:

(a) All input tax can still be reclaimed if the input tax related to exempt supplies is always less than:
   (i) £100 per month on average; or
   (ii) Both £250 per month on average and 50% of all input tax; or
   (iii) Both £500 per month on average and 25% of all input tax.
"On average" means the average over the relevant tax period.

(b) Where the above does not apply then input tax must be restricted in accordance with the ratio of exempt to total supplies.

There are two recommended methods of doing this although other methods may be authorised by the Commissioners.

Method I
The deduction of input tax is restricted to the percentage his taxable supplies bear to the total supplies, e.g.

F. Jones is a jeweller. However, he also has an insurance agency to handle the insurance of his customers' purchases should they require it. His results in a quarter are:

Jewellery sales	£1,000,000	VAT	£150,000
Insurance business	£200,000		
Input TAX £100,000			

The allowable deduction for input tax is:

$$\frac{1{,}000{,}000}{1{,}200{,}000} \times 100{,}000 \quad = \quad £83{,}333$$

This method, though simple to use, can be unjust in that, as in the above example, the majority of input tax relates to the goods being resold and is thus disproportionately disallowed. Method II trys to alleviate the problem.

Method II
In this method those inputs specifically attributable to taxable outputs are allowed in full and only those inputs which cannot be specifically identified as belonging to taxable supplies are apportioned, e.g.

Jewellery sales	£1,000,000	VAT	£150,000
Insurance business	£200,000		
Jewellery purchases	£500,000	VAT	£75,000
General expenses subject to VAT	16,000		2,400
			£77,400

Calculation of allowable inputs:

Jewellery purchases	75,000
General expenses: $2{,}400 \times \frac{1{,}000{,}000}{1{,}200{,}000}$ =	(2,000)
Allowable input tax	77,000
Disallowable input tax	400

Special schemes for retailers

Since retailers generally deal with the consumer and therefore are not required to issue VAT invoices, and also due to the number of transactions, it would not be feasible to expect retailers to calculate tax accurately in the ordinary way, dividing between standard rates, zero rated and possibly exempted supplies. Therefore, a number of special schemes have been devised to help simplify the recording and calculation of the VAT on sales by retailers.

For the purposes of these schemes every retailer has to keep a daily record of his gross takings by one of the following methods:

1. a total of cash received each day, plus the value of goods taken for his and his family's own use. This is known as the standard method, or
2. keep a record of daily cash sales, credit sales and goods taken for own use. This is known as the optional method.

The standard method has the advantage that since only cash receipts are taken into account any bad debts are automatically excluded.

The Customs & Excise have the power to refuse permission to allow a particular retailer to use a particular scheme, such as if they consider it will not reflect the proper liability, but the retailer has a right of appeal to a VAT Tribunal against a refusal to allow him to use a particular scheme.

For a start-up business the Customs & Excise are prepared to accept retrospective changes in schemes back to the initial VAT registration as long as there has been no registration visit from the Customs & Excise. This initial visit is normally within 18 months of registration, but can vary.

The schemes are described in brief below.

Point of sale schemes: A and F

These schemes only require accurate figures for gross takings to be available.

Scheme A is limited to businesses which only make standard rate supplies and includes goods and services. There is no limitation of turnover, it only requires normal records, plus a record of daily gross takings, is simple to operate and calculates the output tax accurately. Typical users are hairdressers, electrical shops and jewellery shops. The calculation of output tax is done by taking daily gross takings and applying the VAT fraction.

Scheme F. This can only be used if goods and services which are supplied at different rates of tax can be separated at the point of sale. This means that either there must be separate tills or coded tills which can cope with such record-keeping. Like scheme A there is no limit on turnover, it can be used for home-made and home-grown goods, it only requires normal records, plus a record of daily gross takings. Typical users are clothing shops, stationers, music shops, book shops, petrol stations and garden centres. The output tax is calculated by taking the daily gross takings of the standard rate supplies and applying the appropriate VAT fraction.

Expected selling price schemes: B, B1, B2, C, E and E1

Scheme B

This scheme is suitable for two rates of tax, there is no turnover limit and it is limited to where zero-rate sales are not more than 50% of the total tax-inclusive turnover for a year. It can include standard rate supplies, but zero-rate services must be dealt with outside the scheme. The method of calculation is to take the gross takings (A), calculate expected selling price of zero-rate goods received or manufactured (B). Calculate the standard rate takings by deducting B from A and applying the appropriate VAT fraction to this figure.

Scheme B1

This is similar in scope and operation to Scheme B except that it dispenses with the 50% limitation on zero-rate sales, but does requires an adjustment for zero-rated stock at the start of using the scheme and at the end of each year.

Scheme B2

This can only be used where standard and zero-rate supplies are made, any services supplied must be standard-rated, annual turnover must be less than £500,000 and none of the zero-rate goods included in the scheme must be home-made or home-grown. A fixed mark-up is applied to different categories of goods supplied.

Scheme C
This scheme is suitable for goods at two or more rates of tax, there is a limitation on turnover of £90,000 and is not available for services or home-made or home-grown goods. The calculation of output tax is based on fixed mark-ups and daily gross takings do not enter into output calculations and therefore there can be a cash flow disadvantage if output tax has to be recognised before the goods are sold. It is limited to certain categories of retailer.

Scheme E
This again is suitable for goods, but not services at two or more rates of tax. Again there is no turnover limit. Output tax is based on expected selling price of standard-rate goods. There are potential cash flow disadvantages in that daily gross takings do not enter into the calculation so that output tax may be recognised before goods are sold. The initial stock of standard-rated goods for resale is included in the first period only. Typical users of this scheme are butchers and bread and milk roundsmen. The output tax for a period is calculated by taking the expected selling price of standard-rate purchases received for retail and applying the appropriate VAT fraction.

Scheme El
This is similar to Scheme E and can operate with the supply of standard or zero-rated goods. Opening and closing stock of either standard-rate or zero-rate goods must be ascertained and any services supplies must be taxable at the other rate. Again, there is no turnover limit.

Apportionment schemes D, G, H, J

Scheme D
This is suitable for both standard and zero-rate supplies of goods and there is a turnover limit, including VAT, of £½m, including any sales outside the scheme. Supplies of services or home-made goods are outside the scheme, it is suitable for two or more rates of tax and is based on apportioning total gross takings into a ratio of the tax-inclusive purchases of standard-rate and zero-rate goods.

Normal records must be kept, plus a record of all goods, including VAT, received for resale and of daily gross takings. The scheme is dependent on gross takings and therefore there is a cash flow advantage, there is also automatic bad debt relief, and there is a requirement to ensure that only goods for resale are entered into the calculation.

Scheme D requires an annual adjustment to cover seasonal variations in purchases of standard or zero-rate goods which may affect specific quarters.

The method of calculation is to take total daily gross takings (A), the total cost price (VAT inclusive) of standard-rate goods received for resale (B) and then calculate the total cost, including VAT, of both standard-rate and zero-rate goods received for resale (C). The calculation of the output tax due is then A × B/C × the VAT fraction.

Scheme G

This is very similar to scheme B, but is not recommended for retailers with a turnover of less than £½m as less tax would then be paid under Scheme D. It is suitable for both standard and zero-rated supplies of goods, but supplies of services and home-made goods are outside the scheme.

The scheme is based on apportioning the tax-inclusive purchase price of standard-rate and zero-rate goods against the gross takings. It differs from Scheme D in that once the output tax has been calculated a ⅛th uplift has to be applied. This works normally against the retailer, forcing him to pay more output tax than would be due under other schemes.

Detailed stock has to be taken prior to commencement of the scheme and normal records have to be kept, plus a record of all goods received for resale, plus a record of daily takings.

It is useful for medium-sized grocers and small supermarkets.

Scheme H

This is suitable for standard and zero-rate supplies, including home-made goods. It is not suitable for services. There is no turnover limit.

It is based on an apportionment of the gross takings against the expected selling price, including VAT, of zero and standard rated goods received, or made for resale. Detailed stock records are required at the commencement of the scheme and normal physical stocktaking is required. Normal records are required, plus a record of daily gross takings and a record of expected selling prices, including VAT, of each class of goods received or made for resale. Good records are required and it would be an advantage to have a computer-based system that evaluates and marks up purchases to expected selling prices. The scheme is dependent on gross takings and there can be a cash flow advantage from money received.

Typical users are department stores with sophisticated accounting systems.

Scheme J

This is suitable for standard and zero-rate supplies and can also include home-made goods. It is not suitable for the supply of services. There is no turnover limit.

It is based on the apportionment of gross takings against the expected selling price, inclusive of VAT, of zero and standard-rated goods in stock received or made. As the scheme is based on a full year's trading, commencing from the first period of use, an annual adjustment is made and the scheme started all over again with the closing stock becoming the opening stock, etc.

Normal commercial records are required, plus details of stock records at commencement and at the year end, and details of total expected selling prices, inclusive of VAT, for each class of goods made or purchased for resale. In view of the complexity of the scheme a computer-based record-keeping scheme is more than likely required. Purchases must be accurately valued at selling price and the correct determination of VAT liability is essential and price reductions must be allowed for.

This scheme is generally only used by large or multiple retail outlets with no point of sale identification of liability.

Secondhand schemes

There are special schemes for traders in: a) Secondhand cars; b) Secondhand boats, etc.; c) Secondhand caravans and motor cycles; d) Secondhand works of art, antiques, etc. (goods over 100 years old); e) Horses and ponies.

These are all basically the same in that the trader keeps a stock book recording the required information, e.g.

a) Stock number.
b) Date of purchase.
c) Purchase invoice number.
d) Seller's name and address.
e) Description and, depending on what scheme is being used, further identification details, e.g. vehicle registration number and chassis number.
f) Date of sale.
g) Sales invoice number.
h) Buyer's name and address.
i) Purchase price (inclusive of any tax).
j) Gross selling price (inclusive of any tax) or method of disposal if not sold.
k) Margin on sale.
l) Tax rate at time of sale.
m) Tax on margin due to Customs and Excise.

Since the secondhand goods dealt with under the scheme are usually acquired from non-registered persons, there would be no charge for input tax which could be claimed back. It would therefore be unjust to charge VAT on the full selling price since this could well be higher than the value being added (i.e. the increase from cost to selling price).

Therefore, VAT is only calculated on the difference between cost and selling price and since both these are expressed at tax inclusive price, the margin must be tax inclusive and so to calculate the VAT the VAT fraction is used, e.g.

Secondhand car –	Cost price	700
	Selling price	930
	Margin	230

Output VAT:

$230 \times {}^{3}\!/_{23} = £30$

It must be remembered that where normally the notices issued by the Customs and Excise are only guides to the interpretation of the law and have no statutory authority, the guides to the special retailers and secondhand goods schemes have a statutory effect, and thus any non-compliance with any of the rules in them is a breaking of the law and allows the Customs and Excise to require the calculation of VAT in the ordinary way. This has especially drastic effects in connection with the secondhand schemes when instead of VAT being calculated on the margin it is calculated with regard to the selling price.

Example

Harry Jones sells secondhand cars but has not kept full details required.

Using the scheme his output VAT would be:

Sale price	930		
Cost price	700		
Margin	230	Output tax	30

But if the strict rules are applied he will pay VAT as though his selling price was inclusive of VAT.

$$930 \times {}^{3}/_{23} = 121$$

Thus he pays £91 more VAT since he still has no input tax available to deduct, and thus his gross profit has been reduced from £200 to £109 on the sale.

It must be emphasised that with regard to the secondhand schemes it is the initial cost price that is used in the calculation of the margin, any additional costs incurred in putting the goods in a saleable condition being ignored, e.g.

Car costs	100
Repair work costs	300
Sale price	500

Margin = 500 − 100 = 400

However, any VAT paid on the repair work can be claimed back as input tax in the normal manner.

Bad debt relief

A new scheme of relief for bad debts has been introduced from 1990. Previously a trader had virtually to prove a debtor was bankrupt or in liquidation to get relief.

Now, if a debt is more than 2 years old and has been written off in the accounts of the business, it is eligible for VAT relief. When the debt is subsequently paid in full or in part, there is a clawback of the relief previously given. The scheme has been operative since July, 1990 and has been backdated to 1st April, 1989 to allow the first claims to be made from 1st April, 1991.

Returns

A trader is required to complete a VAT return for a specified VAT period which is usually every three months (apart from the first period), in which he has to state his output tax, input tax and any adjustments for previous periods, e.g.

Output VAT
Adjustments
Total outputs

Less: Input VAT
Adjustments
Total inputs
Amount due to/or
repayable

Also he has to state the total of his sales excluding VAT, total purchases and expenses, i.e. inputs excluding VAT, but including exempt inputs, e.g. rates, and also indicate which special scheme if any he has used.

Assessments

If a trader fails to complete a return or, after a control visit in which errors on previous returns have been found, or if the Customs and Excise are of the opinion sales have been underdeclared on previous returns, the Commissioners have the power to issue an assessment for the tax underpaid. This amount becomes due unless the trader appeals against the assessment within 30 days, and leave to appeal will not be given unless the disputed tax is deposited with the Commissioners, except in the case of extreme hardship.

Once an appeal has been made it can be settled in a number of ways as follows:

1. By the trader deciding to accept the assessment and withdrawing the appeal.

2. By coming to an agreement with the Commissioners and accordingly the matter is settled.

3. If no agreement is reached the appeal will be heard by a VAT tribunal and they will decide the issue.

Enforcement

Penalties of varying degrees are provided for failure to comply with VAT regulations. The penalties that can be levied can either be criminal or civil. There is a right of appeal to a VAT Tribunal against penalties imposed. Below are listed the civil offences.

Civil fraud

When a person acts dishonestly to evade tax a penalty of 100% of the tax evaded, or attempted to be evaded, can be imposed. However, this can be mitigated by up to 50% in certain cases.

Late registration

Lateness in registering for VAT by a trader results in a penalty which depends on how late registration is, with a minimum of £50.

If the period of delay is less than 9 months the penalty is 10% of the net VAT due since the date the business should have been registered, 20% between 9 and 18 months, and 30% over 18 months.

Default surcharge

If returns or payments connected with VAT are made more than one month after the end of a return period, the taxpayer is in default. If he defaults twice in a twelve month period, he is issued with a "surcharge liability notice" (SLN) which remains in force for twelve months from the date of the second default, and is known as the "default period". If there are further defaults during this period it results in a percentage surcharge which increases for first and subsequent delays. The first offence leads to a 5% surcharge, increasing for second and subsequent offences by 5% a time, to a maximum of 30%. The minimum surcharge is £30.

The surcharge liability notice only lapses once returns and payments have been submiteed on time for a complete period of 12 months. There are also provisions for relief if the taxpayer has sent in a return allowing a reasonable time for delivery, and has a reasonable excuse for the delay.

Serious misdeclaration

When a registered trader has underdeclared his liability and not told the Customs, he has committed a serious misdeclaration. The error must be at least 30% of the tax due, or the greater of £10,000 or 5% of the due tax.

The penalty is 30% of the tax due, but there can be relief if the taxpayer has a reasonable excuse.

Minor errors of up to £1.000 in total may be disclosed in the trader's VAT return, to be treated as tax payable in the period the error is found.

Persistent misdeclaration

This offence occurs when there have been material errors in at least two VAT returns in a two-year period. A penalty liability notice is then issued, and any further offence in the next two years leads to a penalty of 15% of the tax lost.

A material error occurs when the tax lost would have been more than £100 or 1% of the true tax, whichever is the greater. Again, the trader can escape the penalty if he has a reasonable excuse, or if the inaccuracy is corrected before any enquiries are made by C&E.

Breach of regulations

Any trader breaching VAT regulations is liable to a penalty if he has previously been issued with a written warning within two years prior to being issued with an assessment.

Failure to retain VAT records for six years carries a penalty of £500. Other offences such as a failure to submit or keep proper records, or inform the authorities that the making of taxable supplies has ceased, carry a daily penalty which ranges from £5 a day up to £15 a day. The maximum for continued failure is a penalty for 100 days, with a minimum of £50.

Unauthorised issue of tax invoices

If VAT invoices are issued without the trader being VAT registered a penalty of 30% of the tax can be levied, with a minimum of £50.

Reasonable excuse

Except for civil fraud, a penalty can be avoided by a trader if he has a reasonable excuse for what he did. There is no specific statutory definition, but it does say the excuse cannot be a shortage of resources to pay VAT, or dependency on anyone else to carry out the required task. Also not acceptable are ignorance or misunderstanding of the law, a failure to register, or difficulty in estimating turnover, or a lack of intent to evade tax.

Interest on overdue tax

Default interest can be charged on tax underpaid or a repayment overclaimed, in addition to any penalty which may have been levied. The interest is charged from the date VAT should have been paid, or seven days after the authorisation by C&E of an incorrect repayment.

The rate of interest is set by the Treasury, and varies from time to time as commercial rates alter.

Repayment supplement

A supplement of 5% or £50, whichever is greater, when a VAT refund is made more than 30 days after the submission of the VAT return was submitted.

There is no supplement if the return is submitted more than two months after the end of the return period, or if the refund claimed is overstated by more than £250 or 5% of the refundable tax, whichever is the greater.

VAT tribunals

These are completely independent bodies, having no connection with the Customs & Excise and consist of a Chariman sitting either alone or with one or two other members. They are established on a regional basis with centres in London, Edinburgh, Belfast and Manchester.

The tribunals can deal with appeals about the following matters:

1. Registration or cancellation of registration.
2. Assessment of tax by Customs & Excise or the amount of an assessment.
3. Amount of tax chargeable (if any at all) on any supply of goods or services.
4. Amount of input tax which may be deducted by a taxable person.
5. The amount of restriction placed on input tax of a partially exempt person.
6. Refusal to allow the use of a retailer's scheme.
7. A requirement by the Commissioners that a trader should give security as a condition of making taxable supplies.
8. Refusal to allow group registration.
9. Directions by the Commissioners with regard to the value of supplies of goods and services.
10. Amounts of refunds to do-it-yourself builders.

However, disputes about the value of imported goods do not fall within the scope of the VAT tribunals' authority.

Customs and Excise powers

The Commissioners have the power to require the production of documents where a repayment of VAT is involved.

They have the power to require the keeping of records in a form and to a standard they think satisfactory.

Every taxable person has to notify the Commissioners within 21 days of any change in his business circumstances, e.g. change of address or change in partners.

The officers of Customs and Excise have the power to require the production of documents for inspection by an authorised person and that he be allowed to copy such documents or remove them at a reasonable time and for a reasonable period.

Any authorised person, i.e. Customs and Excise officer, has the right, at any reasonable time, to enter any premises used in connection with a trade or business for the purpose of exercising any of the powers conferred on him by the VAT legislation.

In addition to this he has the power to obtain a search warrant from a Justice of the Peace.

However, the Commissioners cannot send an authorised person to subject a taxable person to a prolonged interrogation.

Control visits

These are periodic visits by Customs and Excise officers for the purpose of examining a trader's records and checking such records against the returns supplied, in order to check the accuracy of such returns and correct any errors found, and to assess the adequacy of such records.

Miscellaneous

Self-supply

Since certain traders may provide themselves with goods for use in their business which they have manufactured or produced, and by so doing avoid paying VAT on their purchase, similar persons acquiring from an outside source suffering VAT which they cannot claim back, then the person who supplies himself is obtaining a tax advantage over the other person. In order to avoid this the Treasury have the power to make an order requiring that VAT be paid on goods so supplied.

At present there are only three such orders:

1. Dealing with the printing of stationery by an exempt or partly exempt person, since if he purchased stationery he would pay VAT, but by printing his own he would otherwise avoid VAT. The value of the self-supply must exceed the registration threshold.
2. A manufacturer or dealer in motor cars is able to obtain back the VAT since they are his stock in trade whereas any other person is specifically excluded from claiming back the input VAT on the purchase of a motor car. Therefore, by appropriating from stock the manufacturer/dealer is avoiding paying the VAT on the motor car used in his business. Thus, to correct the position, he is required to account for the VAT on his acquisition.
3. The self-supply of the construction of a building or civil engineering work extending the floor area of an existing building other than for sale or letting.

Import and export

VAT is charged on the importation of goods and certain services into the UK as if it were a customs duty, regardless as to whether or not the importer is a taxable person. Certain importations are relieved from VAT, such as agricultural products and animals, etc.

Certain services provided to a UK person by an overseas business are liable to VAT. The UK importer is deemed to supply himself, and has to account for the VAT, but the tax is also deductible as input tax.

Some temporary importations which are later re-exported are not liable to VAT.

Exports are not liable to VAT unless the goods are in the UK when sold. If the goods are then exported, the sale is zero-rated.

EEC package tours

From 1st April, 1988 a special scheme is to be introduced, bringing the gross profit margins earned by tour operators on their sales and package tours to EEC countries within the scope of VAT.

Holiday accommodation

From 1st November, 1986 the letting of hotel accommodation other than bedrooms is exempt. Service flats used as holiday accommodation are taxable from the same date.

There is a relief under which the VAT value of hotel accommodation is reduced to one fifth after occupation for more than 28 days, but is restricted to cases where the occupation is by the same individual throughout.

Motoring expenses

From 6th April, 1987 the car fuel benefit scale is used to assess VAT due on petrol provided at less than cost for private journeys by registered traders or their employees when the petrol has been provided from business resources. The scale is halved when business mileage exceeds the quarterly or monthly equivalent of 18,000 miles p.a.

	Business miles			
	Quarterly up to 4,500	Monthly up to 1,500	Quarterly Over 4,500	Monthly Over 1,500
Up to 1,400 cc	120	40	60	20
1,400 cc to 2,000 cc	150	50	75	25
Over 2,000 cc	225	75	112.50	37.50

Directors' accommodation

From July, 1990, VAT incurred on repairs, refurbishments and other expenses on the domestic accommodation provided by companies for directors and their families is not eligible for offset as input tax. Neither is the relief available for VAT incurred on the private accommodation of the sole proprietors and partners.

Chapter Eighteen

Inheritance Tax

Introduction and scope

Inheritance tax applies primarily to individuals:

1. Primarily to their estates on death. That is, the property they own at the date of death.
2. It can also apply to gifts they make in the seven years prior to their death.
3. Gifts to discretionary trusts are chargeable immediately they are made if they are large enough.

Inheritance tax can also apply to trusts and settlements:

1. When an individual dies, any trust in which he had a life interest is treated as an extension of his estate on death, and the value of the trust assets is deemed part of the estate. However, the trustees pay their own portion of the tax.
2. When trustees transfer assets to other people there may be an occasion of charge.
3. Discretionary trusts face a periodic charge to tax every ten years.

The tax can also apply to close companies, i.e. family controlled unquoted companies. Transfers by a company can be apportioned among the shareholders and treated as individual transfers by them.

Individuals

As stated, the tax applies mainly to individuals and their property, either on death or on the making of a gift on certain occasions.

The tax applies to property owned by an individual:

1. If the individual is domiciled in the UK it applies to all assets wherever situated in the world.
2. If the individual is domiciled outside the UK it only applies to assets situated in the UK.

The definition of domicile and the situation of assets are dealt with at the end of this section.

The individual can be "deemed" to be domiciled in the UK for inheritance tax purposes only (not for other taxes) in certain circumstances. (See the definition of domicile for more detail.)

There are of course various limitations on the operation of inheritance tax:

1. Various exemptions and reliefs.
2. Various arithmetical limits, which if not exceeded ensure that no tax is payable. These arithmetical limits are updated from time to time, some annually.

Exemptions

Some gifts are automatically cumulated with other special types of gifts within the previous seven years and if the aggregate is over the total of exemptions and the nil rate band of tax the excess is charged at progressive rates of tax. Other gifts are only charged if they are made within the seven years prior to death.

However, there are some exemptions which apply whatever the nature of the gift (those automatically cumulated or those others made within seven years of the death):

1. There is firstly complete or partial relief according to the nature of the property:
   a) Works of art and historic houses.
   b) Business property and agricultural property relief (a reduction of the chargeable value of the property of 50% or 30% depending on the nature of the property – see later).
   c) Commercial woodlands on death if the personal representatives make an election (see later).
2. Certain occasions of transfer. Limited relief (up to certain amounts) on the following occasions.
   a) Transfers between spouses who are living together and domiciled in the UK. If the recipient spouse is not domiciled in the UK the total exemption in a cumulative period of seven years is limited to £55,000.
   b) Gifts in consideration of marriage made to the happy couple.
      i) Parent to child up to £5,000 (the father and mother each have a separate £5,000 relief).
      ii) Grandparent or one party to the marriage to the other party, £2,500 (bear in mind after the marriage the spouses can make transfers between themselves without limit).
      iii) Anyone else £1,000.
   c) Regular gifts out of income which are normal expenditure and do not affect the standard of living of the donor.
   d) Gifts to one recipient which in a year do not exceed £250 from one donor.
   e) Annual gifts not exceeding a certain figure (£3,000 for 1990/91). Any part of the annual exemption unused can be carried forward and used to relieve gifts in the following year. For this purpose the fiscal year (to 5 April) is used.

Example

Burton makes chargeable gifts into a discretionary trust of:

10th October, 1988	5,000
19th July, 1989	3,700

He has never before made any chargeable gifts and it is assumed the annual rate of exemption is 3,000 for all relevant fiscal years.

Gift made 10th October, 1988		5,000
1988/89 (current year) annual exemption		(3,000)
		2,000
1987/88 annual exemption brought forward	3,000	
Utilised	(2,000)	(2,000)
Net chargeable gift		Nil
Unutilised exemption wasted (not carried forward)	1,000	
Gift made 19th July, 1989		3,700
1989/90 (current year) annual exemption		(3,000)
Net chargeable gift		700

f) Gifts and bequests to:
   i) Charities. They can receive exempted gifts of any amount.
   ii) Gifts to political parties. They can receive exempted gifts of any amount.

g) Certain bodies concerned with the preservation of the national heritage or of a public nature and non-profit making.

The charge to tax

Rates of tax

From 6th April, 1990 the first £128,000 of property is charged at a nil rate, and the balance at a standard rate of 40%. Before that date the charge had been progressive, like income tax. The greater the value of the property the higher the percentage marginal rate had been.

The cumulative principle

Under this principle a chargeable transfer is added to other chargeable transfers in a certain period before working out the tax payable. Transfers before that period drop out of the reckoning. At present the "cumulative period" is seven years prior to death, so that only gifts made in the seven years prior to death become chargeable. Therefore, lifetime gifts are generally known as "potentially exempt transfers" or PETs for short. If a gift is made seven years prior to death it effectively is not chargeable. Only certain gifts connected with discretionary trusts are outside this rule, and therefore potentially chargeable immediately they are made. (See the section on trusts for more information.)

Example

Donner makes gifts (after all exemptions):

1/8/87	to his daughter	40,000.
1/9/88	to his son	100,000.
10/8/95	Donner dies, leaving an estate worth	120,000.

As the gift to his daughter was more than seven years prior to his death it is not charged. The gift to his son therefore is charged, taking into account all gifts made in the seven years prior to the gift to the son and is charged as though Donner's "cumulative total" at the time was 40,000 + 100,000 = 140,000.

On Donner's death the chargeable total of his estate is 100,000 + 120,000 = 220,000.

Therefore, any gifts within seven years of death are chargeable, but measuring the chargeable total taking into account the value of that gift plus all other gifts made within the seven years *prior* to that chargeable gift.

Taper relief

When an individual dies within seven years of making a gift, that gift becomes chargeable, but if made more than three years before the date of death only a proportion of the full tax is payable according to the following rates:

Time from gift to death (in years)	% of tax payable
1–3	100
4	80
5	60
6	40
7	20
Over 7	Nil

The rates of tax applied to a chargeable gift made within seven years of death are the rates applicable at the time of death, but the value of the gift is the value at the date of the gift.

Example

Giver dies on 10th April, 1990. He had made a gift on 1st March, 1987 worth 140,000 (after all reliefs). There had been no previous gifts. The charge to tax would be:

140,000 − 128,000 = 12,000 × 40% = 4,800 × 80% = 3,840 payable.

The gift was made between three and four years prior to the death.

Estates on death

General charging rule

The general rule on death is:

1. If the deceased was domiciled (or deemed domiciled) in the UK, all of his assets wherever situated, form part of the chargeable estate, plus the assets of any trust in which he had an interest.
2. If the deceased was not domiciled, then tax is only chargeable on assets situated in the UK.

The general rule is that the estate is chargeable to tax as if the deceased had made a chargeable transfer equal to the value of the net estate.

Valuation of estate

The gross value of the estate includes all the property owned on death. There may be some special rules on the valuation of certain assets. This can include:

1. All property owned anywhere in the world, including land and buildings, business assets, debts owing to the deceased.
2. Assets not owned before death such as the proceeds of a life insurance policy the deceased held on his own life.

Certain deductions are allowed from the gross estate.

1. Some exempt transfers (see the previous section on exemptions).
2. Reasonable funeral expenses.
3. Debts owned by the deceased at the date of death, including unpaid income and capital gains taxes, but not inheritance tax payable on the death, or income tax, etc. arising after the death. However, debts may be disallowed if they are connected with gifts made to creditors, or the debt was not incurred for full benefit by the deceased.
4. Debts due to persons resident overseas are normally only deductible against the value of assets situated abroad.
5. No deduction is allowed for the legal and other costs arising as a result of the death, such as obtaining probate and executors' expenses.

Excluded property

Certain classes of property are left out of account in valuing the deceased's estate. These are:

1. Property situated outside the UK if the deceased is not domiciled in the UK.
2. Reversionary interests in settled property unless it was purchased or it relates to the termination of a lease treated as a settlement.
3. Cash options under approved retirement schemes provided an annuity becomes payable to the dependents instead of the cash.
4. Certain UK government securities if the deceased is not ordinarily resident or domiciled in the UK.
5. Overseas pensions from former colonies including death payments and returned contributions.
6. National savings certificates and premium bonds if the deceased is domiciled

in the Channel Islands or the Isle of Man.

7. Property in the UK belonging to visiting forces and NATO headquarters staff.

Double taxation relief

The UK has entered into several agreements with other countries which operate systems of death duties or tax on lifetime gifts to avoid double taxation by paying such taxes in both countries.

Example

This is a simple example of an estate on death. It does not include some of the specialist rules of valuation and reliefs which are described later.

Dodo dies in 1990, leaving an estate which consists of the following:

Cash	5,000
Bank deposits	8,000
Furniture and chattels	12,000
Investments	85,000
Property – family home	70,000
Rented property	30,000

He also had a life interest in settlement left by his mother, and the value of the trust assets at his death was £40,000.

Between four and five years prior to his death he had also made a gift to his son valued at £150,000 but had not made any other lifetime gifts.

He left the family house and £40,000 of investments and £2,000 cash to his widow, the balance of his estate to be divided equally between his son and daughter. His brother succeeded him as life tenant of the settlement.

He had debts on death of £2,000 ordinary commercial debts, and unpaid tax to the date of death of £4,000. The costs of the funeral were £1,600 and the executors' expenses were £3,000.

Gross value of estate:

Personality (personal property, that is, not land and buildings)

	5,000	
	8,000	
	12,000	
	85,000	110,000
Realty (land and buildings)	70,000	
	30,000	100,000
		210,000
Deductions:		
Debts	2,000	
Tax	4,000	
Funeral expenses	1,600	(7,600)
		202,400

Left to widow (and therefore not taxable):

Family home	70,000	
Investments	40,000	
Cash	2,000	(112,000)
Net estate		90,400
Value of settled property		40,000
Value of chargeable estate		130,400
Gift made within the previous 7 years		150,000

Annual exemptions for year of gift and previous year

	3,000	
	3,000	(6,000)
		144,000
Nil rate threshold		(128,000)
Chargeable		16,000
Gross tax on gift 16,000×40% =		6,400

Net payable, with taper relief: $6{,}400 \times 60\% = 3{,}840$

Tax on balance of the estate:

$130{,}400 \times 40\% =$ 52,160

Responsibility for payment of the tax:

Payable by executors $52{,}160 \times \frac{90{,}400}{130{,}400} =$ 36,160

Payable by trustees of settlement

$52{,}160 \times \frac{40{,}000^*}{130{,}400} =$ 16,000

**Note:* The net chargeable estate is charged at what is known as the "estate rate". In the days when the tax had different progressive rates, this was an average rate of the total tax payable. Now, with a standard rate, the total tax payable is simply divided between the different persons responsible for paying the tax in relation to the proportion of their property value as a percentage of the total value of the chargeable estate.

Responsibility for payment of tax is dealt with later.

Lifetime gifts

Potentially exempt transfers

These are lifetime gifts which are not:

1. Gifts to a discretionary trust.
2. Gifts with a reservation (see later).

If an outright gift is made more than seven years prior to the death of the donor, then no tax is chargeable on the gift. It is only those made within seven years of death that are chargeable. These are known as "potentially exempt transfers" or PETs for short.

However, in arriving at the chargeable amount, they are aggregated with any other chargeable gifts within the seven previous years to the gift to arrive at the cumulative total.

Gifts within seven years prior to the date of the relevant gift are not included in the cumulative total if they themselves are not:

1. Automatically chargeable.
2. Within seven years of the death.

In other words, PETs are completely ignored once they are over seven years old.

Example

Muggins is a kind and generous husband and father, and makes gifts to his family as follows:

7/4/79	to his daughter, Kate	35,000
1/3/86	to his son, Mark	43,000
1/6/86	to his daughter, Kate	60,000
1/9/87	to his wife	5,000
1/9/88	to his son, Philip	43,000

On the 1st July 1992 he dies of a broken heart, the kids having stripped him of everything and abandoned him (sob!). He leaves an estate value at £70,000 (he did not tell the kids everything!) to his favourite barmaid.

On death, all gifts within seven years are specifically exempt. This takes us back to 1st July 1985.

Therefore:

1. The gift on 7th April, 1979 is excluded from charge being over seven years old.
2. The gift to his wife on 1st September 1987 is specifically excluded.

Therefore the chargeable gifts are:

1/3/1986	43,000	
Annual exemptions 1985–96 & 1984–85	(6,000)	37,000

But this is under the nil rate threshold, £110,000, even when combined with the previous gift to his daughter on 7th April 1979 of £35,000. This then drops out of the reckoning as it is over seven years before the next gift is made on 1st June 1986, even though it was chargeable to capital transfer tax.

1/6/86	60,000	
Annual exemption 1986–87	(3,000)	57,000
1/9/88	43,000	
Annual exemption 1987/88 and 1988/89	(6,000)	37,000
Total gifts to date of death	37,000	
	57,000	
	37,000	131,000
Nil rate band		(128,000)
Chargeable (at 40%)		3,000
Gift on 1/9/88 chargeable 3,000×40%=	1,200	
Taper relief (between 3–4 years of death)		
20% relief	(240)	
Tax payable on gift	960	
1/7/92		
Gifts in previous 7 years	131,000	
Estate on death	70,000	
	201,000	
Therefore entire estate chargeable at 40%.		
40%×70,000=	28,000	

Gifts with reservation

When a gift is made where the donor retains an interest in or use of the property, the effect of the gift is nullified for tax purposes – it is still deemed to belong to the donor, and thus chargeable on his death. The gift is deemed only to take place when the reservation is given up, and if this is within seven years of death it becomes taxable.

These rules do not apply to gifts with reservation which are exempt under the following provisions – transfers between spouses, small gifts, gifts on marriage, to charities, political parties, for national purposes, public benefit, maintenance funds for historic buildings and to employee trusts. Note the annual exemption and gifts out of income relief are excluded.

There are exemptions for:

1. Reservations which are enjoyed for full consideration in money or moneysworth, e.g. gift of land which is then tenanted by the donor in return for payment of a full rent.

2. When a donor disposes of property but then later has to have enjoyment of the property because of his/her infirmity, e.g. a father disposes of the family house to the children, but later has to go and live with them because of old age or infirmity.

3. When the reservation is only small – the exclusion of the donor from the property is "virtually to the entire exclusion of the donor".

If the original property is exchanged or substituted for other property and the reservation is transferred to the new property, the restrictions of gift are carried through to the replacement property.

Relief for business property

A reduction is given for both lifetime transfers and deceased's estates on the gross value of "relevant business property". This reduction is applied before any other relief is given such as the annual exemption.

The reduction is either 50% or 30% depending on the nature of the property as follows:

1. The whole or part of a business (sole trader or partnership) – 50%.
2. Qualifying company shares giving a controlling interest (including control through related holdings) – 50%.
3. An interest in an unquoted trading company which gives the transferor over 25% of the voting power, but not if the 25% interest is only exceeded by including "related" property – 50%. USM companies are treated as "quoted".
4. Other minority interests in an unquoted trading company – 30%.
5. Property owned by an individual used by a trading company he controls or a partnership of which he is a member – 30%.
6. Business property owned by a trust transferred by a beneficiary with an interest in possession – 30%.

In general investment, land or share dealing company shareholdings do not qualify, and business property or business property it has directly replaced must have been owned for a minimum of two years prior to the transfer. If an asset is under a contract for sale at the date of disposal then no relief is due.

Example

Witherspoon has 60% of the shares in North West Widgets Ltd, a private manufacturing company. His shares are valued at £300,000.

He also owns personally the company's premises, which he rents to the company at a commercial rental of £600 a week. The premises are valued at £400,000.

On his death the shares and property would be valued at:

Shares (gross value)	300,000	
Business property relief (50%, being a controlled holding)	(150,000)	150,000
Business property rented to company	400,000	
Business property relief (30%, being owned but not traded from personally)	(120,000)	280,000
Net value chargeable to inheritance tax		430,000

Relief for agricultural property

Relief is due when property has been occupied for at least two years for the purposes of agriculture or owned for at least seven years if other people farm it (it is occupied by tenants). There are relaxations of these rules when the property has been inherited or has replaced previous agricultural property. The relief also applies to controlling shareholdings in farming companies.

If the owner has vacant possession of the land or can obtain it within the next twelve months the relief is 50% of the value. Otherwise the relief is only 30%, applying for example to ownership of tenanted farms. The grant of a tenancy for full consideration is not related as a chargeable transfer.

The system of relief changed at 9th March, 1981 and anyone who would qualify for the relief at 50% under the old system but not the new can still obtain 50% relief, but it is limited to £250,000 or 1,000 acres, whichever is greater. The balance only attracts 30% relief.

Relief is given only on the "agricultural value", and where the conditions for both agricultural and business relief are satisfied agricultural relief is given on the agricultural value and business relief can be claimed on the excess value.

Example

Barleycorn owns 200 acres of agricultural land, which he farms himself, He also owns a further 100 acres which he rents to the farmer down the road at a commercial rent. The farmland is valued at £3,000 an acre, but its agricultural value (its value assuming it could only be used for agriculture, and no other purpose) is only £1,700 an acre.

If Barleycorn died, the value chargeable to inheritance tax would be:

Land Barleycorn farms himself:

200 acres at £1,700 an acre (agricultural value)*	340,000	
Agricultural property relief (50% of agricultural value)	(170,000)	170,000
Agricultural land rented to tenant:		
100 acres at £1,700 an acre (agricultural value)	170,000	
Agricultural property relief (30% of agricultural value	(51,000)	119,000
Remaining value of land farmed personally		
200 acres×£1,300 an acre (3,000−1,700)	260,000	
Business property relief (50%)	(130,000)	130,000
Net value chargeable to inheritance tax		419,000

Notes

1. Agricultural property relief is only given against the agricultural value.
2. However, any excess value of land actually farmed by the owner, also qualifies as business property, and attracts business property relief.

Woodlands

If within two years of death the recipient elects, tax is not charged on timber included in the deceased's estate. If however before the recipient dies the timber is disposed of tax is charged on the proceeds or value. The tax rate is calculated as applied at the date of death.

Valuation of assets

General

In general, for inheritance tax purposes, assets are valued at their open market value, at the date of transfer whether that be the date of gift (if a chargeable occasion), or the date of death.

However, in certain circumstances, special rules of valuation apply.

Loss of value

What is taxable on an occasion of charge is not the intrinsic value of the asset itself, but the loss to the donor's estate, that is, the value he forfeits by disposing of property. This is more important in chargeble gifts, rather than on death when all property is automatically disposed of.

Example

Dogsbody made a gift of shares in the family trading company, which is an unquoted private company. The gift becomes chargeable because of Dogsbody's death within seven years of making the gift.

The company has an issued share capital of 1,000 ordinary shares, of which Dogsbody owned 600 before the gift. He gave his son 200 shares, leaving himself with only a minority interest of 400.

Shares in a majority holding are valued at £100 each, those in a minority holding at £40 each.

The son only received value of 200×40=8,000, but the father lost:

Value of 600 shares before gift ×100=	60,000
Value of 400 shares after gift 400×40=	(16,000)
Loss to father's estate	44,000

Therefore £44,000 is the chargeable amount. Note the same rules of valuation do not apply for capital gains tax. In that tax the disposal value is the intrinsic value of the asset given, in this case £8,000.

Particularly in the case of private company shares, the rules of valuation are specialised and not discussed here. The Inland Revenue have a specialist division, the Shares Valuation Division, which deals with such matters.

Related property

If the value of a particular asset or assets is less than the proportionate value of that and "related" assets, then the value used is the appropriate proportion of the total value.

"Related property" is property of the same kind:

1. Belonging to the owner or his spouse.
2. Property in a settlement of which the individual or their spouse referrred to above have an interest in possession.
3. Property transferred, by the individual spouse to a charity or charitable trust.

The most practical application of the rule is to the valuation of shares in unquoted private companies. In order to reduce the value of a controlling shareholding a married couple may split the holding between them into two minority holdings. Again the rule is exclusive to inheritance tax and has no application to capital gains tax.

Example

George Beagle and his wife Floppy own shares in Foxhunting Enterprises Ltd, a private unquoted trading company. There are 5,000 shares in issue of which George owns 2,000 and Floppy 1,000. The remaining shares are owned in small holdings by various other members of the family.

A controlling holding is valued at £200 a share and a minority holding at £90 a share.

George gave his son 600 shares and then was inconsiderate enough to drop dead within seven years of the date of the gift.

The shares held with his wife are valued together being related property:

George	2,000
Floppy	1,000
	3,000 valued at £200 each=600,000
After gift to son:	
George	1,400 (2,000−600)
Floppy	1,000
	2,400 valued at £90 each=216,000

Therefore the total loss of value in related property on the gift to the son was £600,000−£216,000=£384,000.

The amount chargeable to tax is only a proportion of this, as only George made a chargeable gift, not Floppy. The amount taxable is:

$$384{,}000\times\frac{2{,}000}{3{,}000}=256{,}000$$

If related property is inherited on a death, and the property is sold within three years of the death for less than the valuation on death, then subject to various conditions, including that the sale was an arm's length sale, for a commercial price, the seller can claim to have the property revalued at death as if it was not related to any other property.

Quoted investments

Shares and securities quoted on the Stock Exchange are valued at the lower of two alternative figures:

1. The lower closing price for the day, plus one quarter of the difference between the lower and higher closing prices (the "quarter-up" rule).
2. A figure halfway between the highest and lowest recorded bargains on the day (the "half-up" rule).

Units in approved unit trust schemes are valued at the managers' buying price, i.e. the lower of the two prices published.

If a security, such as a government stock, is quoted "ex-dividend", then the interest payable at the next due date, has to be added to the value less any tax deducted at source.

Example

Burney dies on 31 March, owning £10,000 (nominal value) of five per cent Treasury Stock, 1990–97. The interest is payable half yearly on 1 May and 1 October. The value of the stock on 31 March is £7,299 ex-div.

Value of stock		7,200
Plus half-yearly interest payable on 1 May	250	
Less tax deducted at source (25%)	(63)	187
Total value chargeable		7,387

Relief is available when quoted securities are sold for less than their probate value within twelve months of the death. This applies when any quoted shares or securities or holdings in authorised unit trusts are realised within twelve months of the death. The persons liable to pay the tax can claim that the total of the sale prices can be substituted for the probate values. However, if the proceeds are re-invested by the same people in the same shares or unit trusts, after the death and withnin two months of the last sale, the relief can be reduced or lost altogether.

Example

Grimley dies leaving the following estate:

House	100,000
Contents and chattels	40,000
Cash and bank deposits	50,000
Shares in Nat East Bank (quoted)	120,000
Total estate	310,000

Tax chargeable	128,000×Nil=	Nil
	182,000×40%=	72,800
	310,000	72,800

Six months after the death the son, who inherited the entire estate, sold the shares in the Nat East Bank for 70,000.

Revised charge to tax:

Original value of estate 310,000−loss on sale of shares 50,000=260,000.
Loss on shares, 120,000−70,000=50,000.

Tax chargeable	128,000×Nil=	Nil
	132,000×40%=	52,800
	260,000	52,800

Land sold within three years of death
When the person who pays the tax on land inherited on a death sells that land within three years of the death for less than the probate value, he can claim that the sale proceeds be substituted for the original valuation.

There are of course conditions to be satisfied, the main ones being:

1. The sale or sales or land must be at a commercial price in arm's length transactions.
2. The shortfall in the sale price of the land must be at least the lower of £1,000 or five per cent of the probate value.

The relief is extended beyond the three years when there is a compulsory purchase notified before the end of the three years.

Miscellaneous matters on death

Deeds of family arrangement
Inheritance tax is not charged on certain viariations in the destination of property passing on death, or on disclaimers of title to property passing in death.

The variation or disclaimer must be made within two years of the death, and an election made to the Inland Revenue within six months of the variation.

The exemption also applies, but without a time limit, when a surviving spouse's life interest under an intestancy is redeemed. It also applies if an interest in settled property is disclaimed unless some consideration in money or money's worth is received.

Estate duty surviving spouse exemption
When estate duty (charged on deceased's estates prior to March 1974) was charged on the death of a spouse on property in which the other spouse was given a limited interest (for life or widowhood), the property was usually exempt from estate duty on the death of the surviving spouse. In such a case, when the survivor dies

there is no charge to inheritance tax on the settled property if it would have been exempt from estate duty on the survivor's death.

Administration

Returns

Chargeable transfers must be reported to the Inland Revenue Capital Taxes Office within twelve months from the end of the month of transfer or death. Note that only immediately chargeable transfers, such as a transfer to a discretionary settlement, not PETs, have to be reported.

Rates of tax and dates of payment

The nil rate band is index-linked and therefore is increased periodically. From the 6th April, 1990 the threshold of charge is property of £128,000, and then there is a standard rate of charge of 40%. In the past the rates of tax have been progressive.

Tax is chargeable on an estimated figure before probate is granted. Inheritance tax is payable out of the residuary estate unless there is a contrary direction in the will. However, property situated abroad bears its own tax. Recipients of PETs which become chargeable are responsible for paying any tax which arises.

Interest on tax is charged from when the tax is due. The due date is six months from the end of the month in which death occurs. For chargeable lifetime transfers the due date is six months from the end of the month in which the transfer is made. However, in the case of transfers made between 6th April and 30 September, the due date is 30th April in the following year.

The same rate of interest is charged on overdue tax arising on death or chargeable lifetime gifts. The interest does not attract any income tax relief.

Payment of tax on death by instalments

The tax due on certain assets may be paid by ten annual instalments. The classes of assets where this can be claimed are:

1. Land and buildings.
2. Controlling holdings of shares in companies.
3. Certain minority holdings of unquoted shares.
4. Business assets.
5. Property qualifying for agricultural relief.

Instalments paid on time concerning shares and business assets are free of interest. Interest is not charged on the tax payable on land and buildings only if they are held as business assets.

Payment of tax on lifetime gifts by instalments

The payment of tax by instalments is only available if:

1. The donee pays the tax; or
2. Settled property is retained in a settlement.

Only the classes of assets listed as qualifying on death qualify on chargeable lifetime gifts with these additional qualifications:

1. Lifetime disposals of timber.
2. In the case of minority holdings of unquoted shares, they must be worth at least £20,000 and be at least a ten per cent holding.
3. Instalments may also be claimed when payment in one sum would cause undue hardship and the recipient retains the shares.

Settled property

The method and occasions of charge on settled property vary as to whether or not there is an interest in possession by the beneficiaries, i.e. are they entitled to the income or enjoyment of the property.

Interest in possession

When there is such an interest there is a charge on the property when:

1. The interest terminates; or
2. When the property is transferred.

The amount charged is based on the cumulative total of the beneficiary with the interest in possession, although responsibility for actually paying the tax in that of the trustees.

No interest in possession

When there is no interest, e.g. a discretionary trust, the main occasions of charge are:

1. Every tenth anniversary on or after 1st April, 1983 of the date the trust was created.
2. Distributions of capital.
3. On a creation of an interest in possession.
4. On the conversion of the trust into a special trust, e.g. into an accumulation and maintenance settlement.

The amount of the charge depends on the amount of the property originally and subsequently settled. In the case of settlements made on or after 27th March, 1974 the settlor's cumulative total at the date of settlement determines the amount of charge. If the trust was created prior to 27th March, 1974 the settlement is in effect deemed to be a separate individual with its own cumulative total, but without access to annual exemptions, etc.

Definitions

Domicile

Domicile is the country which an individual regards as his natural home, the place he will eventually return wherever he might travel. For most people it is their country of birth, but it can be changed by permanently emigrating. Nobody can have two domiciles, unlike nationality.

There are three types of domicile:

1. Origin.
2. Choice.
3. Dependency.

Domicile of origin

Domicile of origin is created at birth, and is normally that of the father; but in the case of an illegitimate birth or birth after the father's death, it is that of the mother.

Domicile of choice

A domicile of origin can be altered by permanently emigrating to another country. This then becomes the domicile of choice. Most of the contracts with the country of birth would have to be abandoned.

Permanent return to the country of birth would soon re-establish the domicile of origin.

Domicile of dependency

Certain individuals are deemed not to be capable of establishing a new domicile and their domicile is fixed by law.

A child under 16 has that of his father (or mother if illegitimate). However, a girl under 16 who marries acquires the domicile of her husband.

In Scotland a boy has an independent domicile from 14 and a girl from 12.

Prior to 1st January, 1974 a wife took the domicile of her husband, and women married before then still operate by that rule. After even death or divorce she retains that domicile unless it is altered by choice.

From 1st January, 1974 a married woman's domicile is decided independently of her husband.

Deemed domicile

For inheritance tax purposes only, an individual is deemed to retain his UK domicile in certain circumstances:

1. For the first three years after a change of domicile of choice.
2. If an individual has been resident in the UK in not less than 17 fiscal years out of the preceding 20, then he automatically acquires deemed domicile in the UK for inheritance tax purposes.

Location of assets

Assets are located for tax purposes as follows:

1. Immovable property is situated wherever it happens to be.
2. Tangible movable property is situated wherever it happens to be at the moment of charge.

3. A debt, secured or unsecured, is situated wherever the creditor is resident.
4. Government or local authority securities are situated wherever the issuing authority is situated.
5. Shares and securities of companies are situated wherever the register is kept.
6. Ships and aircraft are situated wherever the owner is resident.
7. Goodwill of a business is situated wherever that business is carried on.
8. Patents, trademarks, etc. are situated in the country of registration.
9. A judgement debt is situated wherever it is recorded.
10. A bank account not in sterlng, and owned by a non-UK domiciled individual, is only situated in the UK if the individual is resident here, and the bank branch at which the account is held is in the UK.

Comprehensive example
Jeremy Pass-Tover died recently.

Seven years and two months before the death he had given his son £50,000 of shares in a quoted company. He had not previously made any chargeable gifts.

Five years and two months before the death he had given his daughter £136,000 of quoted company shares.

Four years and two months prior to the death he had given his wife (domiciled in the UK) £60,000 of quoted shares.

Two years before the death he had given his son £40,000 of shares in a quoted company.

On his death he owned the following estate:

	£
Personal chattels	10,000
Cash and bank deposits	27,000
Private houses	140,000
Country cottage	45,000

(There is an outstanding mortgage on the cottage of 21,000).

Quoted shares
2,000 ordinary shares in Washout Laundries plc valued quoted at 100p and 116p for the day. The lowest and highest bargains struck were 98p and 128p.

10,000 ordinary shares in Gazumping Buildings plc quoted at 314p and 326p, with bargains struck at 300p and 330p.

Other investments
20,000 (nominal) of seven per cent consolidated stock, ex-div, interest payable twice yearly. Tax is deducted at source from the interest.

4,000 shares in Frozen Chicks Packing Ltd, an unquoted company. His wife has 2,000 shares, and the total issued shares are 10,000. Majority holdings are valued at £50 a share, and minority holdings at £20 a share.

Other property interests
Jeremy has a life interest in a settlement set up by his father. The trust assets are valued at £150,000.

Jeremy's will leaves the family home and £25,000 in cash to his widow, the balance of the estate to go to his son.

Within eleven months of the death the son sold the Washout Laundries shares for £1,600.

There were outstanding personal debts of £2,000, unpaid income tax of £6,000, and the funeral expenses were £1,000. The costs of the executors were £5,000.

Answer

Potentially exempt transfers
Gift to son (7.2 years prior to death) – not chargeable, made more than seven years before death.

Gift to daughter (5.2 years prior to death) – 136,000 chargeable, but less 6,000 annual reliefs, means £130,000 chargeable.

Value at date of gift, rates of tax at date of death.

128,000 × Nil =		Nil
2,000 × 40% =		800
130,000		800
Taper relief:		
60% × 800	=	(480)
Tax payable		320

Gift to wife (4.2 years prior to death) – not chargeable, gift to UK domiciled spouse.

Gift to son (two years prior to death) – 40,000 chargeable, but less 6,000 annual reliefs, leaving 34,000 chargeable.

Tax payable 34,000 × 40% = 13,600 – no taper relief due, as the gift was made under three years from death.

Estate on death

Personal chattels		10,000
Cash and bank deposits		27,000
Private house		140,000
Country cottage	45,000	
Less mortgage	(21,000)	24,000

2,000 shares Washout Laundries plc:
Valuation quarter up to 104p, half up 113p.

2,000 × 104p	=	2,080

10,000 shares in Gazumping Builders plc:			
Valuation quarter up 317p, half up 315p.			
10,000×315p	=		31,500
20,000 Consolidated Stock		18,000	
Half-yearly interest (ex-div)	700		
Less tax (25%)	(175)	525	18,525
40,000 shares in Frozen Chicks Ltd			
Controlling holding (related property)			
40,000×50	=		200,000
Settled property			150,000
Gross value of estate			603,105
Deductible expenses:			
Personal debts		2,000	
Tax owed		6,000	
Cost of funeral		1,000	(9,000)
Executors' costs are not allowable.			
Net estate			594,105
Exempted property:			
Property bequeathed to surviving spouse:			
Family home		140,000	
Cash		25,000	(165,000)
			429,105
Loss on sale of quoted shares on sale within 12 months of date of death:			
2,080−1,600	=		(480)
Net estate on which tax chargeable			428,625
Gross tax payable:			
428,625×40%	=		171,450
Estate rate:			
$\frac{171,450}{428,625} \times 100 = 40\%$.			
Payable by:			
Trustees of settlement	150,000×40% =	60,000	
Executors	278,625×40% =	111,450	

Tax relating to the shares in Frozen Chickss Packing Ltd, 200,000×40% = £80,000, could be paid, if claimed, by ten annual interest free instalments.

Chapter Nineteen

Anti-Avoidance

General

As will be seen from this chapter there are many sections of the Income and Corporation Taxes Act and various Finance Acts which deal with tax avoidance schemes. They are not mutually exclusive and any particular scheme may be subject to assessment under several sections at the same time.

This chapter only summarises the effects of some of the main anti-avoidance sections, and is not intended to be either a comprehensive or detailed consideration of the subject.

Some of the main provisions are:

1. **Ss.703 to 708, ICTA, 1988.** These sections are generally considered to be the main weapon in the Revenue's anti-avoidance armoury. In theory they are extremely wide and cover many situations. However, their main practical use today is to prevent companies building up reserves out of accumulated retained profits and then distributing them to shareholders as capital (e.g. by way of voluntary liquidation).

Transactions carried out for bona fide commercial reasons are exempted and there is a clearance procedure provided.

The procedure for raising assessments under these provisions is specialised:

a) Assessments can only be raised by the Board under Sch.D, Case VI (local Inspectors cannot use these powers).

b) Before raising such assessments the Board must give prior notification of its intention and there is a special appeal procedure through a body known as the Tribunal.

c) All appeals on the assessments themselves go initially to the Special Commissioners.

2. There are three main sections dealing specifically with deals/income, etc. from overseas:

a) **S.742, ICTA, 1988.** This is designed to prevent individuals ordinarily resident in the UK from avoiding tax in the UK by transferring assets in such a way that the income becomes payable to a person resident abroad, but by various arrangements the UK resident can enjoy that income now or in the future. This could be done, for example, by transferring assets to a non-resident company or trust with himself as a shareholder/beneficiary, etc. Nominees may be used.

Again, assessments are under Sch.D, Case VI and there is a let out for bona fide commercial transactions.

b) **Ss. 765 to 767, ICTA, 1988.** This makes it unlawful (except with Treasury consent, in practice given by the Inland Revenue) for a UK Company to sell a non-resident subsidiary to foreign ownership, or to issue shares in a non-resident subsidiary to a non-resident person, except to enable them to become a director.

A company that becomes non-resident can trigger a capital gains charge on its assets.

c) **S.770, ICTA, 1988.** This is designed to prevent a company (particularly a multinational) from extracting profit from the UK to an overseas company by artificial pricing arrangements. When a UK and foreign company are under common control the Inland Revenue can impose a commercial price in dealings between them in computing profits liable to UK tax.

3. **S.775, ICTA, 1988.** When a high-earning individual attempts to convert his income to capital by transferring his services to a company in exchange for shares, this section allows the Revenue to assess any "capital" profit as income.

4. **S.776, ICTA, 1988.** This section should be read in conjunction with other legislation on land, e.g. development land tax. It allows the Revenue to assess as income (once again under Sch.D, Case IV) a capital gain on land held as stock in trade, purchased with the object of making a gain on sale or developed with the intention of making a gain.

Since the House of Lords decision in Furniss v. Dawson in early 1984, the Inland Revenue and the Courts now have the power to ignore any actions or schemes which are primarily for tax avoidance. Therefore many of the specific anti-avoidance provisions may now be outdated.

Bondwashing

"Bondwashing" involved the conversion of income on gifts and other interest-bearing securities into capital, so that profits came within the capital gains tax rules. These qualified for CGT exemption if the securities were held for more than twelve months rather than be liable to income tax. This was done by selling securities "cum div" (possibly to a tax-exempt institution) shortly before an interest payment date, when the proceeds were treated as capital receipts.

The anti-avoidance rules from 28th February, 1986 treat the interest on all fixed and variable securities (including corporate, bearer and foreign securities) as accruing from day to day. When a security is sold, interest accrued since the last interest payment date is taxed on the vendor as income. There is a corresponding CGT adjustment, and the purchaser is allowed a revenue deduction of the same amount primaruly against the next interest receipt, also with a compensating CGT adjustment on eventual sales.

Coupon stripping

Coupon stripping achieved a tax deferral by allowing the taxpayer to take advantage of the rules regarding deep discount bonds. A coupon strip involved an investor acquiring securities carrying a right to periodic interest payments through a vehicle company which issued a series of zero coupon bonds to the investor with different lengths of maturity. Each bond is designed to match the interest on the underlying security, the last bond representing the final source.

Deep discount bond legislation allows the investor to defer payment of tax until he disposes of his investment or until maturity. The new legislation does not apply when the underlying bond is a UK corporate bond, taxes investors on a year to year basis. This is charged as income on the ''income element'' interest in the stocks issues as part of the entire scheme. Any investor disposing of such stocks is liable to tax, but is given credit for amounts charged annually during his period of ownership.

Questions

Income Tax

1. Work out the tax payable for 1990/91 given the following details.

The tax returns show these details:

Tax return for	**1990/91**		**1991/92**
Husband's business profits as			
a garage proprietor – y/e 30/9/89	19,298	30/9/90	15,273
Capital allowances	1,420		2,632
Husband's rents received	480		510
Wife's earnings as a secretary	7.270		11,200
Wife's bank interest:			
NSB Deposit A/C	40		60
(opened 1968)			
NSB ordinary account	60		82
(opened June, 1990)			
Wife's company dividends received	3,280		3,560
They pay:			
Allowable bank interest (gross) (joint)	502		524
Covenant to aunt (gross) (husband)	100		100

The husband pays retirement annuity premiums of £4,044 per annum. The husband is 52. This means 20% of relevant income can be allowed.

2. Mrs Brown, a widow aged 70, has the following income in the years ended 6th April, 1990 and 5th April, 1991. Calculate the tax payable for 1990/91.

Year ended	**5th April, 1990**	**5th April, 1991**
Retirement pensions	5,000	5,400
Building society interest received	1,200	1,420
Bank interest – deposit account		
(NSB)	2,100	423
Purchased life annuity	3,700	3,700
(agreed capital proportion £2,700)		
Dividends from UK companies	794	1,065
Rents from 1, Acacia Avenue	463	1,281

Expenditure on 1, Acacia Avenue:		
Electricity	97	108
Repairs and maintenance	392	54
Insurance	19	22
	508	184

3. A man and his wife have the following details for a year of assessment. Work out the taxable net income.

The husband is a self-employed garage proprietor born in 1960 who in the relevant basis period makes a tax adjusted trading profit of £35,131.

He claims capital allowances on the following:

a) A "pool" brought forward of £720.
b) He sells machinery (which originally cost £900) for £236.
c) He buys secondhand machinery for £1,800 and a new car for £9,000. Private use is agreed with the Inland Revenue at one quarter of the total mileage.

He also pays retirement annuity premiums in the year of £5,500, having paid in the previous year £1,800 when the "relevant income" was £10,600.

His wife earns £900 a year as a part-time secretary. He received rents from a commercial property he inherited from his father. The rents received in the year are £1,600. The property is let on a 16-year lease dated 1.7.88 for the granting of which he received a premium of £6,000. Before letting he spent £500 on redecoration and £800 on new carpets. After letting he spent £100 on insurance of the fabric and £350 on repairing the roof after storm damage.

He is a beneficiary under a discretionary trust and received in the year £780 (net of tax).

The husband has had built for his garage business a new body repair shop. He spent £25,000 to buy the land (in the previous year), and spent (also in the previous accounting period) £29,000 on the building. During the basis period for the current year of assessment he spent £22,000 on completing the body shop, a further £5,000 on staff toilets and £12,000 on a retail shop to sell car spares, tobacco and sweets to customers.

His wife purchased £10,000 (nominal) of 7% Treasury Stock two years ago. The interest is credited half-yearly on 1st June and 1st December. He sold £4,000 (nominal) during the current year on 18th August.

During the year the husband paid out allowable interest of £690, a covenant to charity of £200 (gross) and interest on a bank loan to purchase a yacht (used privately) of £370.

Do *not* calculate the tax payable.

4. Able and Beckett are in partnership as architects. Their accounts to 31st December, 1989 show:

Office salaries and wages	47,402	Gross fees received	97,730
Rent	9,783		
Repairs	1,649		
Telephone and stationery	4,924		
Motoring expenses	5,662		
Professional fees	1,519		
Bad debts	862		
Miscellaneous	327		
Net profit	25,602		
	97,730		97,730

Repairs include:

Redecoration of offices	762
Electrical repairs	237
Conversion of alcove to toilet	650
	1,649

The motoring expenses do not include any private element.

Professional fees include:

Defence of action for professional negligence	487
Drafting of staff service contracts	502
Renewal of 25-year office lease	320
Defence of drink driving charge against Beckett	210
	1,519

Bad debts show:

Increase in general reserve	340
Specific debts written off	527
Loan to employee written off	100
	967
Bad debts recovered	105
To profit and loss	862

Miscellaneous expenses include:

Subscription to Chamber of Commerce	25
Charitable donations	112
Wedding present to staff member	50
Other allowable expenses	140
	327

The partnership agreement allowed for partners' salaries (charged to office salaries) of:

Able	5,000
Beckett	6,000

The remaining profit was then split ⅔ to Able, ⅓ to Beckett.

Callaghan was admitted to the partnership as from 1st July, 1990 when the partnership agreement was amended to:

	Salaries	**Share of profit**
Able	6,000	⅓
Beckett	6,000	⅓
Callaghan	4,000	⅓

An appropriate election was made for the "continuation" basis of assessment to apply to the partnership change at 1st July, 1990.

Calculate each partner's share of the taxable profit 1990/91.

5. Joe Gill is a self-employed garage proprietor. He has been in business for many years and has these relevant results:

	Tax adjusted profit (loss)	**Capital allowances**
Accounts for 12 months to 31st December, 1987	7,480	1,218
Accounts for 12 months to 31st December, 1988	(10,618)	527
Accounts for 12 months to 31st December, 1990	3,160	482

The other relevant details are:

	1988/89	**1989/90**	**1990/91**
Mrs Ann Gill's earnings	3,000	2,900	2,830
Joe Gill's NSB interest assessed	940	1,010	1,400
Ann Gill's rents received	280	370	660
Allowable bank interest paid	400	400	400

Work out the taxable income for all three tax years, assuming that the Gills claim loss relief as effectively as possible.

6. Jim Maynard is a self-employed fisherman and a bachelor. Advise him on the best loss relief claims given these results:

	Tax adjusted profit (loss)	**Capital allowances**
Accounts for 12 months to 31st March, 1988	1,416	160
Accounts for 12 months to 31st March, 1989	(8,000)	282
Accounts for 12 months to 31st March, 1990	2,512	190

His other income is:

	1988/89	**1989/90**	**1990/91**
Rents received	102	7,000	7,200

7. A farmer, for a twelve month accounting period ended on 31st March, 1990 makes a tax adjusted trading profit of £25,704 before claiming capital allowances. You are required to calculate his net taxable trading profit. He is aged 52.

In the twelve months:

a) He purchased new machinery costing £3,710, secondhand machinery costing £940.
b) He sold machinery for £310 which had originally cost £500.
c) His "pool" was brought forward at a figure of £485.
d) He bought more land at a cost of £50,000 and erected on it a barn costing £14,000 and a cowshed costing £10,000. He also had an extension built on his house which cost £9,000.
e) He bought a new car costing £8,200 and it has always been agreed with the Inspector that one quarter of all motoring expenses are for private purposes.

He paid retirement annuity premiums in the year of £5,000.

8. You are required to state under which schedule and case the following sources of income are assessed. State also any other points of significance about the form of assessment such as if it is current or preceding year.

a) Directors' fees from a company resident in the UK where the recipient is resident and ordinarily resident in the UK.
b) A salary paid to an employee ordinarily resident in the UK who is working in a foreign country for a foreign company on a two year contract.
c) Rents from a furnished flat situated in the UK.
d) The interest from an ordinary account with the National Savings Bank.
e) A winning bet on the Grand National.
f) Building society interest.
g) A dividend from a UK resident company.

9. a) Black takes a job in the Middle East earning £25,000 for the term of the contract. He goes to the Middle East for 170 days, returns to the UK for 40 days, goes abroad for another 200 days and then finally returns to the UK. What is the liability to tax?

b) What conditions have to be satisfied for a car to be classified as part of a pool, and what are the tax effects?

c) The chairman of a large company is supplied with a brand new Rolls-Royce by the company. They also provide a chauffeur who is paid £10,000 p.a. If he uses the car for business for 75% of its mileage how is the Sch.E benefit calculated? Assume an annual mileage of 12,000.

d) Are luncheon vouchers taxable?

10. a) What are the duties of an Inspector of Taxes?
    b) Who are, and what are the functions of, the Commissioners of Inland Revenue?
    c) Who are, and what are the functions of the appeal Commissioners?

11. Bergman started self-employment on 1/1/87 and chose as his accounting date 30th June. His first results were:

6 months to 30/6/87	5,800
12 months to 30/6/88	10,600
12 months to 30/6/89	13,900

Work out the assessments for 1986/87 to 1990/91 inclusive.

12. Carroll became self-employed on 1/7/86 and chose as his accounting date 31st December. Work out the assessments 1986/87 to 1990/91 with these results:

6 months to 31/12/86	6,240
12 months to 31/12/87	11,780
12 months to 31/12/88	13,920
12 months to 31/12/89	15,800

13. Darren ceases trading on 31/12/90 having had 30th September as his accounting date and the following results. Calculate all the relevant assessments.

12 months to 30/9/87	10,700
12 months to 30/9/88	10,980
12 months to 30/9/89	11,410
12 months to 30/9/90	8,480
3 months to 31/12/90	1,450

14. Edmunds ceases trading on 30/6/90 having had 30th September as his accounting date. Calculate all the relevant assessments.

12 months to 30/9/87	7,600
12 months to 30/9/88	6,200
12 months to 30/9/89	8,400
9 months to 30/6/90	5,400

15. Fuller changes his accounting date from 30th June to 31st December in 1990. Work out all the relevant assessments using the accepted Revenue practice.

12 months to 30/6/88	6,400
12 months to 30/6/89	7,600
12 months to 30/6/90	10,800
6 months to 31/12/90	9,700

16. Mr Burton died on 6th November, 1990. His income for the period from 6th April, 1989 to date of death was:

Salary as a manager for Scott Holdings Ltd	12,500
Dividends received (net)	750
Building society interest received	150

Mrs Burton has a job as a teacher which paid her £600 per month, and she received £1,210 (net) in dividends on 12th January, 1991.

Calculate the tax payable by Mr & Mrs Burton and the repayments due to Mrs Burton for 1990–91, assuming no deductions of tax under PAYE.

17. Miss Gordon married Mr Blair on 5th September, 1990. Calculate the tax payable by both of them with these details for 1990–91:

Miss Gordon received £400 a month salary and continued working after marriage.

Mr Blair received a salary of £700 a month.

Mrs Blair received rents of £140 in the year, £80 before 5th September and £60 afterwards.

He paid allowable bank interest of £100 from 6th September, 1990 to 5th April, 1991.

18. a) Mr Hanlan is a widower with a daughter aged 6. Work out his taxable income after personal allowances for 1990–91 given these details:

Salary £1,500 per month.

Bonus for company's year end:

31st December, 1989 2,000 paid 1st June, 1989
31st December, 1990 2,400 paid 1st June, 1990
31st December, 1991 2,800 paid 1st June, 1991

He was also provided with a car costing £27,000 on 1st March, 1986 (2,200cc) and the running costs were £800 all paid for by the employer. Business use was agreed at 8% and the total annual mileage was 10,000. He also received a £200 allowance towards his telephone bills. He estimates business calls cost £60 and it is agreed there is 50% business use of the telephone, of which the normal rental is £80.

b) If he was married on 8th November, 1990 what difference would it make to his personal allowances?

19. Mr & Mrs Collins are in their seventies. Work out tax payable for 1990–91 given these details:

Mr Collins:	Retirement pension	7,200
	Pension from former employer	3,600
	Company dividends (net)	2,250
Mrs Collins:	Retirement pension received as a result of her own NIC & private contributions	13,800

They jointly pay a covenant to charity of £200 (gross).

20. Milton, O'Connor and Dippel have been trading in partnership for many years, making their own brand of gentlemen's shirts called "Mods". They shared profits in the ratio of 5:2:2.

In the year ended 30th September, 1989 they made a profit, adjusted for income tax purposes, of £39,600. Unfortunately, Milton had to retire early from the partnership on 30th June, 1990 because of ill health and went to reside in the west country with his wife, dependent mother and two children, aged 7 and 9 respectively.

However, O'Connor and Dippel continued the business, sharing profits equally, until 30th September, 1990 when Abbott, their leading salesman, was admitted as a partner. Abbott had already earned £12,200 since April, 1990 as their salesman.

The terms of the new partnership agreement were that O'Connor and Dippel should receive salaries of £2,000 per annum, together with interest on their capital accounts of £10,000 and £6,500 respectively, at the rate of 10% per annum, and remaining profits shared in the ratio of 2:2:1.

O'Connor and Dippel are both bachelors whilst Abbott is married. O'Connor pays allowable bank interest of £435 per annum.

None of the partners had any other income except Milton, who retired, and he received £35 war loan interest from the £1,000 3½% stock that he had held for many years. An election was made, within the appropriate time limit, in respect of each change in the partnership for the continuation basis to be applied.

You are required to:

a) Show the division of the partnership assessment for 1990–91.
b) Calculate the taxable income of each partner from the information available in the question.

21. Jackson has been in business many years and is resident in the United Kingdom. He specialises in the manufacture of fluffy toys including miniature "wombles".

	£		£
Administration expenses	3,500	Gross profit B/D	40,000
Establishment costs	5,000	Investment income	650
Royalties payable	2,000	Rents receivable	1,250
Repairs and renewals	4,000	Bank interest	1,000
Motor expenses	1,000	Grants received	1,500
Selling and distributions	2,500		
Entertaining	750		
Loan interest	1,250		
Subscriptions	500		
Legal and professional costs	1,500		
Bad debts	7,000		
General expenses	300		
Depreciation	2,700		
Net profit for year	12,400		
	44,400		44,400

Notes:

1) Grants received consist of:

Advertising grant from suppliers	500
Grant under Industry Act 1972	1,000

2) Investment income entirely consists of dividends from United Kingdom resident companies.

3) Royalties payable comprises:

Patent royalty paid	1,200
Provision for royalty due but not yet paid	800

4) Included in repairs and renewals are:

a) Machinery repairs	2,100
b) Cost of office machinery dealt with on renewals basis	900
c) Factory extension	1,000

5) Entertaining comprises:

a) Entertaining UK customers	400
b) Entertaining overseas customers	350

6) Loan interest was payable to a finance company and only £450 had actually been paid at the end of the accounting period.

7) Subscriptions comprise:

a) Chamber of Commerce	100
b) Association of Toymakers	300
c) Chelsea Football Club	100

8) Legal and professional fees relate to debt collection (£800), claim for breach of contract (£400), and income tax appeal (£300).

9) The charge for bad debts includes actual bad debts £4,800, specific provisions £1,400 and general reserve £800.

10) General expenses include £100 for staff Christmas party.

11) Capital allowances have been agreed at £3.050.

12) He paid £500 of Class 4 national insurance in the year.

You are required to compute the taxable trading profit for the accounting period.

22. Tyler, aged 40, has given you the following information to enable you to prepare his income tax computation for 1990–91.

a) He commenced to trade as a stonemason on 1st January, 1989 and has prepared accounts to 31st December annually. His adjusted results were:

Year ended 31st December, 1989	13,000
Year ended 31st December, 1990	11,600
Year ended 31st December, 1991	16,400

b) His wife was employed as a secretary to 31st January, 1991 at a salary of £500 per month. She ceased working on 1st February, 1992.

c) Mr Tyler receives rent of £6,000 p.a. from an unfurnished leasehold property which was first let on 25th March, 1991 at a full rent under a 31 year lease (determinable by either party at the end of the 7th, 14th or 21st years). The rent is payable quarterly in advance on the normal quarter days and Tyler received a premium of £800 on granting the lease. It is clear that the premium relates to the value of a 7 year lease. He incurred the following expenses in respect of the property:

Redecorating prior to letting	180
Insurance (paid 25th March)	121
Letting expenses	29

d) Both Mr & Mrs Tyler received income from ordinary deposits with the National Savings Bank as follows:

	Year to 5/4/89	**Year to 5/4/90**	**Year to 5/4/91**
Mr Tyler (account opened 1967)	85	80	83
Mrs Tyler (account opened June 1988)	65	78	75

e) Mr Tyler received dividends of £1,526 in 1989/90 and £1,607 in 1990/91. He also received in 1990/91 building society interest of £75, an increase of £14 over the previous year.

The following payments were made in 1990/91:

f) Building society interest is paid on his own house of £280 (gross amount) owned by Tyler in his sole name.

g) £65 interest on a loan taken out in 1986 with a UK insurance company to purchase a yacht is paid.

h) £30 interest on an overdraft taken out in June, 1986 with a UK bank to finance the purchase of a hi-fi system.

i) £150 gross under a deed of covenant to Shelter paid by Tyler himself.

£320 gross under a deed of covenant (executed 8/4/84) to his own widowed mother who lives with him.

j) £1,000 premium under a retirement annuity contract with a recognised UK insurance company.

You are required to compute the taxable income for 1990/91.

23. Johnson and his wife have the following sources of income. Work out the taxable income for 1990/91.

Income recived in year ended:

	5th April, 1990	**5th April, 1991**
Salary from employer	27,000	29,000
Bonus for year ended:		
30th September, 1988 (paid 1/5/90)	10,000	
30th September, 1989 (paid 1/5/91)		16,000

A new car is provided costing £20,000 from March, 1988. He does 20,000 business miles in 1990/91. He pays personally for all private petrol.

His wife has interest from National Savings Bank accounts:

Ordinary (opened 1980)	76	89
Deposit (opened 1981)	170	190
Husband has accounts:		
National Savings Bank (Ordinary A/c) (opened 1979)	82	94

Deposit A/c	200	185
Grimethorpe Building Society	70	142
Wife opened a hairdressing business on 1st July, 1989 and profits were:		
Y/e 30th June, 1990		5,400
Y/e 30th June, 1991		3,600
Profit for Y/e 30th June, 1992 is anticipated to be about 3,000.		
Mr & Mrs Johnson pay jointly:		
Mortgage interest on their family home (election made for Mr Johnson to have full tax relief) (Paid under MIRAS)	570 (net)	675 (net)
Covenant to their 19 year old son who is a full-time student (taken out in 1987)	1,000 (gross)	1,000 (gross)

24. Barnacre commenced a garage business on 6th October, 1987 and his profits as adjusted for taxation purposes have been:

7 months to 5th May, 1988	2,800
12 months to 5th May, 1989	4,848

The profit and loss account for the year ended 5th May, 1990 is:

Gross Profit			21,764
Less:	Rent, light and heat	1,872	
	Staff salaries	12,020	
	Hire purchase interest on plant	400	
	Repairs and renewals	532	
	Professional charges	608	
	Stationery, postage and telephone	948	
	Travelling and entertaining	1,236	
	Sundry expenses	790	
	Bad debts provision	362	
	Depreciation: Lathe	300	
	Car	420	19,488
	Profit for the year		2,276

Notes on the profit and loss account:

(1) Repairs and renewals include, apart from normal decorations and repairs, the cost of a new toilet in the garage amounting to £130.

(2) Professional charges are:

Legal charges (debt collection)	58
Legal charges (contravention of safety regulations)	50
Accountancy	500
	608

(3) Travelling and entertaining expenses are:

Staff travelling	346
Motor expenses	730
Entertaining UK customers	160
	1,236

It has been agreed that the personal use by Barnacre of the car represents 20% of the total mileage.

(4) Sundry expenses are:

Advertising ball point pens for 250 customers at Christmas	410
Staff Christmas party	174
Donation – Dr Barnado's	52
Trade journals	38
Miscellaneous allowable expenses	116
	790

(5) Bad debts provisions are;

In respect of specific debts	152
5% on all other debts	210
	362

Fixed asset purchases and sales have been:

Purchase costs:

10th October, 1987 secondhand lathe	2,230
10th April, 1988 secondhand car	1,680
30th April, 1989 new lathe	3,000

Sale proceeds:

30th April, 1989 original lathe	1,500

You are required to:

Compute the adjusted trading profit for y/e 5th May, 1990 and calculate the taxable profit and capital allowances for 1987/88 to 1991/92.

25. Berkeley opened a National Savings Bank deposit account on 1st June, 1985 and interest is credited:

31st December, 1985	170
31st December, 1986	220
31st December, 1987	180
31st December, 1988	340
31st December, 1989	280
31st December, 1990	420
The account was closed on 30th June, 1991	240

He purchased, through the National Stock Register, 10,000 (nominal) of 10% Treasury Stock 1998 in May, 1988. He purchased a further 4,000 (nominal) in August, 1990. Interest is paid half-yearly on 30th June, and 31st December.

Calculate the assessable interest for all relevant fiscal years on the NSB account, and for 1985/86 to 1991/92 on the Treasury Stock.

26. George Gollan, aged 60, is married to Elizabeth Gollan, aged 66. Calculate the tax payable for 1990/91 given these details:

George:	Pensions	13,000
	Building society interest received	600
Elizabeth:	Pensions	13,500
	National Savings Bank interest	300

They pay a joint covenant to charity of £200 (gross).

27. Mr Blumenthal owns a property which he lets for the first time (having lived in it himself previously) on 1st August, 1990.

The property is let furnished and the rent is £300 a month payable on the 1st of each month in advance.

Blumenthal pays the electricity bills of £220 (from 1st August, 1990) and repairs a damaged window frame at a cost of £70 in November, 1990.

When let, Blumenthal received a premium of £600 for a 5 year lease.

Assess his taxable income under Sch.D, Case IV for 1990/91.

28. Bullock changes his accounting date from 31st March to 30th September in 1990. Following standard Revenue practice work out all the assessments for the relevant years:

y/e 31/3/88	12,600
y/e 31/3/89	8,400
y/e 31/3/90	16,600
6 months to 30/9/90	10,200

29. State six alternative uses of a building which qualify for industrial buildings allowance.

30. Greenwood commences trade on 1st February, 1988 and draws up his accounts to 30th September. His tax adjusted trading results are:

8 months to 30/9/88	8,000
12 months to 30/9/90	15,000
12 months to 30/9/91	18,000

He buys the following items of equipment. You are required to work out the necessary assessments net of capital allowances.

New machinery purchased at 1/2/88	200
Car on 1/3/88 costing	4,956
Machinery purchased 6/11/88	7,000
Machinery purchased 3/4/89	3,000
Machinery purchased 4/3/90	4,500

The car is used 50% for business.

What difference would it make to the capital allowances only if current year basis was claimed by the taxpayer for the second and third years' assessment?

31. Fagan and Gregory have been trading as a partnership for many years. They admit Hartley to the partnership from1st July, 1986. No continuation basis election was made. Work out all the assessments for the fiscal years ended 1983/84 to 1992/93.

Year ended	30/6/82	42,000
	30/6/83	46,000
	30/6/84	48,000
	30/6/85	40,000
	30/6/86	50,000
	30/6/87	54,000
	30/6/88	58,000
	30/6/89	62,000
	30/6/90	70,000
	30/6/91	78,000
	30/6/92	88,000

Answers

Income Tax

1.

Husband			**Wife**			
Sch.D, Case I	19,298		Sch.E			11,200
CA	(1,420)					
	17,878		Sch.D, Case III			
RAR (20%)	(3,576)	14,302	Ord. A/C	82		
			Exempt	(70)	12	
Sch.A		510	Deposit A/C		40	52
			Sch.F		3,560	
			3,560 × ⅓ =		1,186	4,746
		14,812				15,998
Bank interest 524 × ½ =		(262)	Bank interest 524 × ½ =			(262)
		14,550				15,736
SPA	3,005		SPA			(3,005)
MCA	1,720	(4,725)				
		9,825				12,731

9,825 × 25% = 2,456.25   12,731 × 25% = 3,182.75

2.

Sch.E			5,400
BSI		1,420	
1,420 × ⅓ =		473	1,893
Sch.D, Case III			2,100
Life annuity (income portion)			1,000
Sch.F		1,065	
1,065 × ⅓ =		355	1,420
Sch.A: Rents		1,281	
Expenditure	108		
	54		
	22	(184)	1,097
			12,910

Age allowance		3,670	
Income	12,910		
Limit	(12,300)		
Excess	610×½=(305)	(3,365)	
		9,545×25%=2,386.25	

3. Taxable trading profit 35,131

Capital allowances:

	Pool		Car		
B/F	720	Cost	9,000		
Additions	1,800				
	2,520				
Sales	(236)				
	2,284				
WDA (25%)	(571)	WDA	(2,000)×¾=(1,500)		(2,071)
C/F	1,713	C/F	7,000		

Industrial buildings:

Spent in year	22,000		
	5,000		
	27,000		
Prior year's expenditure	29,000		
	56,000×4%=	(2,240)	(4,311)
			30,820

Retirement annuity relief:

Previous year 10,600×17½%	=	1,855	
Premiums paid	=	1,800	
		55	
Present year 30,820×17½%	=	5,393	
Maximum available		5,448	(5,448)
Premiums paid		(5,500)	
Excess premiums unrelieved		52	
			25,372

Sch. A:

Rents		1,600	
Premium	6,000		
6,000×2%×15 years=	(1,800)	4,200	
		5,800	
Expenses:			
	100		
	350	(450)	5,350

Trust income:			
$780 \times {}^{100}/_{65}$	=		1,200
Sch.D., Case III:			
6,000 (nominal) × 7%	=	420	
4,000 (nominal) × 3½%	=	140	560
			32,482
Bank interest	690		
Charitable covenant	200		(890)
			31,592

The wife's earnings of £900 are fully covered by her SPA.

4. Able, Beckett & Callaghan:

Net profit per accounts	25,602
Charitable donations	112
General bad debts reserve	340
Loan to employee	100
Drunk driving expenses	210
Conversion of alcove	650
Partners' salaries	11,000
	38,014

	Able		Beckett		Callaghan		Total
6/4/90 to 30/6/90:							
$38{,}014 \times {}^{3}/_{12} =$							9,504
Salary	1,250		1,500				2,750
Net profit (⅔)	4,503	5,753	(⅓) 2,251	3,751			6,754
1/7/90 to 5/4/91:							
$38{,}014 \times {}^{9}/_{12} =$							28,510
Salary	4,500		4,500		3,000		12,000
Net profit (⅓)	5,503	10,003	(⅓) 5,503	10,003	(⅓) 5,504	8,504	
Total		15,756		13,754		8,504	

5. **1988/89**

	Husband			Wife		
Sch.D, Case I	7,480	Sch.D, Case III	940	Sch.E, 3,000	Sch.A	280
CA	(1,218)					
	6,262					
Bank interest			400			
			540			

Loss relief:

	(10,618)					
CA	(527)					
	(11,145)					
	6,802	(6,262)	(540)	WEIR	(2,605)	
	(4,343)	Nil	Nil		395	
						675
				MA		(4,095)
						Nil

1989/90

Husband				**Wife**			
Sch.D, Case I	Nil	Sch.D, Case III	1,010	Sch.E	2,900	Sch.A	370
Bank interest			(400)				
			610				
				WEIR	(2,785)		
					115		
					1,095		
				MA	(4,375)		
					Nil		

Loss carried forward (4,343)

1990/91

Husband			**Wife**		
Sch.D, Case I		3,610	Sch.E		2,830
CA		(482)	Sch.A		660
		3,128			3,490
Sch.D, Case III		1,400	SPA	3,005	
		4,528	MCA	485	(3,490)
					Nil
Bank interest (Elect to set off the whole against the husband)		(400)			
		4,128			
Loss relief					
B/F	4,343				
Utilised	(4,128)	(4,128)			
C/F	(215)				
		Nil			

6. **1988/89:**

Sch.D, Case I	1,416	Sch.A	102
CA	(160)		
	1,256		
Loss relief	(8,000)		
	282		1,358
C/F	(8,282)	SA	(2,605)
			Nil

1989/90:

Sch.D, Case I		Nil	Sch.A	7,000
Loss relief	(8,282)			
S.380 relief	7,000			(7,000)
	(1,282)			Nil

1990/91:

Sch.D, Case I	2,512	Sch.A	7,200
CA	(190)		
	2,322		
S.385 loss	(1,282)		
	1,040		
		8,240	
	SA	(3,005)	
		5,235 × 25% = 1,308.75	

7. Capital allowances (machinery and plant):

	Pool		Car	Total
B/F	485	Cost	8,200	
Purchases	3,710			
	940			
	5,135			
Sales	(310)			
	4,825			
WDA (25%)	(1,207)	WDA (25%)	(2,000) × 75% = 1,500	2,707
	3,618		6,200	

Capital allowance (agricultural buildings):
Agricultural buildings:

Barn	14,000	
Cowshed	10,000	
Extension		
9,000 × ⅓ =	3,000	
	27,000 × 4% =	1,080
		3,787

Retirement annuity relief:

	25,704	
Capital allowances	(3,787)	
	21,917 × 20% =	4,384

Totals:

Tax adjusted profit	25,704
Capital allowances	(3,787)
	21,917
Retirement annuiyt relief	(4,384)
Net taxable profit	17,533

8. a) Sch.E, current year, receipts basis of assessment.

b) Sch.E, current year basis, but with a 100% deduction, and therefore effectively not assessable in the UK.

c) Sch.D, Case VI, current year basis.

d) Sch.D, Case III, normally preceding year basis, but with a £70 exemption.

e) Not taxable.

f) Taxable on current year basis on grossed up amount of interest received. The credit is limited in its application.

g) Taxable on current year basis, Sch.F, on grossed up amount received. Credit not limited in its application.

9. a) As Black has a qualifying period of over 365 days he is entitled to a 100% deduction. His return visit to the UK does not exceed 62 days or one sixth of the total period overseas.

b) A pool car:

i) Must be available to and acutally used by at least two employees and no one employee must use the car to the exclusion of others.
ii) Any private use must be merely incidental to any business use.
iii) The car must not normally be kept overnight on or near the vicinity of residential premises of the employees.

c) Assessable benefit £7,400
Petrol benefits £900
Benefit of chauffeur £10,000×25% £7,500
£15,800

d) Luncheon vouchers are taxable over 15p per day.

10. a)
i) Issue tax returns and receive the completed return.
ii) Issue assessments and receive appeals against them.
iii) Try and settle appeals informally. If not, place them before the appeal Commissioners.
iv) Attend the appeal hearing and present the Revenue's case.
v) Make repayments of tax.

b) The Commissioners of Inland Revenue constitute the Board of Inland Revenue . Their duties are to advise the Treasury on changes needed in tax law, advise on the effects of likely changes in tax law, and supervise the running of the department in collecting direct taxes.

c) The appeal Commissioners are an appellate body to settle appeals by taxpayers against assessments. Their decision on a finding of fact is final, but an appeal can be made to the High Court on any point of law.

There are two types:
i) The Generals are unpaid local businessmen who act in a local division, appointing a Clerk to help them.
ii) The Specials are full-time paid Civil Servants. They are an alternative to the Generals, but certain specialised appeals must be heard by them.

11.

1986/87					
$5{,}800 \times {}^3/_6$			2,900		
1987/88					
	5,800		$5{,}800 \times {}^3/_6 =$	2,900	
$10{,}600 \times {}^6/_{12} =$	5,300	11,100	$10{,}600 \times {}^9/_{12} =$	7,950	10,850
1988/89		11,100	$10{,}600 \times {}^3/_{12} =$	2,650	
			$13{,}800 \times {}^9/_{12} =$	10,350	13,000
		22,200			23,850

Therefore:	1986/87	2,900
	1987/88	11,100
	1988/89	11,100
	1989/90	10,600
	1990/91	13,800

12.

1986/87		6,240			
$11{,}780 \times \frac{3}{12} =$		2,945		9,185	
1987/88	6,240		$11{,}780 \times \frac{9}{12} =$	8,835	
$11{,}780 \times \frac{6}{12} =$	5,890	12,130	$13{,}920 \times \frac{3}{12} =$	3,480	12,315
1988/89		11,780	$13{,}920 \times \frac{9}{12} =$	10,440	
			$15{,}800 \times \frac{3}{12} =$	3,950	14,390
		23,910			26,705

Therefore:

1986/87	9,185
1987/88	12,130
1988/89	11,780
1989/90	13,920
1990/91	15,800

13.

1990/91		1,450			
$8{,}480 \times \frac{6}{12} =$		4,240	5,690		
1989/90	10,980		$11{,}410 \times \frac{6}{12} =$	5,705	
			$8{,}480 \times \frac{6}{12} =$	4,240	9,945
1988/89	10,700		$10{,}980 \times \frac{6}{12} =$	5,490	
			$11{,}410 \times \frac{6}{12} =$	5,705	11,195
	21,680				21,140

Therefore:

1990/91	5,690
1989/90	10,980
1988/89	10,700

14.

1990/91				
$5{,}400 \times \frac{3}{9} =$		1,800		
1989/90	6,200	$5{,}400 \times \frac{6}{9} =$	3,600	
		$8{,}400 \times \frac{6}{12} =$	4,200	7,800
1988/89	7,600	$8{,}400 \times \frac{6}{12} =$	4,200	
	13,800	$6{,}200 \times \frac{6}{12} =$	3,100	7,300
				15,100

Therefore:

1988/89	7,300
1989/90	7,800
1990/91	1,800

15.

1989/90 (y/e 30/6/88)			6,400
1990/91 (y/e 30/6/89)			7,600
1991/92 (y/e 31/12/90		9,700	
	$10{,}800 \times \frac{6}{12} =$	5,400	15,100

Preceding year 1990/91			
12 months to 30/6/89	7,600	1990/91	
12 months to 30/6/90	10,800	1991/92	
6 months to 31/12/90	9,700		
30 months	28,100	24 months	
$\frac{24}{30} \times 28{,}100 =$			22,480
1991/92			15,100
			7,380

The difference is not significant and therefore the assessment for 1990/91 would not be altered.

7,600		
15,100		
$22{,}700 \times \frac{1}{2} =$	$11{,}350 \times 10\% =$	1,135
Difference	7,600	
	7,380	
	220	

16.

Mr Burton			**Mrs Burton**		
Sch.E		12,500	Sch.E		7,200
Sch.F	750		Sch.F	1,200	
Credit	250	1,000	Credit	403	1,613
BSI	150				8,813
Credit	50	200			
		13,700			
SPA	3,005		SPA	3,005	
MCA	1,720	(4,725)	WBA	1,720	(4,725)
		8,975			4,088
$8{,}975 \times 25\% =$		2,243.75			
Credits $(250+50) =$		(300.00)	$4{,}088 \times 25\% =$		1,022.00
		1,943.75	Credits		(403.33)
					618.67

17. **Miss Gordon/Mrs Blair**

Sch.A	140	Sch.E 400×12=	4,800
		4,940	
SPA		(3,005)	
		1,935	
1,935×25%=		483.75	

Mr Blair

Sch.E 700×12	=	8,400
Bank interest		(100)
		8,300
SPA	3,005	
MCA 1,720×8/12=	1,147	(4,152)
		4,148

4,148×25%=1,037.00.

18.

a) Salary		1,500×12=			18,000
Bonus:					
					2,400
Car					
Scale charge		2,350×1½=		3,525	
Fuel benefit				900	4,425
Telephone			200		
Business use	60				
Rental	Nil		(60)		140
	SPA		3,005		24,965
	APA		1,720		(4,725)
					20,240

b) He would only qualify for restricted marriage allowance and would therefore be better off electing to retain his additional personal allowance for 1990/91.

19.

Husband			Wife	
Sch.E	7,200		Sch.E	13,800
	3,600	10,800		
Sch.F	2,250			
Credit	750	3,000		
		13,800		

Covenant 200×½=				(100)
				13,700
Single AA		3,670		
Net income	13,700			
Limit	(12,300)			
	1,400×½			
		=700		
Limit		(665)	(3,005)	
Excess		35		
MCAA		2,145		
Excess		(35)	(2,110)	(5,115)
				8,585
8,585×25%=				2,146.25
Covenant 100×25%				25.00
				2,171.25

Covenant 200×½=				(100)
				13,700
Single AA			3,670	
Net income	13,700			
Limit	(12,300)			
		1,400×½		
			=700	
Limit			(665)	3,005
			35*	
				10,695
10,695×25%=				2,673.75
				25.00
				2,698.75

* Note: Excess income limit of a wife cannot restrict the married couple's age allowance.

20. Milton, O'Connor and Dippel.
1990/91 Based on preceding year's accounts (y/e 30/9/89) 39,600

	Total	**M**	**O**	**D**
a) Period 6/4/90 to 30/6/90 $^3/_{12}$×39,600=	9,900	5,500	2,200	2,200
b) Period 1/7/90 to 30/9/90 $^3/_{12}$×39,600=	9,900		4,950	4,950
		5,500		
		Abbott		
c) Period 1/10/90 to 5/4/91 $^6/_{12}$×39,600=	19,800			
Salaries	(2,000)		1,000	1,000
	17,800			
Interest	(825)		500	325
Net profit	16,975	3,395	6,790	6,790
	M	3,395	15,440	15,265
	5,500			
Salary		12,200		
Sch.D, Case III (interest)	35			
	5,500	15,595	15,440	15,265
Allowances	(4,725)	(4,725)	(3,005)	(3,005)
Taxable income	775	10,870	12,435	12,260

21. **JACKSON**

Taxation Computation

	Net profit (per accounts)		12,400
Add:	Royalties payable	2,000	
	Repairs and renewals	1,000	
	Entertaining	750	
	Subscription	100	
	Legal costs	300	
	Bad debts	800	
	Depreciation	2,700	7,650
			20,500
Less:	Grant under Industry Act	1,000	
	Investment income	650	
	Rents received	1,250	
	Bank interest	1,000	3,900
	Case I Adjusted profit		16,150
Less:	Capital allowances		(3,050)
			13,100
Less:	Charge paid – Royalty		(1,200)
Less:	Class 4 NIC 500×½		(250)
			11,650

22. Tyler:

Husband			**Wife**	
Sch.D, Case I (current year election)*		12,800	Sch.E 500×10=	5,000
RAR		(1,000)	Sch.D, Case III (3rd year – actual basis)75–70	5
		11,800		
Sch.A (see working)		2,054		
Sch.D, Case I NSB (PY basis) 80–70=		10		
Sch.F	1,067			
Credit	535	2,142		
BSI	75			
Credit	25	100		
		16,106		5,005
Mortgage interest	280			
Covenant to charity	150	(430)		
		15,676		
SPA	3,005			
MCA	1,720	4,725	SPA	(3,005)
		10,951		2,000

Sch.A workings:

Rents 6,000 × ¼ =		1,500
Premium	800	
800 × 2% × 6 years** =	(96)	704
		2,204
Insurance	121	
Expenses	29	(150)
		2,054

* Readers should satisfy themselves that a current year election is beneficial.
** Lease deemed to be 7 years long. 7 − 1 year = 6 years.

23.

Husband

Sch.E			
Salary	29,000		
Bonus	10,000	39,000	
Scale benefit			
4,600 × ½ =		2,300	41,300
Sch.D, Case III 82 − 70 =		12	
		200	212
BSI		142	
Credit		48	190
			41,702
Mortgage interest		675	
Tax deducted		225	(900)
			40,802
SPA		3,005	
MCA		1,720	(4,725)
			36,077

Wife

Sch.D, Case I		
1990/91 (current year basis)		
5,400 × $^3/_{12}$ =	1,350	
3,600 × $^9/_{12}$ =	2,700	4,050
Sch.D, Case III		
76 − 70 =	6	
	170	176
		4,226
SPA		(3,005)
		1,221

Note:

The covenant to the son is left out of the computation as it does not attract higher rate tax relief.

24. BARNACRE

a) ADJUSTED PROFIT FOR INCOME TAX PURPOSES FOR YEAR ENDED 5TH MAY, 1989

Net profit as per accounts			2,276
Add:	Cost of toilet	130	
	Legal charges re safety regulations	50	
	Private motor expenses ($^1/_5$ × 730)	146	

Entertaining	160	
Donation – Dr Barnado's	52	
General provision	210	
Depreciation	720	1,468
Adjusted profit		3,744

b) ORIGINAL AND FINAL ASSESSMENTS UNDER SCHEDULE D CASE I

		Original	Current Year	Final
1987/88	6/10/87 to 5/4/88			
	$\frac{6}{7} \times 2{,}800$	2,400		2,400
1988/89	6/10/87 to 5/10/88			
	$2{,}800 + \frac{5}{12} \times 4{,}848$	4,820		
OR	6/4/88 to 5/4/89			
	$\frac{1}{7} \times 2{,}800 + \frac{1\,1}{12} \times 4{,}484$		4,844	4,844
1989/90	6/10/87 to 5/10/88			
	AGAIN	4,820		
OR	6/4/89 to 5/4/90			
	$\frac{1}{12} \times 4{,}848 + \frac{11}{12} \times 3{,}744$		3,836	3,836
1990/91	y/e 5/5/89	4,848		4,848
1991/92	y/e 5/5/90	3,744		3,744

Note: Barnacre would make a claim for the current year basis because profits on an actual basis total £4,848+£3,836=£8,630 for 1988/89 and 1989/90, compared with £4,820+£4,820=£9,640.

c) CAPITAL ALLOWANCES BASIS PERIOD

Acquisition and disposals during these periods . . .	. . . are first dealt with in these fiscal years
5/10/87–5/4/88	1987/88
6/4/88–5/4/89	1988/89
6/4/89–5/4/90	1989/90
N/A	1990/91
y/e 5/5/90	1991/92

	Pool (25%)	Car (25%)	Allowances given
	£	£	£
1987/88			
Cost (10/10/87)	2,230		
WDA	(558)		558
	1,672		

1988/89			
Addition			
April 1986		1,680	
WDA	(418)	(420) × 4/5 = 336	754
	1,254	1,260	
1989/90			
Addition			
April, 1989	3,000		
	4,254		
Sale	(1,500)		
	2,754		
WDA	(669)	(315) × 4/5 = 252	921
	2,085	945	
1990/91			
WDA	(522)	(237) × 4/5 = 190	712
		708	
1991/92	1,563		
WDA	(391)	(177) × 4/5 = 142	533
	7,172	535	

25.

National Savings Bank (Deposit A/c):

1985/86	170	
1986/87	220	
1987/88	220	180 (Taxpayer's choice)
1988/89	180	
1989/90	340	
1990/91	280	420 (Inland Revenue's choice)
1991/92	240	

Treasury Stock:	**10,000 (nominal)**	**4,000 (nominal)**	**Total**
1988/89	500+500=1,000		1,000
1989/90	1,000		1,000
1990/91	1,000	200	1,200
1991/92	1,000	200+200	1,400

26.

George

Pensions			13,000
BSI		600	
Credit 600 × ⅓ =		200	800
			13,800
Covenant 200 × ½ =			(100)
			13,700
AA – Single		3,670	
Income	13,700		
Limit	(12,300)		
Excess	1,400 × ½ =700		
Restriction	(665)	(3,005)	
	85		
AA – Married couples	2,145		
Excess restriction	(85)	2,060	(5,065)
			8,735

8,735 × 25% =	2,183.75
Tax on covenant	25.00
	2,208.75
Credit	(300.00)
	1,908.75

Elizabeth

Pensions				13,500
Sch.D, Case III				
NSB				300
				13,800
Covenant 200 × ½ =				(100)
				13,700
AA – Single		3,670		
Income	13,700			
Limit	(12,300)			
Excess	1,400 × ½ =700			
Restriction	(665)	(665)		(3,005)
Excess	35*			
				10,695

10,695 × 25% =	2,673.75
Tax on covenant	25.00
	2,698.75

* Note: Excess income of the wife, when the single person's age allowance has been restricted to the maximum, does not further restrict the married couple's age allowance. This is only restricted by excess income of the husband.

27.

Rental	300 × 9 =	2,700
Premium	600	
2% × 4 × 600 =	(48)	552
		3,252
Electricity	220	
Repairs	70	(290)
		2,962

10% deduction for furniture:

Rental	2,700	
Electricity	(220)	
	2,480 × 10% =	(248)
Assessable Sch.A		2,714

28. Original assessments:

1988/89 (y/e 31/3/88)		12,600
1989/90 (y/e 31/3/89)		8,400
1990/91 (y/e 31/3/90)		16,600
1991/92 (y/e 30/9/90)		
	10,200	
16,600 × ½ =	8,300	18,500

Preceding year is 1990/91

y/e 31/3/89	8,400		1989/90
y/e 31/3/90	16,600		1990/91
6 months to 30/9/90	10,200		1991/92
30 months	35,200		36 months
$35{,}200 \times {}^{36}/_{30} =$		42,240	
1989/90	8,400		
1990/91	18,500	26,900	
Potential revised assessment 1990/91		15,340	
Original assessment		16,600	
		15,340	
Difference (over 1,000)		1,260	

Intermediacy test:

y/e 30/9/89	16,600 × ½ =	8,300
	8,400 × ½ =	4,200
		12,500

The new assessment (15,340) is intermediate between 16,600 and 12,500.

29. A building can qualify as an industrial building by being used for the following purposes:

a) As a factory or mill.
b) For the storage of raw materials or finished goods.
c) For certain public utility, tunnel or bridge operations.
d) For mines, oil wells and foreign plantations.
e) For the welfare of staff in a manufacturing industry.
f) As a sports pavilion in any trade.

30. **1987/88**

Profit 8,000 × 2/8 = (1/2/88 to 5/4/88)				2,000
Capital allowances:				
	Pool:		**Car:**	
Cost	200	Cost	4,956	
WDA (25%) 50 × 2/12 =	(9)	WDA (25%) 1,239 × 2/12 =	(207) × 50% = 104	(113)
	191		4,749	1,887

1988/89:

Profit (1/2/88 to 31/1/89)			8,000	
		15,000 × 4/12 =	5,000	13,000
Capital allowances:				
	Pool:		**Car:**	
B/F	191	B/F	4,749	
Cost	7,000			
	7,191			
WDA (25%)	(1,798)	WDA (25%)	(1,188) × 50% = 594	(2,392)
	5,393		3,561	10,608

1988/90:

Profit (1/2/88 to 31/1/89)				13,000
Capital allowances:				
	Pool:		**Car:**	
B/F	5,393	B/F	3,561	
WDA (25%)	(1,349)	WDA (25%)	(891) × 50% = 446	(1,795)
	4,044		2,670	11,205

1990/91:

Profit (1/10/88 to 30/9/89)				15,000
Capital allowances:				
	Pool:		**Car:**	
B/F	4,044	B/F	2,670	
Cost	3,000			
	7,044			
WDA (25%)	(1,761)	WDA (25%)	(668) × 50% = 334	(2,095)
	5,283		2,002	12,905

1991/92:

Profit (1/10/89 to 30/9/90) 18,000

Capital allowances:

		Pool:		**Car:**		
B/F		5,283	B/F	2,002		
Cost		4,500				
		9,783				
WDA (25%)		(2,446)	WDA	(501)	×50%=251	2,697
		7,337		1,501		15,303

Capital allowances on current year basis:

1987/88 (no change) 113

1988/89 (6/4/88 to 5/4/89)

		Pool:		**Car:**		
B/F		191	B/F	4,749		
Cost	7,000					
	3,000	10,000				
		10,191				
WDA (25%)		(2,548)	WDA (25%)	(1,188)	×50%=594	3,142
		7,643		3,561		

1989/90 (6/4/89 to 5/4/90)

	Pool:		**Car:**		
B/F	7,643	B/F	3,561		
Cost	4,500				
	12,143				
WDA (25%)	(3,036)	WDA (25%)	(891)	×50%=446	3,482
	9,107		2,670		

1990/91 (1/10/88 to 30/9/89)

	Pool:		**Car:**		
B/F	9,107	B/F	2,670		
WDA (25%)	(2,277)	WDA (25%)	(668)	×50%=334	2,611
	6,830		2,002		

1991/92 (1/10/89 to 30/9/90)

	Pool:		**Car:**		
B/F	6,830	B/F	2,002		
WDA (25%)	(1,708)	WDA (25%)	(501)	×50%=251	1,959
	5,122		1,501		

31.

Fagan and Gregory:

	Original:	Potential revision		
1983/84	42,000			
1984/85	46,000	$48{,}000 \times \frac{3}{12} =$	12,000	
		$40{,}000 \times \frac{9}{12} =$	30,000	42,000
1985/86	48,000	$40{,}000 \times \frac{3}{12} =$	10,000	
		$50{,}000 \times \frac{9}{12} =$	37,500	47,500
1986/87		$50{,}000 \times \frac{3}{12} =$	12,500	

Fagan, Gregory and Hartley:

1986/87	$54{,}000 \times \frac{9}{12} =$		40,500			
1987/88	$54{,}000 \times \frac{3}{12} =$	13,500				
	$58{,}000 \times \frac{9}{12} =$	43,500	57,000			
1988/89	$58{,}000 \times \frac{3}{12} =$	14,500				
	$62{,}000 \times \frac{9}{12} =$	46,500	61,000			
1989/90	$62{,}000 \times \frac{3}{12} =$	15,500				
	$70{,}000 \times \frac{9}{12} =$	52,500	68,000			
1990/91			62,000	$70{,}000 \times \frac{3}{12} =$	17,500	
				$78{,}000 \times \frac{9}{12} =$	58,500	76,000
1991/92			70,000	$78{,}000 \times \frac{3}{12} =$	19,500	
				$88{,}000 \times \frac{9}{12} =$	66,000	85,500
1992/93			78,000			

Questions

Corporation Tax

In all the following questions assume these rates and fractions unless instructed differently:

Financial year	**1988**	**1989**	**1990**
Standard rate (on profit over 500,000 up to FY 1988, 750,000 for FY 1989, and 1 million for FY 1990)	35%	35%	35%
Taper relief fraction (on profit between 100,000 and 500,000 up to FY 1988, 150,000 up to 750,000 for FY 1989, and 200,000 to 1 million for FY 1990)	1/40	1/40	1/40
Small company rate (on profit up to 100,000 up to FY 1988, 150,000 for FY 1989, and up to 200,000 for FY 1990)	25%	25%	25%
ACT fraction	1/3	1/3	1/3

1. Britton Ltd. has been manufacturing football gear for many years. The company is resident in the UK and has no associated companies. Work out the corporation tax payable given these results and assuming all allowances and reliefs are claimed as soon as possible:

Year ended 31st March	1989	1990	1991
Trading profit	130,000	70,000	1,100,000
Capital allowances	18,000	3,000	10,000
Chargeable gains	14,000	2,400	5,000
Dividend paid (net)	21,000	75,000	210,000

2. Murphy Ltd. had these results for the following periods. Calculate the corporation tax payable assuming that all reliefs are claimed as soon as possible:

Year ended 31st March	1990	1991
Trading profit (less capital allowances)	120,000	140,000
Capital gains	10,000	28,000
Capital losses	(15,000)	Nil
Loan interest paid (gross)	(10,000)	(2,000)
Dividends received from UK companies	75,000	30,000
Dividends paid	90,000	170,000

3. Left Ltd. and Right Ltd. have these results, and although the totals of trading profit, capital allowances and chargeable gains are identical, the totals of tax paid are different. Calculate the various assessments.

Year ended 31st March	**1989**	**1990**	**1991**
Left Ltd.			
Trading profit	1,100,000	30,000	220,000
Capital allowances	6,000	10,000	8,000
Capital gains	7,800	5,200	5,200
Right Ltd.			
Trading profit	496,000	24,000	830,000
Capital allowances	20,000	4,000	Nil
Capital gains	10,400	7,800	Nil

4. Milton Ltd. is a wholly owned subsidiary of Dippel Industrial Ltd. both of which are resident in the United Kingdom and have traded for many years. The recent results of both companies are as follows:

	Milton Limited		**Dippel Industial Limited**	
Year ended 31st March	1989 £	1990 £	1989 £	1990 £
Trading profits (after capital allowances)	16,700	–	40,000	17,000
Trading loss (including capital allowances)	–	(33,300)	–	–
Rental income less expenses	310	310	1,000	1,000
Capital losses	(1,100)	–	–	–
Debenture interest received (gross)	490	490	–	–
Capital gains	–	6,300	–	5,200

On the assumption that all reliefs are claimed as early as possible, you are required to:

a) State what relief Milton Ltd. may obtain for its trading loss of £33,300 giving computations to support your answer.

b) Indicate any further relief available to either Milton Ltd. or its parent company Dippel Industrial Ltd, from the information provided and again giving computations to support your answer.

c) State how your answer to (b) above would differ if Milton Ltd. was not a WHOLLY owned subsidiary of Dippel Industrial Ltd.

5. The managing director of Perrifit Ltd. has passed to you a copy of the company's capital budgets for the year ended 31st March, 1990. From the budgets you have been asked to prepare a statement showing the additional capital allowances available in respect of the accounting period ended 31st March, 1990 assuming all items are purchased according to the budget.

You have extracted the following items of capital expenditure from these budgets:

a) New plant and machinery for £22,000.
b) Extension to existing factory building £36,000.
c) New sports pavilion for staff welfare and recreation £44,000.
d) A patent, from another company, for special tools for £36,000 which was first registered in March, 1989.
e) A new factory which will cost £140,000, made up from:

	£
Land	40,000
Site clearance	20,000
Construction materials	30,000
Architect's fees	10,000
Labour costs	40,000

f) A new extruding machine for £100,000 of which £20,000 will be paid as deposit and the balance over the next five years with interest at 10% p.a.
g) A fleet of seven identical new cars for sales representatives £42,000.
h) A new Rolls-Royce for the managing director £57,249.
i) To spend £70,000 on pure scientific research.
j) To purchase an old factory for £27,000 which originally cost the first owner £4,700 when constructed in January, 1934.

6. A Ltd. has two wholly owned subsidiaries B Ltd. and C Ltd. Work out their corporation tax assessments for y/e 31/3/91 given the following results. A S.247 election has been made to ignore ACT in the paying of inter-company dividends:

A Ltd		B Ltd		C Ltd	
Trading profit	89,000	Trading profit	85,000	Trading profit	9,000
Rents received	8,200	Capital gains	780	Bank interest	2,300
Dividends received	15,000	Company paid:		Company paid:	
Company paid:		Dividend paid in the accounting period	7,000	Dividend paid in the accounting period	5,000
Loan interest	10,000				
Dividend paid	12,000				

7. A company (formed in 1967) for the year ended 31st March, 1991 had a trading profit of £20,000. It also had the following payments and receipts:

9th May, 1990 received a dividend from a UK company of £200.
17th July, 1990 paid £2,000 (gross) loan interest.
5th October, 1990 paid a dividend of £1,800.
10th January, 1991 received debenture interest of £2,300 (gross).

Work out the various payments due to the Inland Revenue (and give the latest dates of payment) and any repayments which could be claimed.

8. XYZ Ltd. is the parent company of a wholly owned subsidiary ABC Ltd. Claiming all possible reliefs work out the corporation tax assessments given these results:

Accounting period	1	2	3
XYZ Ltd.			
Trading profit (loss)	10,000	(15,000)	2,000
Capital gain	520	Nil	Nil
ABC Ltd.			
Trading profit	1,000	3,000	1,800
Loan interest paid	1,200	1,200	1,200

(Assuming a rate of tax of 25%).

9. A company has these results for a twelve month accounting period ending 31st March (assume a rate of income tax of 25%). Work out the corporation tax liability.

Trading profit	10,000
Capital gain	780

Also:

1st May	Dividend received from a UK resident company	700
1st July	Loan interest paid	600 (gross)
1st August	Dividend paid	1,470
1st October	Interest received on 7% Treasury Stock	800 (gross)

10. Work out the necessary corporation tax assessments given the following results of a company:

Accounting period	1	2	3	4
Trading profit	17,800	10,000	8,000	15,500
Capital gain	Nil	520	Nil	780
Loan interest paid	1,000	1,000	1,000	1,000
Dividend paid	2,000	5,700	4,600	20,000

Assume a basic rate of income tax and small company rate of corporation tax of 25%.

11. Work out all the necessary corporation tax assessments for a company with the following results. The company commenced trading on 1st April, 1988.

Accounting period year ended	**31/3/89**	**31/3/90**	**31/3/91**
Trading profit (loss)	20,000	(28,600)	220,000
Rents received	2,400	2,100	2,350
Capital gain	668	Nil	26,000
The company paid:			
Loan interest	1,200	1,000	1,000
Dividends	9,000	Nil	12,000

12. Mr Kavanagh is the secretary of Curtain Poles Ltd. and has received a letter from the Inspector of Taxes which reads thus:

"I consider that the company is a close company because it is both under the control of its directors and is also controlled by five or fewer participators together with their associates."

You are required to draft, in brief outline, a letter to Mr Kavanagh explaining the following points:

a) The definition of a director.
b) What a participator is.
c) The meaning of an associate.
d) Why special provisions are required for "close" companies which are not necessary for other companies.

Answers

Corporation Tax

1. **Year ended 31/3/89:**

Trading profit	130,000	CG	14,000
Capital allowances	(18,000)		
Sch.D, Case I	112,000		
		126,000	

Corporation tax	126,000×35%=	44,100
Marginal relief:		
$(500{,}000-126{,}000)\times\frac{126{,}000}{126{,}000}\times\frac{1}{40}=$		(9,350)
		34,750
ACT offset:		
Dividend paid 21,000×⅓=		(7,000)
MCT		27,750
ACT Brought back from y/e 31/3/90		(7,650)
MCT payable		20,100

Year ended 31/3/90:

Trading profit	70,000	CG	2,400
Capital allowances	(3,000)		
	67,000		
		69,400	

Corporation tax	69,400×25%=		17,350
ACT offset:			
Dividend paid	75,000×⅓=	25,000	
Maximum offset 69,400×25%=		(17,350)	(17,350)
Surplus ACT carried backc to y/e 31/3/89		7.650	
MCT			Nil

Year ended 31/3/91:

Trading profit	1,100,000	CG	5,000
Capital allowances	(10,000)		
	1,090,000		
		1,095,000	
Corporation tax	1,095,000×35% =		383,250
ACT offset:			
Dividend paid 210,000×⅓ =			(70,000)
MCT payable			313,250

2. **Year ended 31/3/90:**

Sch.D, Case I	120,000	CG	10,000	FII	75,000
Loan interest paid	(10,000)	Capital losses	(15,000)	75,000×⅓ =	25,000
	110,000		Nil		100,000
		Capital loss c/f	(5,000)		=210,000 (profit)

Corporation tax:

110,000×35% =	38,500
$(750{,}000-210{,}000)\times\dfrac{110{,}000}{210{,}000}\times{}^{1}/_{40} =$	(7,071)
	31,429

ACT offset:

Dividend paid	90,000	
Dividend received	(75,000)	
	15,000 ×⅓ =	(5,000)
		26,429
Surplus ACT brought back		(6,417)
MCT payable		20,012

Year ended 31/3/91:

Sch.D, Case I	140,000	CG	28,000	FII	30,000
Loan interest paid	(2,000)	Capital loss	(5,000)	30,000×⅓ =	10,000
	138,000		23,000		40,000
					=201,000 (profit)
		161,000			

Corporation tax:			
161,000×35% =		56,350	
(1,000,000−201,000) $\times\frac{161,000}{201,000}\times\frac{1}{40}=$		(16,000)	40,350
ACT offset:			
Dividend paid	170,000		
Dividend received	(30,000)		
	140,000 × ⅓ =	46,667	
Maximum offset:			
161,000×25% =		(40,250)	(40,250)
Surplus ACT (carried back)		6,417	
MCT payable			100

3. Left Ltd.:

Year ended 31/3/89:

Trading profit	1,100,000	CG	7,800	
Capital allowances	(6,000)			
	1,094,000			
		1,101,800×35% =		385,630

Year ended 31/3/90:

Trading profit	30,000	CG	5.200	
Capital allowances	(10,000)			
	20,000			
		25,200×25% =		6,300

Year ended 31/3/91:

Trading profit	220,000	CG	5,200	
Capital allowances	(8,000)			
	212,000			
		217,200×35% =	76,020	
Marginal relief:				
(1,000,000−217,200) $\times\frac{217,200}{217,200}\times\frac{1}{40}=$			(19,570)	
				56,450
Total corporation tax paid over three years				448,380

Right Ltd.:

Year ended 31/3/89:

Trading profit	496,000	CG	10,400	
Capital allowances	(20,000)			
	476,000			
		$486{,}400 \times 35\% =$		
Marginal relief			170,240	
$(500{,}000-486{,}400)\times\frac{486{,}400}{486{,}400}\times\frac{1}{40}=$			(340)	169,900

Year ended 31/3/90:

Trading profit	24,000	CG	7,800	
Capital allowances	(4,000)			
	20,000			
		$27{,}800 \times 25\% =$		6,950

Year ended 31/3/91:

Trading profit	830,000	CG	Nil	
Capital allowances	Nil			
	$830{,}000 \times 35\% =$		290,500	
$(1{,}000{,}000-830{,}000)\times\frac{830{,}000}{830{,}000}\times\frac{1}{40}=$			(4,250)	286,250
				463,100

4. a) Milton Limited may obtain relief for its trading loss of £33,300 in year ended 31st March, 1990 as follows:

Firstly, by setting the trading loss against all other profits of the same accounting period (£6,000) under the provisions of s.393(1) ICTA, 1988.

Secondly, by setting any losses, not so far relieved, against the total profits of the immediately preceding accounting period (£17,500), again under the provisions of s.393(2), 1988 ICTA.

b) Finally, by surrendering any remaining losses (£9,800) to its parent company Dippel Industrial Limited for the same corresponding period, i.e. year ended 31st March, 1990.

The relevant computations would be as follows:

Milton Limited

Accounting period to 31st March, 1989:	£
Schedule D, Case I	16,700
Schedule A	310
Unfranked investment income	490
	17,500
Less s.393(2) relief	(17,500)
	Nil

Accounting period to 31st March, 1990	£	£
Schedule D, Case I		Nil
Schedule A		310
Unfranked investment income		490
Capital gains	6,300	
Less losses b/f	(1,100)	
		5,200
		6,000
		(33,300)
Less s.393(2) Accounting period 31st March, 1990		6,000
		(27,300)
Less s.393(2) Accounting period 31st March, 1989		17,500
Loss available for group relief		(9,800)

Loss surrendered under group relief to Dippel Industrial Limited for its accounting period ended 31st March, 1990 being the corresponding period.

Dippel Industrial Limited

Accounting period to 31st March, 1989	£
Trading profits	40,000
Schedule A	1,000
	41,000

Accounting period to 31st March, 1990	£
Schedule D, Case I	17,000
Schedule A	1,000
Capital gains	5,200
	23,200
Less group relief	(9,800)
	13,400

c) Group relief is only available if one company is a 75% subsidiary of another or where two or more companies are members of a group, the 75% relationship exists directly or indirectly between those companies.

A 75% subsidiary exists where all the following three conditions obtain:

1. Entitlement to 75% control by voting powers or rights.
2. Entitlement to 75% of the profits if all profits were distributed.
3. Entitlement to 75% of the assets on a notional winding up.

5. **Perrifit Limited**

Additional capital allowances for the accounting period ended 31st March, 1990		**Allowances**
a) The plant and machinery will rank for 25% writing down allowance.		5,500
b) Extension Factory Building: Writing down allowance 4% × 36,000	=	1,400
c) New Sports Pavilion: This will rank as an industrial building as used for company's trade. Writing down allowance 4% × £44,000	=	1,760
d) Writing down allowance 25% × £36,000	=	9,000
e) New Factory: Cost (excluding land) £100,000 Writing down allowance 4% × £100,000	=	4,000
f) Extruding Machine: Hire purchase will not affect claim to capital allowances provided asset eventually becomes owned by Perrifit Limited and the machine is "brought into use" in the accounting period: 25% × £100,000	=	25,000
g) Fleet of Cars: Writing down allowances of 25% × £42,000.		10,500
h) Rolls-Royce – Maximum writing down allowance.		2,000
i) Scientific Research – 100% write off.		70,000
j) The factory is over 50 years old and has expired its life for taxation purposes. Therefore no further allowances will be due.		Nil
Total additional capital allowances		£129,200

6. **A Ltd.**

Sch.D, Case I	89,000	Dividends received	15,000	
Sch.A	8,200	Group income	(12,000)	
	97,200		3,000	
Loan interest	(10,000)	3,000 × ⅓ =	1,000	
	87,200	+ FII	4,000 =	91,200 (Profit)

87,200 × 35%	=	30,520
Taper relief:		
$(333,333^* - 91,200 \times \frac{87,200}{91,200} \times \frac{1}{40}$	=	(5,788)
Gross CT		24,732

ACT offset:			
12,000 × ⅓ =	4,000		
FII credit	(1,000)	(3,000)	
MCT		21,732	
B Ltd.			
Sch.D, Case I	85,000		+ CG 780 = 85,780 (chargeable profit and profit)
85,780 × 35%	=	30,023	
Taper relief:			
(333,333* − 85,780) × 1/40	=	(6,189)	
MCT		23,834	
C Ltd.			
Sch.D, Case I	9,000		
Sch.D, Case III	2,300		
	11,300		
Gross CT 11,300 × 25% =		2,825	

* Being three associated companies, the upper limit for marginal relief (1 million) is divided equally between the companies, 1 million × ⅓ = 333,333.

7. Advance corporation tax.

Q/E 30th June, 1990:

FII received 200 × ⅓ = 67 rebate due, but cannot yet be claimed – no ACT yet paid in accounting period.

Q/E 31st December, 1990:

Dividend paid 1,800 × ⅓ = 600 − 67 (on FII) = 533 payable to Inland Revenue by 14th January, 1991.

Income tax:

Q/E 30th September, 1990:

Loan interest paid 2,000 × 25% = 500 payable to Inland Revenue by 14th October, 1990.

Q/E 31st March, 1991:

UFII received 2,300 × 25% = 575 − 500 (on loan interest previously paid reclaimable). 75 offsettable against MCT.

Corporation tax assessment:

Sch.D, Case I		20,000
UFII		2,300
		22,300
Loan interest paid		(2,000)
		20,300
Gross CT 20,300 × 25%	=	5,075

ACT offset:		
600 − 67	=	(533)
MCT		4,542
Income tax offset:		
575 − 500	=	(75)
MCT payable (by 1st January, 1992)		4,467

8. **XYZ Ltd.**

A/P 1		**A/P 2**		**A/P 3**	
Sch.D, Case I	10,000	Sch.D, Case I	Nil	Sch.D, Case I	2,000
CG	520			S.393(1) loss relief	(2,000)
	10,520				Nil
Group relief	(200)				
	10,320				
Loss relief	(10,320)				
	Nil				

ABC Ltd.

Sch.D, Case I	1,000	Sch.D, Case I	3,000	Sch.D, Case I	1,800
Loan interest	(1,000)	Loan interest	(1,200)	Loan interest	(1,200)
	Nil		1,800		600
		Group relief	(1,800)		
Annual charge	1,200		Nil	600×25% =	150
Sch.D, Case I	(1,000)				
	200				
Group relief	(200)				
	Nil				

XYL Ltd. Loss	(15,000)
S.393(2) A/P 1	10,320
	(4,680)
Group relief A/P 2	1,800
	(2,880)
S.393(1) relief A/P 3	2,000
Carry forward	(880)

9. **CT 61s:**

Quarter ended 30th June:				
FII received		700		
Credit	700 × ⅓	233	933	– No repayment due, no ACT yet paid.
Quarter ended 30th September:				
Loan interest paid	600 × 25% =		150	income tax paid to Inland Revenue.
Quarter ended 31st December:				
Dividend paid	1,470 × ⅓ =		490	
FII credit			(233)	257 ACT paid to Inland Revenue.
Quarter ended 31st March:				
Interest received	800 × 25% =		200	150 recovered from Inland Revenue.

Corporation tax assessment:

Sch.D, Case I	=	10,000	CG = 780	
UFII		800		
		10,800		
Loan interest		(600)		
		10,200		
10,200 × 25%	=	2,550	780 × 25% =	195
ACT offset:		(257)		
		2,293		
Income tax credit 200 − 150	=	(50)		
MCT payable		2,243	+ 195 =	2,438

10. **Accounting period 4:**

Sch.D, Case I	15,500	ACT 20,000 × ⅓ =	6,667
CG	780		
	16,280		
Loan interest paid	(1,000)		
	15,280		
15,280 × 25% =	3,820		
ACT offset	(3,820)		(3,820)
MCT	Nil		2,847

Accounting period 3:

Sch.D, Case I		8,000	
Loan interest paid		(1,000)	
		7,000	
7,000×25%=		1,750	
ACT maximum offset	1,750		
ACT on div. paid in period 4,200×⅓=	(1,533)	(1,533)	
	217	217	
ACT offset brought back		(217)	(217)
MCT		Nil	2,630

Accounting period 2:

Sch.D, Case I		10,000	
CG		520	
		10,520	
Loan interest paid		(1,000)	
		9,520	
9,520×25%=		2,380	
ACT maximum offset	2,380		
ACT on div. paid in period 2: 5,700×⅓=	(1,900)	(1,900)	
	480	480	
ACT offset brought back		(480)	(480)
MCT		Nil	2,150

Accounting period 1:

Sch.D, Case I		17,800	
Loan interest paid		(1,000)	
		16,800	
16,800×25%=		4,200	
ACT maximum offset	4,200		
ACT on div. paid in period 1: 2,000×⅓=	(667)	(667)	
	3,533	3,533	
ACT offset brought back		(2,150)	(2,150)
MCT		1,383	Nil

11. **Year ended 31/3/90:**

Sch.D, Case I	Nil	Loss	(28,600)
Sch.A	2,100		
	2,100		
Loss relief S.393(2) loss	(2,100)		2,100
	Nil		(26,500)

Year ended 31/3/89:

Sch.D, Case I	20,000	CG	668	
Sch.A	2,400			
	22,400			
Loss relief	(22,400)		(668)	23,068
	Nil		Nil	(3,432)
		Loan interest 31/3/89		(1,000)
		Loan interest 31/3/88		(1,200)
				(5,632)

ACT to carry forward 9,000 × ⅓ = 3,000

Year ended 31/3/91:

Sch.D, Case I		220,000	CG = 26,000
S.393(1) Loss		(5,432)	5,432
		214,568	Nil
Sch.A		2,350	
		216,918	
Loan interest		(1,000)	
		215,918 + 26,000 = 241,918 (chargeable profit)	
Taper relief:			
241,918 × 35% =		84,671	
(1,000,000 − 241,918) × $\frac{1}{40}$ =		(18,952)	
		65,719	
ACT offset:			
Brought forward	(3,000)		
Dividend paid on 31/3/91			
12,000 × ⅓ =	(4,000)	(7,000)	
		58,719	

12. **Mr Kavanagh**

Vouch, Tick & Watch,
Accountants,
2, Busy Street,
Neverending,
VAT 700.

DATE:

Dear Mr Kavanagh,

Thank you for your recent letter and for enclosing the letter you have received from the Inspector of Taxes.

I have read the Inspector's letter and think it would assist you greatly if the definitions of the various terms used by him were explained to you in the detail laid down by the Taxes Acts.

A Director is defined as:

1. Any person so called and concerned with management of the company; or
2. Any person acting in the like capacity of a director however called (i.e. general manager, president, etc.); or
3. Any person, who by himself or together with his associates, controls more than 20% of the company's share capital.

A Participator is:

1. Shareholder or option holder.
2. Loan creditors (except banks and ordinary trade creditors).
3. Any person with a financial interest in the company.

An associate of a participator is:

1. Husband, wife, brothers, sisters, parents, children and remoter forebears.
2. Business partners.
3. Trustees of any settlement by the participator or his associates.
4. Any participator's co-beneficiaries where shares of the company are comprised in the estate.

As you will appreciate there may be certain taxation advantags to ''Close'' Companies, which are not available to other companies, because the control of the company's affairs is in the hands of a few people. It is these advantages that the legislation tries to remedy and prevent. The main areas in which ''close'' companies would otherwise obtain substantial advantages are:

1. By retaining non-trading profits in the company in excess of its needs.
2. By disguising distributions as business expenses thereby obtaining relief.
3. By disguising a distribution as a long term loan.

Therefore certain ''close'' investment companies are not charged at the small or marginal rates of corporation tax, but at the full standard rate, whatever their level of profit.

Questions

Capital Gains Tax

1. State whether or not the following disposals are chargeable events for capital gains tax:
   1. Compensation received for personal injury.
   2. Sale of business motor vehicle.
   3. Sale of taxpayer's own private residence.
   4. Proceeds on maturity of taxpayer's life policy.
   5. Sale of taxpayer's private motor car.
   6. Sale of Government securities held for many years.
   7. National Savings Certificate redemption.
   8. Gift of shares to taxpayer's wife.
   9. Property transferred to taxpayer's son on death.
   10. Gift of a work of art to British Museum.

2. Eric & Sons Limited have made the following disposals of assets during the year ended 30th June, 1990:
   a) Sold on 31st March, 1990 an item of plant for £14,000 on which capital allowances have previously been claimed. The cost of this plant was £7,800 when purchased on 17th May, 1983. The company intends to replace this item within 12 months by purchasing more sophisticated plant which may cost £12,000 for a small machine or £15,000 for a larger machine.
   b) Sold in March, 1990, 3,000 shares in Terry plc (a quoted company) for £3,600.
      The company's previous transactions in these shares had been.

1st August, 1963	bought 3,000 shares for £1,800
17th July, 1964	bought 2,000 shares for £1,500
1st May, 1969	sold 2,500 shares for £2,100
1st October, 1972	bought 500 shares for £300
10th December, 1984	bought 500 shares for £500

Value at March, 1982 90p per share.

Assume RPI:

March, 1982	79.44	March, 1990 (say)	122.0
May, 1983	84.60	May, 1990 (say)	130.0
December, 1984	90.90		

Terry plc went into liquidation on 1st May, 1990 and the Revenue accept that the shares became of negligible value.

From the information given you are required to prepare a statement of the company's assessable capital gains or losses for the year ended 30th June, 1990.

3. Broome purchased a property on 6/4/74 for £20,000. He used the ground floor as a retail shop and the upstairs as a flat for the use of himself and his family. The upstairs and downstairs are exactly equal in floor area. The value on 31st March, 1982 was £40,000.

On 6/4/90 he sold the entire property for £70,000 and on 7/6/90 bought a new retail shop for £32,000.

The ancillary costs of purchase were £700 and of sale £2,400.

What is the assessable gain? Assume that between March, 1982 and April, 1990 the Retail Price Index increased by 40%.

4. Gornall bought a house for £20,000 in April, 1968. He lived in the whole of it as his private residence up to April, 1982. He then converted one half of it to a shop for his wife to run a business. Its value in March, 1982 was £80,000. He moved out of the entire premises in April, 1988 and it remained empty until April, 1990 when it was sold for £150,000. Indexation between March, 1982 and April, 1990 increased by 40%.

5. Jones has the following transactions in 1990/91. Work out the capital gains (ignore indexation).

a) He purchased a painting for £1,400 in June, 1974 and sold it for £6,600 in May, 1989. Value in March, 1982, £2,000.
b) He purchased £4,000 (nominal) of 7% Treasury Loan for £2,810 on 17/7/83 and sold £2,000 (nominal) for £1,735 on 9/4/89. He purchased a further £3,000 (nominal) for £2,165 on 1/9/84 and sold £4,000 (nominal) for £7,182 on 25/11/89.
c) He purchased 1,500 £1 ordinary shares in Goldenshake plc, a quoted company, for £714 in 1973. In May, 1989 there was a successful takeover bid by Silverarm plc who offered 3.25 shares (valued at 60p each) and 50p in cash per share. He sold 900 Silverarm shares for £6,100 in March, 1991. The value in March, 1982 of Goldenshake shares was £1 per share.
d) He purchased a Rover car for £15,000 in July, 1986 and sold it for £17,500 in November, 1990.

6. Barrett is 64 years old on 16/6/90. On that day he sells his garage business which he founded on 16/6/81.

The details of the sale are:

a) The premises were purchased for £14,000 (including legal costs). He sold one third of the premises in 1980 for £10,000. The value of the remainder in March, 1982 was £30,000. He improved the premises in April, 1985 at a cost of £10,000. The selling price was £180.000.
b) The goodwill cost him nothing, was worth £12,000 in March, 1982 and was sold for £40,000.
c) The plant and machinery which he sold for £6,000 had originally cost £7,500.

Indexation increased by 50% from March, 1982 to date of sale, and by 30% from April, 1985. Calculate the assessable gain.

7. John Price and his wife Mary Price have the following transactions in 1990/91. What is the capital gain?

a) John Price purchased 800 £1 ordinary shares in Smith Ltd. (an unquoted company) for £500 on 6/4/63. Their value on 6/4/65 was 75p each. He sold 600 of the shares for £8,800 on 6/4/90.
Their value at March, 1982 was £2,000.
b) Mary inherited 1,400 50p ordinary shares in Sherratt plc (a publicly quoted company) on 18/6/76 when the quoted daily prices were 120p and 128p. The bargains struck on that day varied from 114p to 138p. On 11/8/90 there was rights issue of one new share for each four already held at a price of 100p per share. Mary did not take up the offer but sold her entitlement for £500. After the rights issue the shares were valued at 110p each.
The value of each share in March, 1982 was 120p.
c) Mary also inherited £10,000 (nominal) of 3½% War Loan valued on the death of her uncle at £2,900. Her uncle died on 21/5/85. She sold the entire holding for £3,850 on 16/8/90.
d) John purchased 3,000 shares in Peterson plc (a publicly quoted company) for £5,000 in 1978 and sold them for £22,000 on 14/4/90. Their value at March, 1982 was £6,000.
She made an election to value all assets at 31/3/82, when purchased prior to that date.

Assume RPI:

March, 1982	79.44
April, 1990 (say)	122.00
August, 1990 (say)	130.00
September, 1990 (say)	132.00

8. Baldrick had dealings in the shares of ABC plc (a quoted company) as follows:

	Transaction	No. of shares	Price
			£
17/11/63	Bought	1,000	800
9/10/64	Bought	700	1,100
11/3/65	Sold	200	600
	Value at 6/4/65 £150 each		
10/8/68	Bought	250	400
30/4/70	Bought	50	100
22/11/77	Sold	1,500	3,200
19/1/83	Bought	500	1,900
27/8/90	Transferred to his ex-wife in a divorce settlement 800 shares when they were quoted at 380p to 388p and bargains struck at 370p, 375p, 380p, 387p and 392p. Value at March, 1982 was 320p per share.		

Calculate the relevant capital gains for 1990/91.

Assume RPI:

March, 1982	79.44
January, 1983	82.60
August, 1990 (say)	130.00

9. A taxpayer has the following transactions in 1990/91. Work out the capital gains tax payable:

a) He sold 1,000 shares in XYZ plc for £12,000 in August, 1990. They had been acquired as part of a takeover bid when XYZ had taken over ABC Ltd. in May, 1984. They had offered 3 XYZ shares (then worth £3 each) for each ABC share. The taxpayer had originally acquired 500 ABC shares for £1,000 in February, 1983.
b) He inherited £2,000 (nominal) of 3½% War Loan in June, 1984. He sold it for £1,400 in June, 1990.
c) He sold a painting for £7,200 in June, 1990. He had acquired it for £1,500 in May, 1982. Indexation added £400 to the cost.
d) He sold 2,000 shares in MNP Ltd. for £8,000 in August, 1990. He had acquired 1,500 shares for £1,000 in June, 1981. Their value at 31/3/82 was £2 each. There was a rights issue of 1 for 3 shares held at a cost of £1 per new share in September, 1983.

His income for 1990/91 was £23,000, and he was married.

Assume RPI:

March, 1982	79.44
February, 1983	82.97
September, 1983	86.06
May, 1984	88.97
June, 1990 (say)	126.00
August, 1990 (say)	130.00

10. A taxpayer sells 2,000 shares in Carey plc for £24,000 in August, 1990. They were acquired:

Date	Shares	Price
Bought 1/4/64	500	900
Value at 6/4/65	Per share	£2 each
Bought 9/8/78	300	£2,400
Value 31/3/82	Per share	£10 each
Bought 1/2/83	1,000	3,000
Bought 1/9/83	400	1,400

Work out the capital gain, 1990/91. Use the RPI figures in question 9.

11. McDonald purchased a piece of land in September, 1983 for £80,000. He sold part of it for £19,800 in August, 1990 when the remaining part was valued at £100,000.

Calculate the gain, or comment on any other treatment. Use the RPI figures in question 9.

Answers

Capital Gains Tax

1.1. Damages or compensation received for personal injury or wrongs are not generally assessable to capital gains tax.
2. If a business asset on which capital allowances have been claimed is sold for more than original cost then a capital gain can arise.
3. A taxpayer's main or only private residence is normally exempt.
4. Maturity proceeds of a taxpayer's own life policy are exempt from capital gains tax.
5. Private motor vehicles are specifically exempted from capital gains tax.
6. Government securities are specifically exempted from charge.
7. Monies received on the redemption of National Savings Certificates are not chargeable to capital gains tax.
8. Transfers between husband and wife are disregarded for capital gains tax purposes.
9. There would normally be no liability to capital gains on the death of the taxpayer. However, there are exceptions in cases where the taxpayer is a life tenant or has the benefit of assets in trust.
10. Gifts to museums and places of National Heritage (National Trust) are exempt from capital gains tax.

2.a)			
	Sale of plant		14,000
	Cost	7,800	
	Indexation $7{,}800 \times \frac{120-84.6}{84.6}$ (0.418) =	3,260	(11,060)
	Gain		2,940

If replaced by plant costing 12,000 there would be cash retained of 2,000 (14,000 − 12,000) which would be assessed to capital gains tax, and rollover relief given of 940 (2,940 − 2,000), giving an acquisition cost to the new machine of 11,060 (12,000 − 940).

If the machine purchased cost 15,000, full rollover (or depreciatory) relief would be given and the cost of the replacement for the new machine would be 12,060 (14,000 − 2,940).

b) Sale of shares in March, 1990:

New pool:

Sale price (500 shares)	$3{,}600 \times \frac{500}{3{,}000} =$	600	
Cost	500		
Indexation $500 \times \frac{120 - 90.9}{90.9}$ (0.320)	160	(660)	(60)

1982 pool:

Sale price (2,500 shares)	$3{,}600 \times \frac{2{,}500}{3{,}000} =$	3,000	
Value at 31/3/82 2,500×90p=	2,250		
Indexation (from March, 1982) $2{,}250 \times \frac{120 - 79.44}{79.44}$ (0.511)=	1,150	(3,400)	(400)
		Loss	(460)

Negligible Value claim, May, 1990:

1,000 shares, disposal value		Nil	
Value at 31/3/82 1,000×90p=	900		
Indexation $900 \times \frac{130 - 79.44}{79.44}$ (0.636)=	572	(1,472)	
		Loss	(1,472)

3.

Sale of shop portion:	70,000×½=			35,000
Value at 31/3/82	40,000×½=	20,000		
Indexation (40%)	20,000×40%=	8,000	28,000	
Costs of sale			1,200	
				(29,200)
Gross gain				5,800

Proceeds reinvested, 32,000. Cash retained 35,000−32,000=3,000 gain assessed. Therefore 5,800−3,000=2,800 rolled over.
Therefore deemed cost of new premises 32,000−2,800=29,200.

4.

Sale price		150,000
Value at 31/3/82	80,000	
Indexation 80,000×40%=	32,000	(112,000)
Gross gain		38,000

Business use:
Owned for 8 years from 1/4/82. Exclusive business use 50%.

38,000×50%=19,000.

Therefore assessable gain 19,000.

Private portion not assessable – private occupation (of half) 1982 to 1988, last two years' ownership always exempt in private accommodation.

				Total:
5.a)	Sale price	6,600		
	Value at 31/3/82	(2,000)		
		4,600		
	Excess of sale price over 6,000=600×$\frac{5}{3}$=1,000			1,000
b)				Exempt
c)	May, 1989 – takeover			
	Cash received 1,500×50p=		750	
	Value at 31/3/82			
	$1{,}500\times\frac{750}{750+2{,}925^*}$		(306)	444
	* Note: 2,925 is 3.25 shares×1,500×60p.			
	Sale of shares			
	Sale price		6,100	
	Remaining value at 31/3/82	1,500		
	Less:	(306)	(1,194)	4,906
d)				Exempt
	Total capital gains			6,350

6.a)	Sale of premises			180,000	
	Value at 31/3/82	30,000			
	Indexation (50%)	15,000	45,000		
	Improvements	10,000			
	Indexation (30%)	3,000	13,000	(58,000)	122,000
b)	Sale of goodwill			40,000	
	Value at 31/3/82	12,000			
	Indexation (50%)	6,000		(18,000)	22,000

c)

		Exempt
Gross gain		144,000
Retirement relief	$125{,}000 \times {}^{9}/_{10}{}^{*} =$	(112,500)
		31,500
Half retirement relief		
	$31{,}500 \times \frac{1}{2} \times {}^{9}/_{10} =$	(14,175)
Taxable gain		17,325

* Note: Only in business for nine years.

7.a) **John:** Total:

Sale price 8,800

Value at 31/3/82 $2{,}000 \times \frac{600}{800} =$ 1,500

Indexation from March, 1982

$1{,}500 \times \frac{122-79.44}{79.44}$ (0.536) = 804 (2,304) 6,496

b) **Mary:**

Sale price of rights 500

Value of shares at 31/3/82

$120 \times 1{,}400 = 1{,}680 \times \frac{500}{500+1{,}540^{*}}$

(1,940)

= 411

$411 \times \frac{130-79.44}{79.44}$ (0.636) = 261 (672)

Loss (172)

(indexation)

*Value of shares retained after rights issue is:
$1{,}400 \times 110p = 1{,}540$

c) **Mary:**			Exempt
d) **John:**			
Sale price		22,000	
Value at 31/3/82	6,000		
Indexation			
$6{,}000 \times \frac{122-79.44}{79.44}$ (0.536)=	3,216	(9,216)	12,784
Gains of John			6,496
			12,784
			19,280
Annual exemption			(5,000)
Chargeable gains			14,280
Losses of Mary			(172)

Losses cannot be offset against the gains of a spouse for 1990/91 onwards.

8. Disposal value calculation: Total:

¼ up rule=388−380= 8×¼= 2. 380+ 2=382p

½ up rule=392−370=22×½=11. 370+11=381p

Disposal value 800×381p		3,048	
New pool:			
Sale price (500 shares) $\frac{3{,}048 \times 500}{800}$=		1,905	
Cost price	1,900		
Indexation			
$1{,}900 \times \frac{130-82.6}{82.6}$ (0.574)=	1,091	(2,991)	(1,086)
1982 Pool:			
Sale price (300 shares) $\frac{3{,}048 \times 300}{800}$=		1,143	
Value at 31/3/82 300×320p=960			
Indexation (from 31/3/82)			
$960 \times \frac{130-79.44}{79.44}$ (0.636)=	611	(1,571)	(428)
Total loss			(1,514)

		£	£
9 a)	Sale price		12,000
	Original cost		
	$1{,}000 \times \frac{1{,}000}{1{,}500} =$	666	
	Indexation:		
	$666 \times \frac{130-82.97}{82.97^*}$ (0.567)=	378	(1,044)
	Gain		10,956

* Note: Indexation figure at February, 1983. On the takeover by XYZ plc in May, 1984, as it was entirely for shares, the XYZ shares would be deemed to have been acquired for the original cost of the ABC shares.

b)			Exempt
c)	Sale price		7,200
	Cost 1,500+400=		(1,900)
	Gross gain		5,300
	Gain limited to $7{,}200-6{,}000=1{,}200\times \frac{5}{3}=2{,}000$		
d)	Split of shares sold: 1,500 originals 500 rights		
	Sale price of originals		6,000
	Value at 31/3/82: 1,500×2=	3,000	
	Indexation:		
	$3{,}000 \times \frac{130-79.44}{79.44}$ (0.636)=	1,908	(4,908)
			1,092
	Sale price of rights issue		2,000
	Cost 500×1=	500	
	Indexation:		
	$500 \times \frac{130-86.06}{86.06}$ (0.511)=	256	(756)
			1,244
	Total gain 1,092+1,244=		2,336

Total gains in year:

10,956
2,000
2,336
15,292

Gross income			23,000	
SPA		3,005		
MCA		1,720	(4,725)	
			18,275 × 25% =	4568.75
Capital gain			15,292	
Annual exemption			(5,000)	
			10,292	
2,425	(20,700 − 18,275) × 25% =		606.25	
7,867	× 40% =		3,146.80	
10,292			3,753.05	

10.

		Price	£	£
New pool:				
Sale price (1,400 shares)				
$24{,}000 \times \frac{1{,}400}{2{,}000} =$			16,800	
Shares		**Price**		
1/2/83	1,000	3,000		
Index to Sept. 1983:				
$3{,}000 \times \frac{86.06 - 82.97}{82.97}$ (0.037) =		111		
		3,111		
1/9/83	400	1,400		
	1,400	4,511		
Index to August 1990:				
$4{,}511 \times \frac{130 - 86.06}{86.06}$ (0.511) =		2.305	(6,816)	9,984
1982 pool:				
Sale price (600 shares)				
$24{,}000 \times \frac{600}{2{,}000} =$			7,200	
Value at 31/3/82:				
$800 \times £10 = 8{,}000 \times \frac{600}{800} =$		6,000		
Index from 31/3/82:				
$6{,}000 \times \frac{130 - 79.44}{79.44}$ (0.636) =		3,816	(9,816)	(2,616)
Net capital gain				7,368

11.

	£	£
Sale price		19,800
Cost price		
$80{,}000 \times \dfrac{19{,}000}{100{,}000+19{,}000} =$	12,773	
Indexation:		
$12{,}773 \times \dfrac{130-86.06}{86.06}\ (0.511) =$	6,527	(19,300)
Gain		500

But: The sale price of £19,800 is less than 20 per cent of the total value at the date of sale (20% ×£119,000=£23,800).

Therefore the taxpayer could claim if he wished to offset the sale price against the cost carried forward:

	£
Original cost	80,000
Indexation to Aug., 1990:	
80,000×0.511=	40,880
	120,880
Less: Sale price	(19,800)
Value carried forward	101,080

Index